Overcoming the Persistence of Inequality and Poverty

Overcoming the Persistence of Inequality and Poverty

Edited by

Valpy FitzGerald
Oxford Department of International Development (Queen Elizabeth House), UK

Judith Heyer
Somerville College, University of Oxford, UK

Rosemary Thorp
Oxford Department of International Development (Queen Elizabeth House), UK

First published 2011 by
PALGRAVE MACMILLAN

Palgrave Macmillan in the UK is an imprint of Macmillan Publishers Limited,
registered in England, company number 785998, of Houndmills, Basingstoke,
Hampshire RG21 6XS.

Palgrave Macmillan in the US is a division of St Martin's Press LLC,
175 Fifth Avenue, New York, NY 10010.

Palgrave Macmillan is the global academic imprint of the above companies
and has companies and representatives throughout the world.

Palgrave® and Macmillan® are registered trademarks in the United States,
the United Kingdom, Europe and other countries.

ISBN 978–0–230–24970–7 hardback

This book is printed on paper suitable for recycling and made from fully
managed and sustained forest sources. Logging, pulping and manufacturing
processes are expected to conform to the environmental regulations of the
country of origin.

A catalogue record for this book is available from the British Library.

Library of Congress Cataloging-in-Publication Data
Overcoming the persistence of inequality and poverty / [edited by]
  Valpy FitzGerald, Judith Heyer, and Rosemary Thorp.
     p.   cm.
  Includes index.
  Summary: "International experts evaluate new policy directions in economic
development and poverty reduction, building on the ideas of a pioneer in the
new discipline of Development Studies, Frances Stewart. Combing ideas and
evidence on technological change, human development and conflict prevention
to address the issue of the persistence of inequality"— Provided by publisher.
  ISBN 978–0–230–24970–7 (hardback)
  1. Economic development.   2. Income distribution.   3. Poverty.
  4. Equality.   I. Fitzgerald, E. V. K. (Edmund Valpy Knox), 1947–
  II. Heyer, Judith.   III. Thorp, Rosemary.
  HD82.0915 2011
  338.9—dc22   2010050730

10   9   8   7   6   5   4   3   2   1
20   19   18   17   16   15   14   13   12   11

Printed and bound in the United States of America

Contents

List of Figures and Tables

Figures

Tables

Acknowledgements

The epigraph to Chapter 2 is taken from "Snow" by Louis MacNeice, published by Faber and Faber.

Figure 8.5 is taken from Gasparini, L., G. Cruces, L. Tornarolli and M. Marchionni. 2009. A Turning Point? Recent Developments on Inequality in Latin America and the Caribbean. *CEDLAS Working paper* No. 81, La Plata.

Notes on Contributors

Giorgio Barba Navaretti is Professor of Economics at the University of Milan, Director of the Graduate School in Social, Economic and Political Sciences of the University of Milan and Scientific Director of the Centro Studi Luca d'Agliano. He has a PhD in economics from the University of Oxford and a degree in economics from Bocconi University in Milan. He has been a consultant for the World Bank, the Organisation for Economic Co-operation and Development (OECD), the European Commission, the United Nations Children's Fund (UNICEF) and the Italian Ministry of Foreign Affairs. He specialises in international and development economics and has worked extensively on the economics of multinational firms, on the link between trade, foreign direct investment and technology diffusion, on international economic policy and on firm dynamics in developing countries. His publications include books and several papers published in academic journals and international working paper series. He is the co-author of *Multinationals in the World Economy* with Anthony J. Venables (2004; *Le multinazionali nell'economia mondiale,* 2006). He also writes a column for Italian newspaper *Il Sole 24 Ore.*

Graham K. Brown is Director of the Centre for Development Studies and Senior Lecturer in International Development at the Department of Social and Policy Sciences at the University of Bath. He is also a Research Associate at the Centre for Research on Inequality, Human Security and Ethnicity (CRISE) at the University of Oxford. His research is primarily concerned with the nexus of inequality, identity, and political mobilisation, including violent conflict, with a focus on the Southeast Asian region.

Giovanni Andrea Cornia is Professor of Development Economics in the Faculty of Economics at the University of Florence. He was the External Research Coordinator for the sub-project on Macroeconomics and Social Policy within the Social Policy in a Development Context project at the United Nations Research Institute for Social Development (UNRISD). He has also taught at the University of Pavia, the University of Helsinki and the European Institute in Florence. He was

Director of the World Institute for Development Economics Research of the United Nations University (UNU/WIDER), based in Helsinki, between 1995 and 1999, and also the Director of the Economic and Social Policy Research Programme at the International Child Development Centre in Florence between 1988 and 1995. His current research focuses on pro-poor macroeconomics, globalisation and inequality, and the socioeconomic impact of AIDS on children. Key publications include *Adjustment with a Human Face* with Richard Jolly and Frances Stewart (Vol. 1, 1987 and Vol. 2, 1998); *Transitions and Institutions: The Experience of Gradual and Late Reformers* with Vladimir Popov (2001); and 'Poverty and Inequality in the Era of Liberalization and Globalisation' in *Human Development and the Environment* by H. Van Ginkel et al. (eds) (2001). He has also published some thirteen chapters for different edited books, and some forty articles in economic journals and working paper series. He has also coordinated four research reports for the United Nations Children's Fund (UNICEF).

Séverine Deneulin is a lecturer in International Development at the University of Bath, where she teaches for the Masters course on Wellbeing and Human Development. Her research specialism is in development theory and ethics. She holds a DPhil in Development Studies from the University of Oxford and an MA in Economics from the University of Louvain (Belgium). She is the author of *The Capability Approach and the Praxis of Development* (2006) and co-edited *Transforming Unjust Structures: The Capability Approach* (2006). She has published numerous articles which have critically examined the freedom focus of the human development and capability approach. She is the Education Officer of the Human Development and Capability Association, coeditor of its e-bulletin, *Maitreyee*, and convener of the thematic group 'religion and human development'. She is finalising the editing of a textbook on human development and the capability approach. Her current research focuses on religion and values and her latest book, *Religion in Development: Rewriting the Secular Script*, was published by Zed Books in 2009.

Gianfranco De Simone is an economist at Fondazione Giovanni Agnelli. He holds a PhD in economics from the University of Turin. His publications focus on FDI and migration.

Valpy FitzGerald is Professor of International Development and Head of the Department of International Development at the University of

Oxford. His research interests cover determinants of capital flows from developed to developing countries, macroeconomic policy in emerging markets, long-run economic growth and welfare in Latin America, and conflict economics. He was educated at Oxford (PPE, BA 1968) and Cambridge (Economics, PhD 1972). He was Assistant Director of Development Studies at Cambridge (1973–80) and then Professor of Development Economics at the Institute of Social Studies, The Hague, until returning to Oxford in 1993. He is also a Professorial Fellow of St Antony's College, Oxford, and Visiting Professor of International Finance at the Universidad Complutense, Madrid. He has in recent years conducted advisory work for international agencies on international investment regulation (Organisation for Economic Co-operation and Development, OECD); debt sustainability (United Nations Conference on Trade and Development, UNCTAD); macroeconomic policy and children (United Nations Children's Fund, UNICEF); and financial development (United Nations-Department of Economic and Social Affairs, UN/DESA).

Barbara Harriss-White is Professor of Development Studies at the University of Oxford. Her research interests have developed from the economics of agricultural markets to India's socially regulated capitalist economy and corporate capital; and from the malnutrition caused by markets to many other aspects of deprivation: notably poverty, gender bias and gender relations, health and disability, destitution and caste discrimination. She has a long-term interest in agrarian change in South India and has also tracked the economy of a market town there since 1972. She has held research posts in the Centre for South Asian Studies, Cambridge, the Overseas Development Institute, London, and the London School of Hygiene and Tropical Medicine, before coming to Queen Elizabeth House (QEH) (now the Department of International Development) at the University of Oxford in 1987 to teach rural development and peasant economy. In 1995, she became the founder-director of the MPhil in Development Studies and was Director of QEH from 2003 to 2007. Since 1969 she has spent a total of six years in the field in South Asia and six months in francophone West Africa. She has carried out policy research for seven UN agencies – including on food, disability, social security and post-harvest technology. She has been a trustee of Action Aid for many years, and Board of Trustees member of the International Food Policy Research Institute (IFPRI) since late 2006. She was the first chair of the subpanel assessing Development Studies for the 2008 Research Assessment Exercise.

Judith Heyer is an Emeritus Fellow of Somerville College, an Honorary Associate of the Oxford Department of International Development, and an Associate of the School of Interdisciplinary Area Studies, all at the University of Oxford. She has a doctorate from London University. Her research interests are primarily rural poverty and social formations and she has worked extensively in Kenya and in India. She taught at the Department of Economics and Institute of Development Studies, University of Nairobi, from 1964 to 1975, and was a Fellow and Tutor at Somerville College from 1975 to 2005. Her published works include *Rural Development in Kenya*, with D. Ireri and J. Moris (1971); *Agricultural Development in Kenya, An Economic Assessment*, edited with J. K. Maitha and W. M. Senga (1976); *Rural Development in Tropical Africa*, edited with P. Roberts and G. Williams (1981); *Kenya: Monitoring Living Conditions and Consumption Patterns* (1991); *Groups, Institutions and Development*, edited with F. Stewart and R. Thorp (2001); and *Comparative Political Economy of Development, Africa and South Asia*, edited with B. Harriss-White (2009).

Yanjing Huang received an MA in International and Development Economics and a Master of Environmental Management from Yale. She was a research fellow at UNITAR, the Yale Center for Environmental Law and Policy as well as the Economic Growth Center. Her research interests include natural resource economics, energy markets and economics and development. She currently works as an equity analyst at Huatai United Securities covering environmental services and renewable energy.

Mallory Irons graduated from Yale University in 2009, where she was an economics and international studies double major focusing primarily on the political economy of developing countries. She is currently an analyst in public finance at an investment banking firm in New York City.

Arnim Langer is University Lecturer in International Relations and Director of the Center for Peace Research and Strategic Studies at the University of Leuven in Belgium. He was formerly a Research Officer at the Centre for Research on Inequality, Human Security and Ethnicity (CRISE) at the University of Oxford where he was involved in research on group identity and group behaviour in a range of African countries, cultural status inequalities and group mobilisation, the persistence of socioeconomic horizontal inequalities, and the relationship between multidimensional horizontal inequalities and violent conflict.

Bruno Martorano is a PhD candidate at the University of Florence working on taxation and inequality in Latin America.

Thandika Mkandawire is Professor of African Development at the London School of Economics. He was director of the United Nations Research Institute for Social Development (UNRISD) from 1998 to 2009. A Swedish national of Malawian origin, he is an economist with many years' experience in the promotion of comparative research on development issues. He studied economics at Ohio State University and the University of Stockholm and has taught at the Universities of Stockholm and Zimbabwe. He holds a Doctorate in Letters from Rhodes University. From 1986 to 1996, he was Executive Secretary of the Council for the Development of Social Science Research in Africa (CODESRIA) based in Dakar, Senegal. Prior to taking up his appointment with UNRISD, he was Senior Research Fellow at the Centre for Development Research in Copenhagen. He has published broadly on the social sciences in Africa and on problems of policy-making, adjustment and democratisation. He is a member of the editorial boards of *Africa Development; Africa Review of Books; Development and Change; Feminist Economics; Global Governance; Journal of Development Studies; Journal of Human Development and Oxford Development Studies* and has recently served on the executive committees of the International Institute for Labour Studies, the Swedish NGO Fund for Human Rights, the Comparative Research Programme on Poverty (CROP) of the International Social Science Council, Care International, the Steering Committee of the UNU Project on Intellectual History, and the African Gender Institute.

Abdul Raufu Mustapha is University Lecturer in African Politics at the University of Oxford and Kirk-Greene Fellow in African studies at St Antony's College. His current research focuses on the politics of rural societies in Africa, ethnicity and identity politics and the politics of democratisation in Africa. He studied political science at Ahmadu Bello University, Nigeria, and St Peter's College, Oxford. He has held teaching and research positions at Beyero University, Kano, and Ahmadu Bello University, Zaria, Nigeria. He is a member of the editorial advisory group for the *Review of African Political Economy*, an adviser for the 'A Democratic Developmental State in Africa?' project for the Centre for Policy Studies (CPS) in Johannesburg, South Africa, and a member of the Board of Trustees of the Development Research and Projects Centre (DRPC), Kano, Nigeria. He has also been appointed to the Scientific Committee of the Council for the Development of Social Science Research in Africa

(CODESRIA), Dakar, Senegal. Recent projects have included research on 'Ethnic Structure and Public Sector Governance' for the United Nations Research Institute for Social Development (UNRISD) in Geneva. He also completed fieldwork and initial analysis of data for a project for the Centre for Research on Inequality, Human Security and Ethnicity (CRISE) at the University of Oxford on the effectiveness of the Federal Character Commission in Nigeria.

Gianluca Orefice is a PhD student in economics at the University of Milan. His research interests include labour migration, foreign direct investment and international economics.

Gustav Ranis is the Frank Altschul Professor Emeritus of International Economics at Yale University. He was Director of the Yale Center for International and Area Studies from 1995 to 2003, a Carnegie Corporation scholar from 2004 to 2006, Director of the Economic Growth Center at Yale from 1967 to 1975, Assistant Administrator for Program and Policy at the US Agency for International Development (USAID) from 1965 to 1967, and Director of the Pakistan Institute of Development Economics from 1958 to 1961. Professor Ranis has more than 20 books and 300 articles on theoretical and policy-related issues of development to his credit.

Sunali Rohra heads external relations for a leading management consulting firm in India. Her research interests lie in Indian energy policy, politics, and foreign policy. She is currently researching the impact of solar energy development and diffusion on India's foreign policy.

Angelica Salvi is a fellow at the Centro Studi Luca d'Agliano and has been a consultant for the World Bank and the Asian Development Bank. She holds a PhD in economics from the University of Milan. Her publications focus on the investment climate, trade facilitation and poverty reduction.

Nigel Singh graduated from the University of Oxford in 2009 with an MSc in Contemporary India, for which he researched the solar industry and the Indian government's negotiating position at climate talks. He has also written on technology transfer and intellectual property issues for Policy Network. He is a producer for the BBC and Channel Four. He will be a Visiting Fellow at the Institute of Defence Studies and Analysis in New Delhi from January 2011.

Rosemary Thorp is Emeritus Reader in the Economics of Latin America and an Emeritus Fellow of St Antony's College at the University of Oxford. She was for three periods Director of the Latin American Centre. During 2003–04 she was director of Queen Elizabeth House (QEH) (now the Department of International Development) at the University of Oxford. In December 2001 she became for five years the Chair of Trustees of Oxfam GB. Her *Progress, Poverty and Exclusion: An Economic History of Latin America in the Twentieth Century* (2000) was written at the invitation of the Inter-American Development Bank. Three companion volumes are entitled: Vol. 1: *The Export Age: The Latin American Economies in the Late Nineteenth and Early Twentieth Centuries* (co-edited with Enrique Cárdenas and José Antonio Ocampo), Vol. 2: *Latin America in the 1930s: The Role of the Periphery in World Crisis* (2nd ed) and Vol. 3: *Industrialization and the State in Latin America: The Postwar Years* (co-edited with Enrique Cárdenas and José Antonio Ocampo). As well as contributing two chapters for the *Cambridge History of Latin America* on the Latin American economies (1913–19 and in the 1940s), she has written an economic history of Peru (Macmillan), on social policy in Peru and Venezuela, and on decentralisation in Chile and Colombia (2001) with Alan Angell and Pamela Lowden. She is now participating in the Centre for Research on Inequality, Human Security and Ethnicity (CRISE) at QEH.

John Toye is Chair of the Advisory Council of the Oxford Department of International Development. He has an MA in history from Jesus College, Cambridge, and a PhD in economics from the School of Oriental and African Studies (London University). He began his career in the British Treasury in the 1960s, where he worked on the development of the UK Public Expenditure Survey. Since then, he has been successively a professor of development economics at the universities of Wales, Sussex and Oxford. He has also worked for the United Nations (as director of the Globalisation Division of UNCTAD, the UN Conference on Trade and Development, from 1998 to 2000). He has authored seven books, his first being *Public Expenditure and Development Policy in India* (1981) and his most recent being *The UN and Global Political Economy* (2004), which he wrote with Richard Toye. He was managing editor of *Oxford Development Studies* from 2006 to 2009. He is currently a head of region for Africa for Oxford Analytica.

Ukoha Ukiwo, DPhil (Oxon), is a lecturer in the Department of Political and Administrative Studies, University of Port Harcourt, Nigeria. He was a CRISE scholar at St Cross College at the University of Oxford. He has held research positions at the Centre for Advanced Social Science (CASS), Port Harcourt, and the Institute of International Studies at the University of California, Berkeley. Dr Ukiwo was nominated for and served as Co-Leader of the 2009 American Political Science Association (APSA) Africa Democracy Workshop. He has researched and published widely on democratisation, identity politics, conflicts and the Niger Delta region of Nigeria.

List of Acronyms

AC	Advanced Country
ANC	African National Congress
ASLI	Asian Strategy and Leadership Institute
ASSOCHAM	Association of Chambers of Commerce and Industry of India
BEE	Black Economic Empowerment
B-BBEE	Broad-Based Black Economic Empowerment
BMF	Black Management Forum
CEE	Commission for Employment Equity
CGIAR	Consultative Group on International Agricultural Research
CII	Confederation of Indian Industry
CO_{2e}	Carbon Dioxide Equivalent
COSATU	Congress of South African Trade Unions
CPPS	Centre for Public Policy Studies
CRISE	Centre for Research on Inequality, Human Security and Ethnicity
DC	Developing Country
DFID	Department for International Development
DSA	Development Studies Association
EEA	Employment Equity Act
ELF	Ethnolinguistic Fractionalization
FCC	Federal Character Commission
FCP	Federal Character Principle
FCS	Federal Civil Service
FDI	Foreign Direct Investment
FICCI	Federation of Indian Chambers of Commerce and Industry
FODESAF	Fondo de Desarrollo Social y Asignaciones
FSG	Food Studies Group
GEAR	Growth Employment and Redistribution
GOI	Government of India
HDCA	Human Development and Capability Association

HDR	Human Development Report
HINDRAF	Hindu Rights Action Front
HI	Horizontal Inequality
HIPC	Heavily Indebted Poor Countries
ICS	Institute of Commonwealth Studies
IDS	Institute of Development Studies
IISc	Indian Institute of Science
IIT	Indian Institute of Technology
ILO	International Labour Organization
IMF	International Monetary Fund
IP	Intellectual Property
IPR	Intellectual Property Rights
IRAE	Institute for Research in Agricultural Economics
IS	Innovation Systems
ITRI	Industrial Technology Research Institute
LOC	Left-of-Centre
MDG	Millennium Development Goals
MNRE	Ministry of New and Renewable Energy
NASSCOM	National Association of Software Services Companies
NDSF	Niger Delta Strike Force
NDVS	Niger Delta Volunteer Service
NGOs	Non-Governmental Organizations
NEDC	National Economic Development Council
NEF	National Empowerment Fund
NEP	New Economic Policy
NTUI	New Trade Union Initiative
OECD	Organisation for Economic Co-operation and Development
PLN	Partido Liberación Nacional
PV	Photovoltaic
QEH	Queen Elizabeth House
RDP	Reconstruction and Development Programme
RE	Renewable Energy
RSC	Refugee Studies Centre
SANAS	South African National Accreditation System
SCBA	Social Cost–Benefit Analysis
TERI	The Energy Research Institute
TFP	Total Factor Productivity
TRIPS	Trade-Related Aspects of Intellectual Property Rights
UNICEF	United Nations Children's Fund
UNIDO	United Nations Industrial Development Organisation

UNRISD	United Nations Research Institute for Social Development
USAID	United States Agency for International Development
WB	World Bank
WTO	World Trade Organization
WVS	World Values Survey
WISE	World Institute for Sustainable Development

Part I
Introduction

1
Presenting the Book

Valpy FitzGerald, Judith Heyer and Rosemary Thorp

Some three-quarters of human beings live in developing countries, and half the world's population are victims of inequality, poverty and insecurity. Yet, despite historically unprecedented advances in global technology, productivity and communications, the 'international policy community' of democratic states, intergovernmental institutions, non-governmental organisations and academic bodies still seems unable to address this injustice directly. The issue has recently been thrown into stark relief by the global economic crisis, which makes clear not only that the market alone cannot maintain employment and incomes, but also that the commitment to dignified welfare standards as a citizen entitlement can be questioned even in industrialised countries. Increasing conflict on the grounds of ethnic, religious, environmental and property inequality in the developing world further underlines the need for fundamental institutional change in order radically to reduce social, political and economic injustice.

This book aims to contribute to the construction of a new policy framework to address these issues, by building on the foundations established by a pioneer in this field of development studies, Professor Frances Stewart. During her academic career Frances opened up new fields in appropriate technology, human development and social conflict; and this volume has been designed to demonstrate how her colleagues and students have carried forward these lines of enquiry into current research and policy debates. The individual chapters were commissioned from the authors with this objective in mind. The drafts were presented at an international conference in September 2009, to mark Frances's official retirement from Oxford, and were then rewritten in response to the lively debate that ensued. This is, therefore, no ordinary *festschrift*, but rather a substantial contribution to an ongoing research and policy conversation of vital importance to all our futures.

The book has three main sections. The first (Part II) focuses on technology, employment and growth: this was the first major topic on which Frances did pioneering work in the 1960s and 1970s, and the creation of technology and its relation to employment remains central to questions of poverty and inequality today. The second (Part III) concerns human development, income distribution and poverty, a topic to which Frances made major research and policy contributions in the 1980s and 1990s. This, too, is a subject with enormous resonance today, as we approach the target date for the Millennium Development Goals. The third main section (Part IV) moves on to issues relating to conflict, ethnicity and inequality, a topic which Frances has pioneered more recently in her work on 'horizontal' or group inequalities and political violence.

The Introduction outlines the volume and its key insights in the present chapter, which is complemented by an intellectual biography of Frances Stewart provided by John Toye in Chapter 2. This chapter demonstrates not only her enormous creativity as a scholar, but also the key role she has played (and continues to play) in international development policy debates over some four decades. Indeed, the growth of her own ideas reflects (or perhaps is reflected in) the evolving debates – particularly within the United Nations system, where her influence has perhaps been greatest – on the broadening of the concept of development itself, from one focused mainly on economic growth and structure, through concepts of human development and inequality, to notions of human security and social inclusion. Last but not least, Toye underlines Frances's remarkable contributions as a teacher of development studies and a builder of research institutions, not only in Oxford but across the world.

Part II: Technical change and economic development

Technology is clearly central to economic development: not only as a key driver of economic growth, but also as one of the central characteristics of society itself since the Enlightenment – the social application of knowledge to improving the human condition. Development is about knowledge embedded in people or in firms (in the broad sense of collective human endeavours). Technical change has generally been understood to be about firms – who are the agents who undertake investment and embody technology – and these in turn are the main actors in markets, which largely define modern society. It is not surprising, therefore, that the study of technical change in both developing and developed countries focuses on institutions rather than on drivers such as relative prices or demand expectations, which are central to neo-classical and Keynesian views of economic behaviour in general and investment decisions in particular.

However, as Frances pointed out some forty years ago in her seminal contribution on technology and development (Stewart, 1972), firms cannot be considered in isolation because externalities, indivisibilities, scale economies and, above all, technological discontinuities are so extensive in developing (and indeed in developed) countries. These dimensions are precisely those which make economic development so difficult and require public intervention. Moreover, the indiscriminate transfer of current Western technology (designed for capital-intensive and labour-scarce economies) to developing countries was then felt by most practising development economists to reduce employment creation and to burden the balance of payments. Thus 'intermediate' or 'appropriate' technologies were then widely thought to be more desirable in order to raise economic growth, generate remunerative employment, and reduce import requirements.

Neither the process of industrialisation nor the attack on poverty in developing countries followed this course during the succeeding decades for a number of reasons. These included the global trend towards more open, market-led economies; the shift of poverty-reduction focus by aid agencies away from employment towards basic needs provision; the international financial institutions' emphasis on export-led growth rather than import substitution; and the enthusiasm among newly industrialising nations for moving up the modern technology ladder. Meanwhile academic research and policy debate on the economics of technology and development also moved away from the original interest in choice of technique, as the three chapters in this volume by Frances's colleagues clearly demonstrate. This is partly due to the real world changes just mentioned, but also to the far greater availability of comparable quantitative data than was the case when Frances embarked on her research. Nonetheless, the influence of her work on each of the three main approaches has been fundamental.

The first approach has been to track the process of technical change in the aggregate, conventionally measured by changes in total factor productivity (TFP), with particular regard to social development driven by the education of young people (and thus by workforce skills or research capacity), and to the institutions that regulate the market (such as innovation systems or foreign investment law), which in turn determine the success of industrialisation strategies (Stewart, 1987). The long-term effect of these structural factors in East Asia and Latin America is the subject of Chapter 3 by Gus Ranis, Frances's research colleague over many years. The second approach has been to track this process using micro-level databases for individual firms (or 'clusters' of firms), to see how local institutions in the form of infrastructure provision, labour markets or financial access affect their productivity and growth, and to derive from these results the implications for appropriate government policies (Stewart and James, 1982). The quantitative impact of migrant labour markets on the productivity of firms, by size, in Europe at this micro level is taken up by Frances's erstwhile doctoral student, Giorgio Barba Navaretti, in Chapter 4. The third approach has been to examine the qualitative relationship between institutions and firms directly, allowing for a two-way influence, of firms on policy-makers and of policy-makers on firms, so as to understand the 'interest' of both government and business in the process of technical change (Stewart, 1977). This critical focus is applied by Frances's colleague Barbara Harriss-White in Chapter 5 on the political economy of technology and development in the Indian energy sector.

In Chapter 3, Gus Ranis, Mallory Irons and Yanjing Huang examine the sources of technology change, that is TFP growth, at the national level over the long term: research and development (R&D), physical investment, patents, foreign direct investment (FDI), and openness on the one hand; and science and technology (S&T) personnel and education indicators on the other. The empirical analysis of six diverse developing countries – Brazil, China, India, Mexico, Taiwan and South Korea – reveals how the Asian countries have performed more strongly than their Latin American counterparts, not only with respect to TFP growth itself, but also in relation to the key causal factors. The chapter argues convincingly that the benefits of investment in educating and retaining adaptively motivated S&T personnel domestically are substantial. Without such investment, developing countries risk losing such individuals to developed nations with strong programmes and more formal education and research structures.

Japan is a key example of technical education (e.g. in reverse engineering), achieving appropriate adaptation by carefully analysing imported machinery and then changing key elements in consonance with local factor and institutional endowments. Brazil and Mexico, in contrast, have given priority to academic over vocational education at the secondary level and to the humanities over science and engineering at the tertiary level. Low-threshold and short-protection types of patent were useful in converting tacit into explicit technical knowledge for Korea and Taiwan and are correlated with TFP growth, and have also been instrumental in China's later catch-up process. Domestic patents also seem to promote TFP growth in Brazil and Mexico – possibly due to their less dynamic manufacturing export sectors.

Although economic theory would suggest that a high level of domestic capital formation is essential in order to embody new technologies (imported, local or adapted) into production, Ranis's results do not reveal this to be the case. Only in Mexico is the relationship between TFP growth and the investment rate both close and positive; Taiwan seems to have maintained stability in TFP growth at much lower investment rates, while there seems to be little linkage between TFP growth and investment in Korea and Brazil. Indeed, for China and India he argues that high investment rates are not necessarily associated with high rates of TFP growth at all, possibly because very high savings rates have led to rising capital-output ratios and to declining returns on investment in new technologies. He concludes, therefore, that in new theories of endogenous growth the emphasis on human development, and specifically on education, in developing countries is correct, as Frances had argued – but not so much because education affects labour productivity directly as because it improves the *absorptive capacity* of domestic firms. In other words, universal primary education is not enough for sustained growth – which requires increased emphasis on vocational secondary education and, subsequently, on science and technology-oriented tertiary education.

In Chapter 4, Giorgio Barba Navaretti, Gianfranco De Simone, Gianluca Orefice and Angelica Salvi examine the interaction between migrant labour use and offshoring across Europe as alternative strategies to raise firm-level productivity in the manufacturing sector. The chapter employs several data sets on migration, outward investment and firm-level productivity within the EU27 area. These allow the linkages between capital and labour movements and firm-level productivity to be identified in terms of the correlation between the two factor movements and of their relationship to regional productivity at the industry level; and, crucially for the findings on firm size, in terms of the shape of productivity distributions within industry and regions. Analytically, outsourcing and immigrant labour can be usefully seen as alternative means of sourcing foreign labour with a more efficient (from the point of view of the firm) wage-productivity ratio.

However, the overall labour market effects of firm-level decisions (and consequently the implications for wage costs, and thus for the sourcing decision itself) are far from clear. The common supposition is that an increase in the supply of foreign migrants reduces local wages; but this chapter argues that it may instead improve labour productivity, by expanding the variety in the supply of skills in the local labour market and by enhancing complementarities with local capabilities. Indeed, Barba Navaretti also shows that the uses of these two labour sources are highly correlated by region (those with more foreign-born workers also have more offshoring projects), but that the relationship to productivity differs markedly according to the size of the firm. Firm-level productivity is thus clearly affected by migration and offshoring through many different channels, which can operate in opposite directions. For example, the availability of migrants provides less efficient firms with an opportunity to reduce production costs and to avoid exit even in fairly competitive environments. Equally, offshoring is a strategy pursued by the most productive firms to reduce labour costs in their routine operations while retaining research and design skills at home.

Chapter 4 concludes, therefore, that immigration promotes the industrial survival (and convergence) of weaker firms and regions within Europe, so that immigration restrictions may undermine the very sectors that government policy aims to support through measures ostensibly designed to promote small and medium enterprise in order to sustain domestic employment and local economies. In contrast, policies limiting offshoring might slow down productivity improvements driven by the most productive firms, and thus technological progress in the stronger sectors and regions of Europe.

In Chapter 5, Barbara Harriss-White addresses the political economy of solar energy in India, in a bold attempt to situate technical change in the politics of markets – themselves embedded, in turn, within state policies and social institutions. This approach goes not only beyond the firm-level decision model criticised by Frances forty years ago, but also beyond the 'national innovation systems' approach to industrial policy espoused by organisations such as the United Nations Industrial Development Organisation (UNIDO). It also contrasts sharply with the approaches taken in Chapters 3 and 4, which see state intervention and social structures as largely exogenous to the industrial sector itself. The author's analysis of the extremely slow pace of technical change represented by solar energy uptake in India – a particularly appropriate technology for developing countries – is explicitly aimed at identifying the 'political' (as opposed to the 'policy') dimension of the market. Specifically, renewable solar energy represents a superior 'choice of technique' over fossil fuels (oil, gas and coal), but also a difference of capital intensity, because solar has large upfront fixed costs and very low running costs compared with fossil fuels. The established vested interests in capitalist markets can then determine how technical change is embodied.

India has an impressive engineering establishment by international standards, and technological change is not obstructed by patent law, as observed by Ranis in Chapter 3. Rather it is the pattern of domestic subsidies, the reluctance of banks to lend for solar projects, unstable tariff prospects and coordination failures between different parts of the generation and distribution system which lock India's energy system into fossil-fuel technologies, which in turn dominate public support and infrastructure. In Chapter 5, Harriss-White argues that an appropriate (i.e. renewable) energy strategy would require an 'alternative political economy', because non-marginal structural change is needed due to a technological system that has developed internal structural and social inconsistencies through incremental change. Market forces alone cannot create the new institutions (and destroy the old ones) for a change tantamount to a 'new industrial revolution'.

The response to global climate change given by India and other developing countries clearly requires a radical and rapid shift in technology. What Harriss-White shows is that the macro-level strategy changes required imply a confrontation with technological systems constructed by specific political interests vested in existing arrangements – reflected not just in policy statements (indeed the Indian government's discourse is committed to solar energy), but rather in a vast and interlocking array of regulations, subsidies, tariffs in the public sector and, perhaps even more importantly, practices of bank lending, profit extraction and asset ownership in the private sector. Much the same might be said for the failure to invest in vocational and scientific training in Latin America identified in Chapter 3, or for the belief that immigration controls will benefit local employment in Europe, discussed in Chapter 4.

Part III: Human development, income distribution and poverty

The move from a focus on income poverty to a focus on human development represented a radical shift in international thinking about development that took place from the late 1970s to the early 1990s. This shift changed views regarding both the meaning of development and ways of achieving it. In this move, human development was seen first and foremost as having intrinsic value, and this was continuously stressed by Frances and others. The fact that it also had instrumental value had equally important implications for development strategies and policies.

From the mid-1970s to the early 1990s, development economists were heavily influenced by the work on human development and poverty that was led by Amartya Sen, Mahbub ul Haq and Frances Stewart, in partnership with Andrea Cornia. Their work helped shift development thinking from a focus on income poverty, with all its limitations, to a much broader concern with human development and human capabilities. The 'sea-change' from the earlier decades was the explicit questioning of values and conceptions of poverty. Two strands developed, in productive dialogue with each other: one was pragmatic and policy-focused (Stewart), and is perhaps best represented by the well-known statement 'Adjustment with a Human Face' (Cornia et al., 1987); the other (led by Sen) sought to understand the philosophical and ethical grounding of people's choices and their implications for welfare. Frances's contributions focused on the links between human development and growth strategies and on the design of policies that would foster them, while Sen and others focused more on the definition and meaning of human development. Many of Frances's students benefited from the creative tension between these two influential bodies of work.

Chapter 6 by Séverine Deneulin, which opens Part III, is by another of Frances's doctoral students who took Sen-type insights forward, with a Stewart-style drive for practical outcomes. Deneulin opens with a theoretical discussion of the dynamics of the formation of values that underpin the human development approach and of the way in which these values influence policies and vice versa – a somewhat neglected topic in the literature on human development and capabilities. She shows how different sets of values lead to different sets of policies and therefore to distinct human development outcomes. Values are themselves determined by political, economic and social processes; groups act as drivers of value changes because people draw their values from groups to which they belong. The author proceeds to show how value changes occur through the changing power of different groups in society and through conflicts between these different groups, making the Stewart-like point that value changes are often the result of conflict between groups, conflict which may or may not be violent in any particular case.

Deneulin argues perceptively that groups and the power configurations within which they operate are shaped by the wider macro-environment, as Frances had suggested earlier (Stewart, 2002). She uses this framework to analyse the introduction of policies fostering human development at four critical historical junctures in Costa Rica since the late nineteenth century. The introduction of each set of new policies fostering human development came about through a particular configuration of groups, in which those with values conducive to human development dominated. This approach has fascinating implications for the determinants of 'policy ownership' in terms of nurturing the groups which hold these values, and thus the political role of NGOs in developing countries.

The value set that is dominant in a society as a whole at any one time clearly frames social policy, as the latter is expressed in government welfare programmes. In Chapter 7, Thandika Mkandawire addresses the implications of the fact that the literature on social policy in developing countries was constructed pragmatically, in response to evident material shortcomings and in relative isolation from the theory of social policy and welfare regimes in European countries. He argues that these two literatures would benefit from more interaction, and he shows that debates going back to the 1950s are still highly relevant in the context of contemporary neoliberalism and reactions to it. He discusses a number of reasons for mutual neglect between the two literatures. The first set of reasons, discussed under the heading 'OECD biases', comes from what Mkandawire calls 'normative dissonance' regarding instrumentalism on the one hand and top-down approaches to social policy on the other. Another 'OECD bias' is the fact that social policy is defined rather differently in developing countries, where policies such as land reform are included in social policy side by side with more familiar themes such as health and education. The paucity of statistics to measure the impact of social policy in the developing countries context is another barrier to communication, because of the epistemic role of 'evidence-based policy' in social democracies. The second set of reasons for mutual neglect, grouped under the heading 'developing country biases', includes the view that development requires the suppression of consumption in the interest of investment and growth, a view inimical to social policy. This view dominated mainstream thinking in the 1950s and the 1960s, notwithstanding critical contributions by leading theorists such as Lewis, Myrdal and Sen. It was not helpful that cross-country comparison showed developing countries with progressive social policies (e.g., India) doing much less well in terms of economic growth than those without (e.g., a number of East Asian countries) at that time.

Mkandawire next addresses the linear view of history, which holds that social policy is the culmination of development, with the implication that social policy is unaffordable in poor countries. This in turn requires re-examination of the tension between productivist views of social policy (such as those held by the World Bank) on the one hand and progressive views that privilege non-instrumentalism (i.e. citizen rights) on the other, the latter being almost an axiom of the European literature on social policy and welfare regimes. A related factor is that, historically, social policy has been much easier to introduce in association with wage labour, not only due to trades union influence but also because it is easier to provide social services to employees organised around factories or their associated towns. In consequence, there is a real danger of segmentation if such policies are introduced for wage labour in developing countries, despite the historical fact that these policies have usually been extended to become universalist at a later stage.

Chapter 7 closes with a discussion of the failure to link economic strategy with social policy in the developing country literature, despite the lessons of endogenous growth theory on the one hand, and those of the empirical links between human development and growth (Ranis et al., 2000) on the other. It is ironic, therefore, that those defending the welfare state against current attacks in Europe highlight the extent to which welfare state policies have supported economic growth and stability, while those defending social policy in developing countries are arguing that reduced state welfare provision threatens citizen inclusion and ultimately leads to civil unrest.

The third chapter in Part III, Chapter 8, by Giovanni Andrea Cornia and Bruno Martorano, revisits a theme brought to the fore in *Adjustment with a Human Face*, on which Cornia worked with Frances for UNICEF in the mid-1980s (Cornia et al., 1987). It examines the effects of recent policies to improve human development and to reduce poverty in Latin America in the early twenty-first century. The authors explore the extent to which the reduction of inequality, recorded in Latin America between 2002 and 2007, after a long period of continuous increase, has been induced by domestic policy as opposed to favourable external circumstances. They discuss the drivers of the observed reduction in inequality suggested by economic theory, and they then attempt to provide econometric support for these drivers. The variables reflecting present favourable external conditions (terms of trade, migration and remittances, and the availability of external finance) do not appear to be statistically significant themselves, although they may be so through their effect on GDP. In contrast, the policies of 'Left-of-Centre' governments seem to have had a significant impact: these include managed exchange rates, counter-cyclical fiscal policies, reduced dependence on foreign capital, accumulation of foreign exchange reserves and active labour and social policies.

The authors' analysis leads them to conclude that recent gains in inequality reduction have been due more to public policy than to external conditions, and that Left-of-Centre governments have achieved greater reductions than others. The chapter ends with a discussion of the 2008/09 financial crisis, which does not appear to have raised inequality as much as might have been feared, but which does imply that some of the changes that have taken place are structural and provide a basis for future gains. However, Cornia underlines the need for a continuation and deepening of the policies embarked upon, if the trend of decreasing inequality is to be sustained during a period of low growth. He is cautiously optimistic – raising the real possibility of reversing the increase in inequality that has dogged Latin American countries since Independence. This analysis clearly has considerable implications for other middle-income regions, where there is policy space for this kind of shift.

The three chapters in Part III thus make very different contributions to the discussion of the pursuit of human development and inequality and poverty reduction in developing countries that has been central to Frances's work throughout her career. Chapter 6, with its emphasis on changing societal values as a prerequisite to changing policies and with its analysis of how these changing values might come about, suggests an area which policy-makers and analysts tend to neglect. The emphasis in Chapter 7 on the need for a better understanding of the links between social policy and development strategy, and thus on the improved design and implementation of policies that build on these links, makes a strong case for considering social policy as an integral part of a successful development strategy. Chapter 8, by revealing the factors behind recent decreases in inequality in Latin America, suggests that significant improvements in human development and reductions in inequality and poverty are achievable through the right mix of public policies, but that a corresponding political stance in government is also necessary.

Part IV: Conflict, ethnicity and inequality

The chapters in the final section all focus on inequality, and all reflect a deep concern that inequality, particularly that between groups of people, is a prime source of violent conflict. All are written by members of the Centre for Research on Inequality, Human Security and

Ethnicity (CRISE), a research centre funded by the Department for International Development (DFID) and led by Frances until 2010.[1] Three of the authors (Graham Brown, Arnim Langer and Ukoha Ukiwo) have completed their doctorates with Frances, within the CRISE framework, and the fourth (Raufu Mustapha) is a senior colleague in the CRISE programme.

The work of the centre brings together two developing strands of Frances's thinking and research. First, there is her work on war and its economic causes (Stewart, Fitzgerald, and Associates, 2001), and, second, her conviction about the importance of groups (already signalled in Deneulin's preceding chapter). As Frances makes clear (Stewart, 2002), economics has done the world little service historically by its pretence that reality can be modelled 'as if' all actors were individuals. The need to pay attention to group identities and the inequalities between groups – horizontal rather than vertical inequalities – has important implications for understanding the root causes of violence and therefore for policy in relation to conflict – both with respect to how policy is shaped and with respect to how it is implemented. This conviction has shaped Frances's leadership of an essentially multidisciplinary team, as is evidenced in the chapters in this section. Each member comes principally from a politics and political economy perspective, but each one reflects an awareness which has grown with time within the team: if we want to understand how policy gets made (which is indeed fundamental to shifting horizontal inequalities), then we need to study not only policies, the theory behind them and the public sector from which they spring, but also civil society, a neglected aspect of conflict work. The first chapter, by Graham Brown, focuses directly on this issue, with a reflective piece on the nature of civil society. The second, by Arnim Langer and Ukoha Ukiwo, explores the perceptions of different groups in civil society, to understand better the contribution of the horizontal inequalities (HI) framework. The third, by Abdul Raufu Mustapha, reflects on a controversial equity strategy, namely affirmative action, and shows how such policies need a responsive civil society if they are to be effective.

Thus the first chapter, by Graham Brown, confronts directly the role of civil societies in providing and contesting a public understanding of HIs. Brown develops a useful conceptual discussion of civil society and social capital, using it to distinguish two broad approaches to thinking about the relation between horizontal inequalities and civil society. The first he describes as a 'social capital approach', which leads to a framing of the issues in terms of the causal relationship between horizontal inequalities and the level of 'social capital'. This approach, he suggests, sees civil society as 'mediating' the impact of horizontal inequalities on conflict. The alternative, less explored, but for him, we suspect, the more interesting, is to see civil society's role as one of contesting and shaping a public understanding of horizontal inequality. In his analysis, this contestation is composed of challenges to accuracy, meaning and tolerability – the degree to which inequality is seen as socially tolerable.

Brown then uses empirical work to explore each conceptual approach more concretely. The first approach can be explored econometrically. He tests the relation between horizontal inequalities and the level of 'social capital' in society (social capital being measured by levels of trust), finding a suggestive negative relationship between horizontal inequality and social trust. The second approach requires case study investigation. He explores a potent example of how civil society, in this case Malaysian, may contest and shape the public understanding of horizontal inequalities. Throughout, the complexity and internal divisions of 'civil society' are highlighted. Beginning in the 1960s, he traces the processes of contestation of a pivotal component of Malaysian affirmative action: equity between ethnic groups in company shareholding. He finds that contestation around accuracy of data and tolerability has probably had more impact, but contestation over meaning has been more deeply progressive in nature.

The next chapter, by Arnim Langer and Ukoha Ukiwo, evaluates the role of HI analysis in helping us understand (i) what makes young people join a group overtly practising political violence; and (ii) what is the role played by their communities. It studies the Niger Delta as an instance of severe conflict and inequality, and it reports the results of two surveys, one of ex-militants (for obvious reasons the authors did not survey militants) and a second one of community members. The principal aim in the first survey was to find out why the militants chose the route of militancy. In the second, the aim was to detect the degree of support for militants and the community's view of their motivation. The sampling of two different groups, ex-militants and community members, allows a fine-tuned exploration of apparent differences and contradictions. The HI approach, by opening up the discussion so as to take in both group and individual perceptions and motivations, allows for a richer examination and a more solidly based set of policy prescriptions than those afforded by essentially single-factor analyses, such as what have become known as 'greed' or 'grievance' models. Those ex-militants interviewed were frequently concerned to improve their own and their family's position, but *at the same time* they had a structural view of injustice and the sources of poverty and felt motivated by that. Over 80 per cent of the community members saw 'unfair distribution of oil resources' and 'socioeconomic marginalisation' as very important causes of militancy, even if they *also* understood that some young people were acting from self-interest. The community was not entirely supportive of the militants – a finding contrary to that of earlier work – but not over-whelmingly negative, nevertheless. Given a binary choice over whether they saw the militants positively or negatively, 40 per cent saw them as 'Niger Delta heroes', 50 per cent as 'greedy criminals'.

The highest consensus on all sides was over the importance of creating jobs as the key policy towards reducing militancy: employment is valued within a greed or grievance framework anyway, but under-pinning the view was, typically, quite a structuralist understanding in terms of justice. The authors use this perception to underline the value of the HI approach: 'unlike the "greed" model that would result only in a recommendation that employment be provided for youths...the horizontal inequalities perspective would support youth employment alongside fundamental changes aimed at promoting more social inclusion'.

A key CRISE finding is that inequalities between groups, or HIs, make political violence more probable. In the final chapter, there-fore, Abdul Raufu Mustapha tackles the issue of what to do about HIs, taking the controversial policy of affirmative action and exploring two recent programmes, in Nigeria and South Africa. Affirmative action is always controversial, since it is feared it will have perverse consequences, increasing awareness of ethnic differences and thereby resentment. The cases of the two countries are very different in the nature of their HIs, as South Africa's historically overlaps with class, while Nigeria's overlap with region. Mustapha shows how this difference has led to very different affirmative action policies, one focused on political inequality and one on economic inequality. In South Africa it was implicitly assumed that equity of political representation would be ensured once apartheid was ended, while economic opportunity was clearly anything but evenly distributed, so the 'Broad-based Black Economic Empowerment' programme put in place four mechanisms to increase economic opportunity for black people from 2003. In Nigeria, the key sensitivity was, historically, the equalisation of political representation for the different regions, so a quota system as developed and implemented through the Federal Character Principle was the logical measure to take for building equity.

Mustapha shows that, according to the quantitative indicators, neither programme has been particularly successful so far; however, to focus only on such indicators would be to miss the point. In both cases, the political commitment represented by the policies has been fundamental in shifting the culture and thereby in reducing the risk of political violence. Such results justify the risks – which, he says, must indeed be evaluated and countered. The quantitative indicators, he argues, need time to shift significantly – indeed, Nigeria's own experience in the 1970s with measures to increase the place of nationals in the economy demonstrates just this. Finally, Mustapha returns to the civil society theme: state action needs to be complemented by civil society through its commitment to developing the necessary skills and to monitoring and consolidating the shift in culture.

Three characteristics stand out in the chapters in this final section, and they represent well the evolution of the discipline of development studies. First, all are multidisciplinary in approach; second, all draw on qualitative and quantitative evidence; and, third, all point to the importance of collective identity in shaping outcomes. We are both individuals and members of groups, usually several groups, and the fortunes of 'our' group – its affirmation or discrimination against, the injustices it may suffer – matter to us. The need to pay attention to group identities and to inequalities between groups – horizontal rather than vertical inequalities – has important implications both for how policy is shaped and for how it is implemented. Finally, the work in this section shows how contemporary development studies is evolving; it also demonstrates the role that Frances still plays as an intellectual mentor. This latter theme is developed by Toye in the following chapter.

Note

1. It has now become an international research network (www.crise.ox.ac.uk).

References

Cornia, G.A., R. Jolly and F. Stewart (1987) *Adjustment with a Human Face* (Oxford: Clarendon Press).

Ranis, G., F. Stewart and A. Ramirez (2000) 'Economic Growth and Human Development'. *World Development* 28 (2): 197–219.

Stewart, F. (1972) 'Choice of Technique in Developing Countries'. *Journal of Development Studies* 9 (1): 99–121.

Stewart, F. (1977) *Technology and Underdevelopment* (London: Macmillan).

Stewart, F. (1987) *Macro-Policies for Appropriate Technology* (London: Westview).

Stewart, F. (2002) 'Dynamic Interactions Between the Macroenvironment, Development Thinking and Group Behaviour'. In J. Heyer, F. Stewart and R. Thorp (eds) *Group Behaviour and Development* (Oxford: Oxford University Press).

Stewart, F., V. FitzGerald and Associates (2001) *War and Underdevelopment* (Oxford: Oxford University Press).

Stewart, F., and J. James (eds) (1982) *The Economics of New Technology in Developing Countries* (Oxford: Frances Pinter).

2
Social Wellbeing and Conflict: Themes from the Work of Frances Stewart

*John Toye**

> *World is crazier and more of it than we think,*
> *incorrigibly plural.*
>
> Louis MacNeice

2.1 Early years

Frances Stewart was born in Kendal in August 1940. She had a famous father, the economist Nicholas Kaldor, who in 1950 moved his family from London to a new home in west Cambridge. As a young woman, Frances came to feel that having a famous economist as a father was not wholly a blessing if one was interested in economics oneself. She preferred not to discuss her opinions on economics with her father, because she feared he would say either 'I have thought of that myself already' or 'it is wrong', and she was not anxious to hear either message. At the same time, her father repeatedly insisted that she was clever enough to think out problems for herself, and this positive message was confidence-building and intellectually empowering for her.

Her mother was Clarissa Goldschmidt, daughter of a stockbroker, herself a brilliant history graduate of Somerville College, Oxford, whom Kaldor had married in 1934. Clarissa's gift to Frances was her social and political commitment and her willingness to campaign publicly for what she believed in: she was a lifelong active supporter of the Labour Party. Even after Nicky had been elevated as Lord Kaldor, she was still Comrade Clarissa.

After doing well at Cambridgeshire High School for Girls, Frances went to Oxford to study politics, philosophy and economics (PPE).

Following her mother to Somerville, she had economics tuition from Margaret Hall, a Fellow and a University Lecturer,[1] and from Paul Streeten. She had philosophy tuition from Elizabeth Anscombe and Philippa Foot; philosophy was exciting for Frances, and at one time she contemplated becoming a philosopher. Paul Streeten was asked by her father to discourage this enthusiasm, and eventually Frances concluded that philosophising all day and every day might be rather too much of a good thing. She decided to stick with the economics option, won both Junior and Senior Webb Medley Prizes and was awarded a First Class in her Finals. Frances was offered a tutorial post at Lady Margaret Hall while she was still in her third year, but she turned it down. A second academic offer was a studentship at Nuffield College, but she decided that at that point she wanted to do something other than take more exams.

She joined the Economic Section of the Treasury in 1961. Her motivation was clear, if overambitious: it was to change single-handedly the economic policy of the Conservative government of Harold Macmillan. Initially, she was assigned to work with Ralph Turvey on taxation issues, but she did not find him to be a good boss. She quickly realised that it was not easy for one person, on her own, to influence government policy. After an unsatisfactory four months she was recruited by Sir Donald MacDougall to work with him and two others at the National Economic Development Council (NEDC). It was an eventful period, when the NEDC was concerned with setting target growth rates for the UK economy and with exploring possible strategies to raise the UK growth rate. She moved with MacDougall into the newly established Department of Economic Affairs, after Labour's election victory under Harold Wilson in 1964.

2.2   Research in Kenya

There are many different ways in which a lifelong interest in development economics can be acquired. Women economists who have economist husbands sometimes find themselves living in a developing country on his account. That was what had happened to Joan Robinson, when her husband Austin was resident tutor to the Maharajah of Gwalior in 1926–27. Something similar happened with Frances, who before 1967 had never worked on questions of economic development.

She had met and married Michael Stewart, an Economic Adviser in the Treasury, who was transferred to No. 10 Downing Street when

Thomas Balogh moved there from the Cabinet Office.[2] Michael had long advocated the devaluation of sterling, and by 1967 both he and Balogh had lost patience with Harold Wilson's refusal to devalue, so Michael resigned. On the advice of Dudley Seers, he took a post as Economic Adviser to the Finance Minister of Kenya. Frances and the children went to Kenya with him, as dependants. Michael did not know the Minister beforehand and in the event found that he did not really get on with him.

Kenya was the place where Frances's interest in the economics of development crystallised. She joined the University of East Africa (Nairobi) as a Lecturer in the Economics Department. Judith Heyer, a friend from undergraduate days, was already there and organised the appointment. Judith and Frances have been lifelong friends and associates. Judith introduced Frances to Philip Ndegwa and Dharam Ghai. There was a constant stream of interesting development economists who gave seminars at the university, such as the young Joseph Stiglitz, Gerry Helleiner, Richard Jolly and others. While in Nairobi, Frances read Gunnar Myrdal's mammoth *Asian Drama* (1968) and was greatly impressed by its perspectives. She now regretted that she had not embarked on a doctorate. She decided that it was something that should be tackled and began the task even without having a supervisor appointed.

Development economics was at a moment of change. The neoclassical growth model's assumption of a single, universally available technology and the paradigm of modernisation through industrialisation on the Western pattern were both losing their credibility with development economists. George McRobie, a great friend of Michael and best man at his and Frances's wedding, was a disciple of E. F. Schumacher and had enthusiastically discussed the idea of intermediate technology as a solution to the development problem with the Stewarts when they were still in London. So an important theme of the moment was the development potential of a technology that was intermediate between the modern technology imported from the West and the existing labour-intensive but low-productivity technology used by the traditional sector. Frances decided to investigate the validity of the ideas that George McRobie had advocated. She chose to undertake case studies of the cement brick industry and maize-grinding industry, and began to collect data on them that would be needed for her planned doctorate. She put forward her research plans at Nairobi seminars, to gather reactions from the development economists to what she was doing.

2.3   Choice of technique

Returning to Britain, Frances registered for a DPhil at Oxford and embarked on a research project on technology and development funded by the Ministry of Overseas Development. Paul Streeten, himself a recent convert to the study of developing economies through his association with Gunnar Myrdal and *Asian Drama*, became her doctoral supervisor. Streeten, like Myrdal, was critical of many of the existing practices of development planning in poor countries and of the intellectual narrowness of a purely economic approach to the study of development.

Frances herself was certainly critical of the neoclassical model and of its implications for the theory of the choice of technique. Its assumption that the number of efficient techniques available is unlimited, permitting any combination of capital and labour and thus (given flexible prices of these factors) the attainment of full employment, seemed to her quite unrealistic in the context of developing countries. Basing herself on the history of technological development and on her industry case studies from Kenya, she argued that the vintage of machinery was important, because older machines were more labour-intensive and thus in older industries the choice of technique was greater. Yet later machines tended to be more productive on account of scientific and technical advances. Since later machines were normally designed to produce a greater scale of output, earlier machines could sometimes remain efficient when the required scale of output was small. Thus she concluded that the range of efficient techniques available to developing countries was likely to be more restricted than the neoclassical model assumed, although less restricted than a technological determinist would assert – there was usually more than a single efficient method, the one currently installed in the West.

En passant, Frances made a number of important conceptual points about the choice of technique debate. She saw that the question of the choice of technique was rarely separable from that of the choice of product: different machines tended to produce somewhat different products. So the definition of the 'product' mattered in the debate. If 'product' was defined widely, say, in terms of function or of the ability to fulfil needs such as shelter or food, the choice of technique might seem extensive (Stewart, 1973: p. 117). If 'product' was defined narrowly, say, in terms of a precise physical specification, the choice of technique would seem very restricted.

The proposition that older machines were more labour-intensive was derived from the belief that most innovation takes place in developed countries, where labour is scarce relative to capital. It implies that transfer of current Western technology to developing countries may have adverse consequences for employment. This was not a novel proposition (see for example Henry Bruton, 1955: pp. 322–36), but it meant that the theme of employment was already encompassed in Frances's work on choice of technique. The policy objective of intermediate technology advocates was to create additional employment, but employment that was more productive, and therefore more remunerative, than was possible with the traditional technology.

The 1972 International Labour Organization (ILO) Employment mission took her back to Kenya, with a team of economists led by Richard Jolly and Hans Singer, which included Dharam Ghai and Keith Griffin. Her contribution was relatively minor, as one would expect from a junior member of the team – a paper on Kenya's tripartite mechanism – but she found the whole process, including the non-stop team discussions, most exciting.

2.4   Social cost–benefit analysis

In 1972 Frances became a Senior Research Officer at the Institute of Commonwealth Studies (ICS) in Oxford, the appointing committee consisting of Wilfrid Knapp, Thomas Balogh, David Fieldhouse and Ian Little. This appointment was followed by a non-stipendiary fellowship at Somerville College in 1975, which meant that she was not on the treadmill of undergraduate economics teaching. The Oxford economics scene in the early 1970s was rather sharply divided politically. Streeten and Balogh were both on the left of the spectrum, while others – like Walter Eltis, Maurice Scott and Ian Little – were on the right. Ian Little and James Mirrlees had just produced, for the OECD Development Centre, their manual on industrial cost–benefit analysis for developing countries (1968). The manual acted as something of a lightning rod for the ideological divisions of Oxford economists, which were displayed in a special issue of the *Bulletin of the Oxford Institute of Economics and Statistics*. Together with Streeten, Frances wrote an article that faulted the Little–Mirrlees method on a variety of grounds: its limited applicability, its assumption of full capacity working of capital equipment, its ignoring of externalities and so on (Stewart and Streeten, 1972). Their critique of neoclassical applied welfare economics was taken badly by some of Frances's and Streeten's economist colleagues in Oxford. Frances thought that these colleagues' displeasure was an obstacle to the progression of her career, but other factors may have played a part in obstructing it. Her wish to live in London and to work half-time from 1976 to 1984 may have given the university an impression of semi-detachment. The rising tide of algebra and econometrics in economics also pushed political economists in Oxford, as elsewhere, towards the margins of the subject.

She followed up with another critical article on social cost–benefit analysis (SCBA) (Stewart, 1975). Having contested some of the technical assumptions behind the recommended SCBA calculation procedure, Frances now went straight to its heart – the incoherent political rationale for SCBA. Starting from Kenneth Arrow's theorem on the impossibility of aggregating diverse preferences while satisfying minimum democratic criteria, she noted that both Little–Mirrlees and the rival United Nations Industrial Develoment Organisation (UNIDO) manual relied on governments to establish the social valuations that were to be used to adjust cash flow calculations based on market prices. She then asked: if governments could enforce decisions made on the basis of their social valuations, why could they not adjust actual prices by fiscal and regulatory measures and thereby render social cost–benefit analysis redundant? Her answer was that they could not do the latter because they were constrained by a multitude of political pressures. However, if that was so, she concluded, they would be no more able to make Olympian social valuations stick in their project selection procedures, once the politically powerful had realised what the cost–benefit technicians were up to.

The significance of this paper in Frances's thinking lies in its assertion that there is no realm above the political fray from which decisions that maximise social welfare can be conjured. Such a radical view has consequences both for planners and for free market advocates. If SCBA is envisaged as the microeconomic extension of a system of aggregate planning, micro-planners are revealed as relying on a naïve assumption of omnipotent and benevolent governments. If that assumption is rejected in favour of the claim that markets maximise social welfare when allowed to operate freely, such a claim requires a prior social agreement that the current distribution of income is optimal – an agreement that rarely exists. Her rejection of the idea of benevolent governments thus gives no warrant for the theories and policies of neoliberalism. Instead, it puts a premium on the economist acting as an advocate, consciously operating as part of the political fray rather than trying to stand above it. This key insight informed the rest of Frances's career.

2.5 The basic needs approach

When Frances was granted a sabbatical year in 1978–79, she chose to work with Paul Streeten, who had left Oxford for the World Bank (WB) in 1976. At the WB, the President, Robert McNamara, was then on the lookout for new ideas and had picked up the ILO theme of basic needs. The WB's work on basic needs was not located in Hollis Chenery's Research Department, but in the Policy Planning Division, run by the Pakistani economist Mahbub ul Haq. Paul Streeten had persuaded Mahbub ul Haq of the importance of the basic needs idea and suggested that Frances be involved in it.

This was the starting point for two important intellectual collaborations in Frances's professional life. The first was with Mahbub ul Haq, with whose qualities she was quickly impressed. He was a powerful animator of teamwork, who picked up interesting developmental ideas, had a way of conveying their excitement to others and was able to synthesise the contributions that others made to developing them. He could draw others into energetic participation and yet maintain the overall organisation of the project intact. He always had some new, grand project on the horizon. Frances enjoyed working with him and continued to do so, even during the time he was President Zia's Finance Minister in Pakistan, until his death in 1998.

On basic needs, Frances worked with Gus Ranis, John Fei and Norman Hicks. Ranis and Fei contributed to the macroeconomic and planning framework of the Basic Needs (BN) approach (Stewart, 1985b: chapters 2 and 3). This was the start of an enduring research partnership with Gus Ranis. Ranis might not have seemed the obvious lifetime professional collaborator for Frances, since he was (and is) more of a mainstream economist than she. Nevertheless, they have a shared field of interests – in poverty reduction, inequality and redistribution, and the human development paradigm. Further, successful collaboration is based as much on knowing how to collaborate and on sharing an open mind about how exactly development takes place as on a pre-existing identity of views about development economics. There is no fixed pattern for their collaboration; both work on theoretical and on empirical material, as the task requires.

Initially, Dharam Ghai and the ILO had generated the idea of 'basic needs'. The original idea had a strong Aristotelian flavour; it was specified as comprising all the components of a full life, including personal autonomy, as well as commodities. However, the application of this idea was, as befits a Policy Planning Department, aimed at getting the condition of the poor onto the international agenda. For this purpose the phrase 'basic needs' sounded more urgent and more likely to get political attention than 'basic desires' or 'basic wants'.

At roughly the same time Amartya Sen started developing his notion of capabilities as a measure of positive freedom. He was critical of the basic needs strategy as a form of commodity fetishism, since different people consumed more commodities in order to achieve the same level of functioning. Physically disabled people, for example, would need more commodities (e.g., mobility scooters) than the able-bodied to achieve the same level of mobility functioning, and there were other conditions that caused differences in individuals' needs for commodities relative to achieved functioning (Sen, 1984: p. 280). Sen argued that an increase in human capabilities was the true objective of development; thus he thought that the basic needs strategy was misconceived, because it focused on means rather than ends. Yet Sen parried requests – received from those convinced of the rightness of this view – that he should develop the capabilities approach as an operational programme.

By contrast, the basic needs strategy was primarily a practical endeavour. Unlike Sen's capabilities, it was intended to be made into an operational policy programme. The idea was to construct a meta-production function for the purposes of economic planning that would relate a set of specific inputs to a measure of welfare distinct from average income, setting up a series of basic needs to be remitted to government departments, in order for the latter to formulate appropriate policies for meeting them. The intention was never essentially philosophical, as was Sen's. It was an attempt to advise planners and government ministries on how to do something for the poor, rather than to change the way that people applied ethical principles to issues of distribution.

The dissonance between the basic needs approach and the capabilities discourse was thus, in part, caused by crossed purposes. That was not the whole of it, however. Even in relation to changing people's thinking, Frances found something unresolved about Sen's capability approach. She struggles with Sen's concept of 'capabilities that one has reason to value', wondering whether it functions as a device to block off the possibility of people wanting to do crazy things and making 'wrong' choices in pursuit of the fully human life – a device similar in purpose to the device of the ghostly auctioneer in Walrasian general equilibrium theory. She also questions whether problems of power can be adequately dealt with by Sen's appeal to the existence of 'a democratic consensus'. In her view of politics, social consensuses hardly ever exist and, when they do, they may or may not be democratic and they may or may not be ignored by those who currently hold the power.

2.6 Adjustment with a human face

Around 1979, the international political tide, which, for decades, had run in favour of social democracy, suddenly turned. Political support for the type of planning approaches Frances had been promoting, and indeed for the whole development planning enterprise, began to ebb. The basic needs strategy lost impetus in the face of the election of Western governments of various degrees of liberalism and conservatism. Their response to the problems of developing countries was to insist on structural adjustment, meaning that developing countries should be told to adjust their economic policies and management to their macroeconomic circumstances in ways to be specified by the International Monetary Fund (IMF) and by the WB.

Poverty reduction as a subject dropped off the international research and advocacy agenda at this time, as economic growth was given priority over income and wealth redistribution. However, child welfare was still widely regarded as a legitimate topic; and this was very important, because the welfare of children was, and remained, highly salient politically for the general public in Western countries. So research on the effect of structural adjustment on children was adopted by the United Nations Children's Fund (UNICEF) as a way of indirectly questioning the validity of IMF/WB forms of structural adjustment itself.

During another sabbatical year in 1985–86, Frances went to UNICEF as a Special Adviser, to work on structural adjustment. Jim Grant acted as the political protector of the work and rebuffed attacks on the group. Because Richard Jolly was too busy to do much of the writing, the main work was done by Andrea Cornia and Frances, with some assistance from collaborators such as Per Pinstrup-Andersen, Richard Longhurst and Gerry Helleiner. In fact, the group had different views about whether structural adjustment was desirable in principle, and the issue was never fully resolved internally. What united them was a tactical belief that, if they publicly attacked the principle of structural adjustment head-on, the rug would be pulled from underneath their project, Jim Grant's protection notwithstanding. Their tactics were therefore to begin by conceding the necessity of structural adjustment at the macro-level, as previous UN expert groups had done (e.g. UNCTAD, 1965: pp. 1–8). Then they argued that it should not be undertaken as a 'big bang' – the liberalisation of everything, all at once – as had happened, with negative social consequences, in Bolivia. Rather, it should be implemented in a phased manner, which would reduce the costs of adjustment. Phasing would give people time enough to make their own adjustments to announced measures of liberalisation before the government policy changes came into effect.

Frances's main conceptual contribution was the idea of the 'meso-level', an intermediate domain of decision-making, which lay below macro-policy but above micro-policy. Questioning orthodox macro-economic policy prescriptions might be off limits for the UNICEF team, but at the meso-level its members could point to many types of policy-making that, if properly used, could improve the lives of vulnerable groups. Examples were changes to the composition of public expenditure and to regulatory policies that affect the distribution of incomes in the private sector.

The UNICEF team's proposals for the modification of the orthodox approach to structural adjustment were published under the title *Adjustment with a Human Face* (Cornia et al., 1987). This study was dedicated to the memory of Nicky Kaldor. While the book was careful not to claim that the decline in economic growth and in welfare indicators in the 1980s were wholly attributable to the implementation of adjustment measures, the question of whether the situation would have been worse without the adjustment measures was not really explored. The book caught a public mood of growing disenchantment with the results of a decade of adjustment. In retrospect, its publication can be seen as the highest point to date of UNICEF's influence on international policy. It also changed the nature of the debate on structural adjustment, leading to the reinstatement of poverty reduction onto the international agenda in the 1990s.[3]

Frances did further work on this topic with Gus Ranis and A. Ramirez. In the course of examining the chains that link economic growth to human development and human development to economic growth, in a process of mutual causation, and in the course of examining empirical data, they argued against the view that economic growth must occur before human development expenditure is undertaken. They concluded, 'Our findings do not deny the importance of economic reforms, but emphasize that a focus on human development must be included from the beginning in any reform programme' (Ranis et al., 2000: p. 213).

This challenged the neoliberal wisdom of the 1980s that the sequence of reform had to be economic stabilisation and adjustment first, and human development only later.

2.7   The human development report

The North–South Roundtable was set up in the 1970s by Barbara Ward, and taken over first by Maurice Strong and then by Mahbub ul Haq and Khadija Haq. Frances went to Pakistan in the early 1980s for a Roundtable on foreign debt. One Roundtable was also held on 'Human Factors in Development'; an important stepping stone, leading Mahbub ul Haq to persuade the Administrator of the UNDP to launch the Human Development Report (HDR), so as to publicise the UNDP's new vision of development – 'human development'. The HDR project brought together the advocates of the capabilities approach and of the basic needs strategy, putting them under the common banner of human development, defined as 'a process of enlarging people's choices' (UNDP, 1990: p. 10). Amartya Sen contributed chapter 1 and Frances contributed chapter 2 to the first report.

In fact neither of them was in favour of including in the report the statistical innovation of the Human Development Index, which combined measures of income per head with measures of life expectancy and literacy, to create a composite indicator of human development. It was only Mahbub ul Haq who really championed its inclusion, though others, including Sen, worked on its construction. Mahbub ul Haq correctly foresaw that the index would attract great attention, both on the political scene and from the media (even if most of the academic attention came from those who criticised its method of construction), and that this would give some additional leverage to NGOs' advocacy for diminishing the plight of the poor.

In subsequent research on the theme of human development, done with Gus Ranis and Emma Samman, Frances has moved beyond the confines of the Human Development Index (HDI), which they now describe as 'a reductionist measure', in favour of measures which include political freedom, guaranteed human rights and self-respect (Ranis et al., 2005). This is not an attempt to provide a comprehensive specification of the components of the good life, in the style of Aristotle and Martha Nussbaum (see Goodin, 2000); rather it is the use of a broader range of indicators to investigate whether, in countries or regions, good things go together, and if not, why not. Like Amartya Sen (1999: p. 286), the authors doubt that there can be an overall rule by which development outcomes can be unambiguously ranked.

2.8   War and underdevelopment

Nevertheless, it was her work for the HDR that led Frances into her big project of the 1990s, on the topic of war and underdevelopment.

Having drawn up a table of best performers and worst performers in terms of HDI relative to GNP per capita – that is, a table of the difference between a country's GNP and HDI position – she noticed that the worst performers were mainly countries at war. Although the HDR did not follow up this result, Frances thought that there was much more to be said about this particular correlation.

At this point, Frances became the director of Queen Elizabeth House (QEH) at the University of Oxford (see below). The research project on war and underdevelopment was designed as the academic centrepiece for the re-launch of QEH, an institution that rather badly needed to improve its intellectual standing. Frances's collaborator in this enterprise was Valpy FitzGerald, who had recently joined QEH after being in charge of research at the Institute of Social Studies in The Hague.

Heretofore war had not had a central place in development studies; it tended to be assumed that a poor country at war needed the international community to provide humanitarian relief, while only in peacetime did it need development aid. There had been little academic probing of whether that dichotomy was still valid in the 1990s. Research was beginning at the Centre for the Study of African Economies, Oxford, on the economic incentives that led to outbreaks of civil war (Collier and Hoeffler, 1998). That line of research did not seem likely to address the policy question of the role of development aid during wartime, a topic of interest to some bilateral aid donors, to the Carnegie Endowment and to the UN, which was reappraising its modes of intervention after the Rwanda genocide of 1994. The research focus was placed not on the causes of war, but on its social and economic consequences and their implications for development aid.

Little systematic information existed on the indirect costs of war in terms of declines in output, exports, investment, food production and social expenditures during conflicts. It was valuable in itself to assemble these data, but additionally the study demonstrated, through a series of country case studies, that country experience was quite varied. Where countries' economies and social systems were being eroded by the costs of conflict, however, the study argued that development aid (although in altered form and with varied conditionality) still had a role to play in reducing these costs (Stewart et al., 2001). This was a major new insight, which affected public opinion and government policy.

The war and underdevelopment project was significant as another watershed in Frances's professional development. Up to this point, Frances could be clearly defined as an economist, engaging with central issues of development economics, although not from a mainstream position. Thereafter she moved more into cross-disciplinary areas of research. This was important in institutional terms, because it set up collective tasks on which a new generation of development researchers at QEH could cut their teeth. It also provided an opportunity for sociologists, political scientists and those with a philosophical and conceptual bent (like Sabina Alkire) to work with economists towards providing insights from a range of disciplinary perspectives. More generally, it facilitated the nurturing of a whole new generation of scholars, as the QEH-trained students have gone out to other universities, UN agencies and national governments. The war and underdevelopment project should thus be seen as part of a new chapter, in which Frances's intellectual broadening coincided with her guidance of the reform of QEH.

2.9 Reforming QEH

To be properly understood, Frances's key role in reforming QEH requires a brief flashback to earlier events. When Frances arrived at QEH in 1972,[4] Paul Streeten was by no means a conventional directorial figure. There were no plans for the future development of QEH, which operated as an institution where those in the university working on Commonwealth studies could meet visitors from the Commonwealth. When on sabbatical leave in 1973, Streeten arranged for Keith Griffin, a Fellow of Magdalen College, to deputise for him; but, partly due to pressure from Griffin for a decision about his future and also for personal reasons, Streeten decided to join the World Bank in 1976. During the Streeten era there were only a few Research Officer posts at the ICS – occupied by, apart from Frances, Stanley Trapido working on South Africa and Neville Maxwell working on India and China. Colin Newbury, an economic historian of Commonwealth African states, and Tommy Balogh, recently returned from the Cabinet Office, also had offices at QEH. The main collective academic activities were the weekly QEH seminar in term time, plus a once a term staff meeting at which staff explained to each other their current work. The only students were those on the Foreign Service Programme and on a programme for visiting fellows.[5] QEH became a livelier place when Griffin took over as warden/director in 1977 and generated research project grants that brought in temporary research officers; but he quickly moved back to Magdalen College as President in 1979.

The 1980s were a difficult period for QEH. There were weaknesses in its organisational structure, its financial control and its management.

The Governing Body set up a 'working party' for which Frances wrote a report on reforming QEH (Rainbird and Stewart, 1984). The university decided to develop a centre for international studies and to merge QEH with the ICS and with the Institute for Research in Agricultural Economics (IRAE), making it a university department within the Social Studies Faculty. Robert Cassen from the Institute of Development Studies (IDS), Sussex, was recruited as the new director, on the promise of a very substantial fundraising drive. Much managerial responsibility was placed on the shoulders of the pro-director whom he brought in, Gowher Rizvi. Before very long the university's vice-chancellor was again increasingly drawn into QEH affairs. In a new externally funded unit, a research report was not delivered to the sponsor because of an internal clash over claims to authorship. On investigation, it turned out that one of those involved was using the title of 'Senior Fellow', although he was not an academic and was not employed by the university. He was also operating a QEH bank account independently of the University Chest. Perhaps these were minor misdemeanours, but, for the second time within a decade, QEH had attracted high-level university intervention.

In 1991, the university appointed a committee under Colin Crouch to evaluate QEH and make suggestions for its future. The Crouch Report said that, if its recommendations were not implemented urgently, the ultimate option would be to close down QEH and to disperse the staff to other departments (paragraphs 87–8 and 112, pp. 26 and 31–32). This option was stated to induce the 'necessary commitments' to follow the report's central recommendation that a strong interdisciplinary core of development studies should be built up. In the event, staff dispersal did not happen. However, QEH governance was effectively placed under 'special measures'. Cassen was replaced by a triumvirate of which he was but one member; the vice-chancellor himself chaired the university committee responsible for QEH. The directorship was then advertised in a form that effectively restricted it to internal Oxford applicants.[6]

Up to this point Frances, although asked previously to put herself forward, had been clear that she did not want to take on any administrative functions, because of her family commitments. By 1993, however, her children had grown up, Michael was in a position to act as house husband and she decided to apply and was appointed. Prompted by Rosemary Thorp to prepare an agenda, Frances identified three major elements of change before her interview. The most important was to raise academic standards, including by detaching from QEH the entities that were not strictly academic in nature. The second was to develop QEH as a multidisciplinary institution, firmly integrated into the university. The third was to create a taught course in development studies, partly to facilitate interaction and the integration of academics from different disciplines, and partly because it seemed probable that future finance would be linked to student numbers.

In terms of raising academic standards, Frances opened the door of QEH to staff who wanted to transfer from other, related departments. Rosemary Thorp and Sanjaya Lall responded enthusiastically by transferring from the Institute of Economics and Statistics. Other faculty members who did not have the option of transfer became associates, closely involved with Frances's QEH. Judith Heyer was one of these. Apart from these distinguished incomers, critical early appointments of new staff were made. A system of Senior Research Associates successfully linked with QEH many other Oxford academics working on development issues. The appointment of outstanding younger scholars gave a signal that the next generation was being built up that would be capable of leading QEH in the future.

QEH had always been dependent on external fundraising, and some units in it were close to operating as consultancies and/or NGOs. One of these, the Food Studies Group (FSG), had run up a deficit, and in July 1993 was forced by the university (some thought precipitately) to call in a guarantee of £173,723 that had been obtained from the Sainsbury family trust, the Gatsby Foundation. The detachment of the Food Studies Group was perhaps Frances's most difficult act as director. Walking into a meeting and telling colleagues that they were about to be cut adrift from the university was quite a challenge. Many in the FSG, however, were willing to go, to gain release from the university's restrictions on their freedom of action. The separation was eased by allowing the FSG to leave with its current research projects and with £50,000, to defray its legal and other employment-related transfer costs.

Other loosely articulated units, dependent on external funding, were dealt with in a different way. These included the Refugee Studies Centre (RSC), which was set up in 1983 by Barbara Harrell-Bond. Its outputs were primarily addressed to the external world rather than to other university academics. Apart from not wanting another grand row, Frances saw the academic potential and importance of the subject and adopted a different approach. When Barbara Harrell-Bond retired in 1996, her successors were recruited to meet a more academically oriented job specification. This option was pursued with the appointment, first, of David Turton and then of Stephen Castles. The RSC offered a one-year non-degree course, which was well attended, especially by US students. As the university came to favour Master's degrees more in the 1990s, this course was converted to an MSt by David Turton, and subsequently to an MSc in Forced Migration by Stephen Castles.

An existing MSc (now defunct) in Agricultural Economics was inherited from the IRAE, but new vehicles for the recruitment of Master's students were needed. A Diploma in Development Economics had been started by Frances, Rosemary Thorp, Judith Heyer and John Knight in 1984. Upgraded to an MSc in Economics for Development, this degree was formally placed under the joint control of QEH and the Economics Department, and Christopher Adam joined QEH to teach the quantitative methods component. The most important development in teaching was a new two-year MPhil in Development Studies, which started life under the outstanding care and protection of Barbara Harriss-White. This required some careful attention to be paid to the concerns of the Oxford anthropologists and of the politics and international relations faculty, whose members feared that the new degree might draw students away from their courses – fears that soon turned out to be groundless. The degree was intended to teach students both in a multi-disciplinary and in an interdisciplinary way, basically incorporating the topics and disciplines that Frances, Barbara and the others involved would have liked to have been able to learn, in a sort of PPE for grown-ups. The degree was outstandingly successful in attracting very high-calibre students, as well as in bringing QEH academics together on the project.

Whereas the top graduates of the Economic Development MSc had a path of progression to doctoral studies in the Economics Department, this was not equally true of the graduates in Development Studies, who were barred from most of the available disciplinary doctorates by their multidisciplinary background. So a DPhil in Development Studies was set up, and a large number of students were attracted into it – possibly a number that initially exceeded the capacity of the staff to ensure their timely progress to completion. The university's agreement that QEH should have its own DPhil programme marked the culmination of the task of institutional renewal.

With these changes completed, QEH began to look much more like a normal university department than it had when it became one in 1986. It had a much stronger focus on teaching and research. The university was reassured by the reforms, and saw its policy of upgrading rather than closure and dispersal to be justified in the event. This was timely, because the university's help would soon be needed. The fifty-year lease on the QEH premises at 21 St Giles expired in 2005, and the owner, St John's College, would not renew it. Where else to turn? Various alternatives were formulated and explored by Frances, Rosemary Thorp and Barbara Harriss-White together with Julia Knight, but all of them were found wanting. Eventually, through the good offices of Donald Hay, head of the university's new Social Sciences Division, the university offered the former Geography Building in Mansfield Road. The department itself had already been renamed the 'Department of International Development'.

2.10   Groups, horizontal inequalities and violent conflict

One of Frances's moves to raise the academic profile of QEH was to re-launch the journal *Oxford Agrarian Studies*, inherited from the old IRAE, as *Oxford Development Studies* in 1996. Writing the first article for the new journal, she noted that, because of its emphasis on optimisation by individuals, for many years neoclassical development economics had had relatively little to say about the role of groups in development and about economic conflicts between groups. As a matter of fact, pertinent questions had been raised by Peter Bauer in the 1950s, but throughout the Cold War years they hung in the air as so many conundrums (Bauer, 1954: pp. 580–85). Frances's own insistence on the irreducibly conflictual nature of politics clearly implied the clash of groups and not just of individuals, but in the 1970s the relevant groups appeared to be social classes. By the time of the 1996 article, the groups given prominence were those entities that appear in the national accounts – families or households, firms in the private sector, governments at different levels and community organisations. Among these the good groups – in the sense of groups raising efficiency and distributing equitably – operated in a mode of trust and reciprocity, a norm that was orthogonal to the neoclassical motive of rational self-interest. If that motive were to be encouraged excessively, she warned, 'groups will still emerge, but they will increasingly be more destructive than constructive' (Stewart, 1996: p. 23).

In subsequent work on groups, done jointly with Judith Heyer and Rosemary Thorp, definitional emphasis shifted again – to local grass-roots groups. Examples included producer co-operatives, saving and credit associations, management groups for common resources, and groups formed to advance claims, self-empowerment and identity formation. The compilation of this wide range of case studies was used to show what collective action could do to improve the lot of the poor – from economic efficiency to a more many-sided self-realisation (Heyer et al., 2002; Stewart, 2005). Although the primary concern was not to tackle the analytical problem of specifying the conditions of successful and unsuccessful group formation by the poor, some of the factors that handicap the poor in forming groups were pointed out (Thorp et al., 2005: pp. 913–15).

The genocide in Rwanda in 1994, along with the humanitarian emergencies associated with the civil wars in Sudan, Sierra Leone and the Democratic Republic of Congo, gave a sudden powerful impetus towards a serious investigation of conflict between groups defined by their ethnicity. While acknowledging the modelling work of Collier and Hoeffler (1998), in neoclassical style, on the economic causes of civil war, Frances embarked on a more comprehensive and multidisciplinary path. She incorporated into her analysis of group mobilisation the construction of group identities and their instrumental use in the pursuit of political ambitions by group leaders. She argued, however, that different group identities would not lead to conflict unless significant economic differences between groups were present, and these differences were not modulated by the exercise of political power. Group differences were labelled 'horizontal inequalities', as distinct from the 'vertical inequalities' in the incomes of an undifferentiated national population. They were seen as having four dimensions: not just incomes and employment, but also political participation, economic assets and social goods. Frances's hypotheses were that group conflicts were not caused by ignorance, but by deliberate manipulation; that they testify to a preference for relative group advantage over absolute advantage; and that relative group advantage is believed to be achievable by means of a drive for political power. The policy implications of this analysis were that policies need to be framed in the light of an understanding of the nature and intensity of the horizontal inequalities that exist in a country, with the aim of reducing them (Stewart, 2000). She noted that the conditionality imposed by international aid donors usually did not include that aim.

This line of research continued, with funding from the Carnegie Foundation, with an examination of the role of diaspora and other international influences on the outbreak, prolongation and resolution of conflicts (FitzGerald et al., 2006). Frances then applied successfully for the resources to direct a Department for International Development (DFID) Development Research Centre specialising in inequality, human security and ethnicity. Given the acronym CRISE, the new centre was set up in 2003 in the Oxford department, but it works with an international network of scholars in Bolivia, Côte d'Ivoire, Ghana, Guatemala, Indonesia, Malaysia, Nigeria and Peru. Such an extensive network put

Frances as its director in a relatively novel position – not of directing an entire department, with its congeries of semi-competitive interests, but of animating a disparate team contributing to a common research objective. The experience of working with Mahbub ul Haq must have stood her in good stead. Like him, she has been able to motivate her team to give its best, while she exercised enough intellectual leadership to deliver a coherent account of the variegated segments of country research which have been undertaken under the CRISE umbrella.

All this is demonstrated by Stewart (2008), in an edited volume that brings together, in an ordered form, the contributions of various members of the CRISE team on the topic of horizontal inequalities and conflict. Groups are there further defined as cultural groups, mainly ethnic or religious. Accordingly, the discussion ranges more widely than just over the developing countries, to include Bosnia, Northern Ireland, the black community in the US and Jews and their fate under the Nazi regime. A chapter co-authored by Frances tackles the difficult issues of defining and measuring horizontal inequalities. Here one senses that finding an appropriate statistical measure for describing group inequality is more tractable than drawing appropriate boundaries around groups when ethnic identities are both objective and subjective, and both self-adopted and attributed by others. All the same, the statistical tests presented appear not to contradict Frances's initial hypothesis that horizontal inequalities are conducive to violent conflict.

Statistical analysis also contributes the interesting finding that this effect may be stronger in societies with democratic political institutions. Democracy does not cause violent conflict, it is argued, but it does not automatically produce a democratic consensus either. In the presence of egregious inequalities, the democratic political fray may descend into violence.

2.11 Conclusion

Frances has been consistently dismissive of neoclassical versions of development economics. She regards comparative statics as a useless technique for analysing dynamic processes of development. The phenomena of economies of scale, technological gaps, externalities, and indivisibilities are crucial to our understanding of the real world and cannot be assumed away. However, her rejection of comparative statics did not lead to a concomitant rejection of microeconomics. It was an important part of her thesis and it reappeared in her work on grassroots groups.

Equally, her dismissal of neoclassical economic theory did not prompt her to reject out of hand economic policies that are often recommended on neoclassical grounds, such as trade and domestic economic liberalisation. She acknowledges that these could often be very effective in generating economic development. In many poor countries they succeeded because they reduced X-inefficiency, they speeded up structural change and they helped to transfer technology and skills. All this had nothing to do with improving resource allocation in a static context.

Above all, the initial distribution of income in poor countries is unacceptable, so that market processes proceeding from it cannot produce optimal outcomes (Stewart, 1985a). In her recent important contributions, Frances has broadened the question of distribution beyond incomes and wealth to include other dimensions, and she has analysed distribution not just vertically, but also in terms of the horizontal inequalities that have the power to wreak social and political havoc.

Her view of politics as inherently conflictual is consistent with her view of her own work as active partisanship for the poor. Several of her contributions, for example to the basic needs strategy and to the campaign for 'adjustment with a human face', had a marked tactical element in their design, building in features that would give them leverage in the political marketplace. Frances's writings are certainly notable for their strong empirical approach. Her early days as a government economist encouraged her interest in economic statistics. She found that the Blue Books provided her with an ever ready source of data, from which she could quickly get a sense of relative economic dimensions. In this she resembled her father, of whom someone said that he could (in the words of Trollope) 'occupy himself with a blue book for hours together without wincing'.[7] For her part, Frances has the impressive skill, when opening up a new research topic, of quickly assembling and laying out the relevant economic, social and political data.

This coupling of pro-poor advocacy and a strong empirical emphasis led to the criticism, coming from the more academically minded, that empirical descriptions do not somehow speak for themselves and that the interpretation of facts inevitably implies some kind of counterfactual scenario (however difficult that may be to define).

Underlying all of her tireless efforts has been a personal commitment to understand poverty in developing countries and a will not just to empathise, but to do something about it. Her career from the mid-1970s on has been devoted to an activity labelled by international relations scholars as 'norm entrepreneurship': the promotion of a set of moral values as the basis for international development policy (Finnemore and Sikkink, 1998). Her achievement in the wider world has been to move the international policy discourse forward on many fronts – towards meeting basic needs, towards achieving a more socially sensitive macroeconomic adjustment, towards humanising war and towards reducing inequalities. She did all this by producing simple ideas out of a sophisticated understanding, ideas that policy-makers could then seize upon and put to use.

Her long-standing engagement with the United Nations, including through membership of important UN committees, has helped to extend the influence of her research. She has been the UK member on the UN University Council and a member of the Governing Body of the United Nations University World Institute for Development Economics Research in Helsinki. After serving on the Council of the United Nations Research Institute for Social Development in Geneva, she became a member of the Committee on Development Policy at UN headquarters in New York in 2007. Outside the UN, she has been President of the Development Studies Association (DSA) (1990–92) and is currently President of the Human Development and Capability Association (HDCA). Organisations that have appointed her to important governance positions include IDS, Sussex, Brown University in Providence and the International Food Policy Research Institute in Washington. Academic journals to which she has given her time include *World Development*, the *Journal of International Development*, the *Journal of Human Development*, the *Journal of Development Economics* and *Development and Change*. In all of these forums her research ideas have circulated fruitfully.

Frances is, after all, an indefatigable communicator. Her stamina for producing and spreading ideas is amazing. Colleagues marvel at her cheerful willingness to go to yet another international gathering to expound the essence of her latest research, and to do so in a way that makes yet another influential audience suddenly feel 'yes, that's it!'. It is fascinating to see it happening, and it is humbling to realise that it is done always with one overriding aim: 'to do something for the poor'.

Oxford University held off from recognising Frances's achievements in the field of international development studies – to the point where she began to contemplate moving elsewhere. Then, relatively late in her career, Frances turned to academic administration, and she proved to be so much more than just a good administrator. Right from the start she was an excellent academic institution builder by recruiting talent, managing change, gaining the confidence of those whose confidence was needed and inspiring all those involved with her to contribute to the collective enterprise. Her decade as director witnessed a most remarkable improvement in the academic fortunes of QEH. Her commitment to raising academic standards has continued since, in the form of research team leadership and of encouraging young researchers – a task on which she thrives, building an academic network dedicated to a central global issue and harvesting the fruit from the co-operative effort.

In 1995, Oxford University awarded her the personal distinction of professorial status, a recognition that many of us felt was already long overdue by that time. Frances's other distinctions now include being cited as an 'outstanding leader' in 2003 by the journal *Scientific American*; receiving the 2009 Mahbub-ul Haq Award for Human Development from the UNDP; and being given an honorary degree by the University of Sussex in January 2010.

Notes

*This paper is based on a series of conversations with Frances Stewart, and has benefited in preparation from comments by Valpy FitzGerald, Judith Heyer, Julia Knight and Rosemary Thorp, to whom I am most grateful.

1. Margaret Hall was at that time the wife of Sir Robert Hall, and was later to become the wife of Sir Donald MacDougall. In 1965, she and Ursula Hicks became the first women members of the Oxford University Political Economy Club (MacDougall, 1987: p. 236).
2. Michael Stewart was the son of J.I.M. Stewart, the English Literature don at Christ Church who also wrote detective novels pseudonymously. Michael became an academic at University College, London, and is the author of several popular books on economics, including *Keynes and After*, which expounded Keynesian economics and its implications for economic policy.
3. However, under the leadership of Carol Bellamy, UNICEF moved back to a more traditional strategy of child-centred medical and nutrition interventions, although in the years since 2005 UNICEF has begun to recruit socio-economists as advisors in its regional offices.
4. The ICS, to which Frances was appointed in 1972, operated inside Queen Elizabeth House at this period, although it was a separate entity. QEH was a portmanteau organisation bringing together a variety of different operations.
5. For a brief account of the Foreign Service Programme at Queen Elizabeth House, see Anthony Kirk-Greene (1994).
6. Because Robert Cassen did not relinquish his professorial position, the directorship as advertised no longer had a full salary attached to it, only an additional allowance. This change meant that external recruitment (as had happened with Cassen) was no longer possible, and that only those who already enjoyed Oxford University salaries were able to apply. There were four applicants from within Oxford, including Frances.

7. From Anthony Trollope, *Phineas Finn, the Irish Member* Vol. 1, Chapter 31, 'Lady Laura Kennedy's Headache'.

References

Bauer, P.T. (1954) 'Book Review'. *Economic Journal* 64 (255): 580–85.

Bruton, H. (1955) 'Growth Models and Underdeveloped Economies'. *Journal of Political Economy* 63: 322–36.

Collier, P., and A. Hoeffler (1998) 'The Economic Causes of Civil Wars'. *Oxford Economic Papers* 50 (4): 563–73.

Cornia, G.A., R. Jolly and F. Stewart (1987) *Adjustment with a Human Face* (Oxford: Clarendon Press).

Finnemore, M., and K. Sikkink (1998) 'International Norm Dynamics and Political Change'. *International Organization* 52 (4): 887–917.

FitzGerald, V., F. Stewart and R. Venugopal (eds) (2006) *Globalization, Self-Determination and Violent Conflict* (Oxford: Oxford University Press).

Goodin, R.E. (2000) *Symposium on Martha Nussbaum's Political Philosophy* (Chicago, IL: Chicago University Press).

Heyer, J., F. Stewart and R. Thorp (eds) (2002) *Group Behaviour and Development: Is the Market Destroying Cooperation?* (Oxford: Oxford University Press).

Kirk-Greene, A.H.M. (1994) *Diplomatic Initiative: The Foreign Service Programme 1969–1994* (Oxford: University of Oxford).

Little, I.M.D., and J.A. Mirrlees (1968) *Manual of Industrial Project Analysis*, Vol. 2 (Paris: OECD Development Centre).

MacDougall, D. (1987) *Don and Mandarin: Memoirs of an Economist* (London: John Murray).

Myrdal, G. (1968) *Asian Drama* (London: Allen Lane, The Penguin Press).

Rainbird, S., and F. Stewart (1984) 'Queen Elizabeth House: The New Phase', Mimeo, Oxford University archives.

Ranis, G., F. Stewart and A. Ramirez (2000) 'Economic Growth and Human Development'. *World Development* 28 (2): 197–219.

Ranis, G., F. Stewart and E. Samman (2005) 'Human Development: Beyond the HDI'. *Economic Growth Center Discussion Paper* No. 916 (New Haven, CT: Yale University).

Sen, A.K. (1999) *Development as Freedom* (Oxford: OUP).

Sen, A.K. (1984) *Resources, Values and Development* (Oxford: Basil Blackwell).

Stewart, F. (ed.) (2008) *Horizontal Inequalities and Conflict: Understanding Group Violence in Multiethnic Societies* (Basingstoke: Palgrave Macmillan).

Stewart, F. (2005) 'Groups and Capabilities'. *Journal of Human Development* 6 (2): 185–204.

Stewart, F. (2000) 'Crisis Prevention: Tackling Horizontal Inequalities'. *Oxford Development Studies* 28 (3): 245–62.

Stewart, F. (1996) 'Groups for Good or Ill'. *Oxford Development Studies* 24 (1): 9–25.

Stewart, F. (1985a) 'The Fragile Foundations of Neo-classical Development Economics'. *Journal of Development Studies* 21 (2): 282–92.

Stewart, F. (1985b) *Planning to Meet Basic Needs* (London: Macmillan).

Stewart, F. (1975) 'A Note on Social Cost-Benefit Analysis and Class Conflict in Less Developed Countries'. *World Development* 3 (1): 31–9.

Stewart, F. (1973) 'Choice of Technique in Developing Countries'. *Journal of Development Studies* 9 (1): 99–121.

Stewart, F., and P.P. Streeten (1972) 'Little-Mirrlees Methods and Project Appraisal'. *Bulletin of the Oxford Institute of Economics and Statistics* 34 (1): 75–91.

Stewart, F., V. FitzGerald and Associates (2001) *War and Underdevelopment* (Oxford: Oxford University Press).

Thorp, R., F. Stewart and A. Heyer (2005) 'When and How Far is Group Formation a Route out of Chronic Poverty?' *World Development* 33 (6): 907–20.

UNCTAD (United Nations Conference on Trade and Development) (1965) *International Monetary Issues and the Developing Countries: Report of the Group of Experts* (New York: United Nations).

UNDP (United Nations Development Programme) (1990) *The Human Development Report* (New York: Oxford University Press for UNDP).

Part II

Technical Change and Economic Development

3
Technology Change: Sources and Impediments

Gustav Ranis, Mallory Irons and Yanjing Huang

3.1 Introduction

The relationship between technology change and economic growth has been of interest to economists for centuries, but especially since Robert Solow made his seminal contribution to the neoclassical model of economic growth in the 1950s, which has led to an explosion in the follow-up literature. Interest in technology change waned perceptibly in the 1980s. However, with the arrival of the 'new growth theory', a notable revival of focus on the subject can be observed. Overall, there remains little doubt that there is a consensus that technology change, in terms of both its process and its quality dimensions, represents the principal driving force in explaining comparative economic performance at the micro- and macro-levels. That said, exactly *how* technology change is generated and what impedes it remains less clear.

The standard neoclassical approach assumes the rate of technological change to be exogenously determined. Solow's model predicts that rich and poor countries alike will, in the long term, converge to steady rates of growth that are determined by technological progress, the savings rate and the growth of the labour force. While the model confirms that higher savings rates lead to higher rates of growth, capital accumulation takes a back seat to technological change (Solow, 1956). This is not to deny that investment is likely to be required to 'carry' technology change.

The 'new growth theory' attempts to render technology change endogenous and, by asserting that externalities permit the maintenance of sustained growth in spite of an increase in the rate of investment,[1] thus avoids the diminishing returns to investment issue that troubled the Solow model. Consequently, 'endogenous growth theory' authors have reinvigorated the debate over the role of technology change in economic growth and have endeavoured to construct macroeconomic models built upon microeconomic foundations. The forces that are generally seen to give rise to endogenous technological progress include education, research and development, external influences and domestic government policies. While empirical evidence in support of endogenous growth theory is still relatively weak, the main contribution of the model to date has been to reinvigorate the discussion surrounding the sources of technological progress.

In the context of this renewed contemporary interest surrounding technology change and economic growth, it seems less useful to differentiate between technology choice and technology change, in the recognition that the two are really indistinguishable, in other words any 'choice' is almost always modified to be rendered a 'change'. Technologies are rarely ever successfully taken off the shelf and deployed as they are; rather, a considerable amount of adaptation must inevitably occur in order for them to be utilised effectively in any given environment. Frances Stewart recognised the importance of the appropriateness of technology early on. As she put it, 'what is needed above all is local technical innovation directed towards local needs' (Stewart, 1977: p. 278).[2]

A closely related dimension of research focuses on the links between economic growth, technology change and human development. Human development and economic growth have been analysed as affecting each other through two 'channels': the first, running from economic growth to human development, is fuelled by household and government expenditures as well as by technology change. It is not as well understood as the second channel, which runs from improvements in human development, is fuelled by foreign and domestic savings as well as (once again) by technology, and leads to the enhancement of growth in gross domestic product (GDP) (Ranis et al., 2003). The first represents a production function converting public and private expenditures on health, education and nutrition, and so on into increases in life expectancy, reductions in infant mortality, educational achievement and the enhancement of other human capabilities. This conversion, of course, depends on technology, but it has thus far proved harder to understand exactly *how* technology change affects human development.

We do know, for example, that per capita income significantly affects life expectancy levels (Preston, 1975) and that human development is positively affected by household and government expenditures on health and education. However, as Behrman has carefully pointed out, there are many interrelated inputs – including home schooling, home health inputs and the distribution of income and nutrition – as well as the relevance of a variety of household characteristics and alternative organisations of the public sector, which render it difficult to get a good fix on this production function (Behrman, 1990). This difficulty reminds one of the early problems encountered in properly defining the agricultural sector production function, given multiple quantitative inputs and the somewhat mysterious role of international and domestic adaptive technology.

The second production function, linking human development to economic growth with the support of domestic and foreign investment and, significantly, of technology change, is better understood; and this is where most of the 'new growth theory' literature has been focused to date. It is in this context that we intend to examine the sources of technology change (total factor productivity, TFP) and the impediments to the full realisation of technological opportunities, both in the abstract and in the context of a comparison between six typologically diverse developing economies. Among the sources of TFP we will examine research and development (R&D), investment, various types of patents, foreign direct investment (FDI), openness, science and technology (S&T) personnel, and other education-related human development indicators. Among impediments, we will analyse public and private policy frameworks that tend to block the realisation of existing technological opportunities.

Throughout, we will focus on the non-agricultural sector. We proceed as follows: in Section 3.2 we conduct a general discussion of the sources of, and impediments to, the full realisation of the opportunities for technology change in the developing countries, broken down into external factors (foreign patents, openness to trade, the role of the multinational corporation, etc.) and internal factors (domestic patents, R&D, investment, education, etc.). The empirical analysis of six diverse developing countries – Brazil, China, India, Mexico, Taiwan and South Korea – is then brought to bear, demonstrating why the Asian countries seem to have exhibited a relatively stronger performance than their Latin American counterparts. In Section 3.3 we summarise the results and discuss some implications for policy.

3.2   Sources and impediments

3.2.1   External sources and impediments

3.2.1(a)   Openness to trade and FDI

A cursory look at the relative economic performance of rich and poor countries highlights, in many cases, large income and productivity gaps between the developed and developing worlds. It is well understood, by neoclassical and new growth theorists alike, that TFP, with all its shortcomings, is the best measure of technology change and has the dominant influence on an economy's growth performance. Accordingly, we accept the TFP estimates provided by UNIDO[3] and try to understand what lies behind them. We also acknowledge the well-known weaknesses of the TFP variable, which constitutes a residual containing considerable 'noise', for instance economies of scale, terms of trade effects and the like, in addition to pure technology change.

While our data set was not large enough to render it meaningful, we tried panel analysis, with exports, FDI, investment, R&D, regular patents and utility models on the right-hand side. Only patents, investment and exports proved significant, at the 5 per cent level. Moreover, we do not claim to present a behavioural model here, but we restrict ourselves to observing differential country trends over time. Nor do we assert that such correlations imply causation. As our six-country data indicate (see Figure 3.1), a particular country's openness to trade seems to be highly correlated with technology change. Four of our countries, Brazil, Mexico, Taiwan and South Korea, initially enjoyed relatively high TFP growth. Later on, the Latin American countries in particular suffered from much lower rates of technology change, while China and, still later, India joined the other East Asian countries. On the other hand, except in the case of China and, to a lesser extent, Korea, FDI does not seem to have had much of an impact on TFP.

Keller (2004: p. 752) argues that, overall, foreign sources of technology account for about 90 per cent of the growth in most countries, and further notes that technology change worldwide is determined in large part by technology diffusion, carried by trade and FDI across borders. The impact of a country's relative openness to trade is clearly by no means limited to the import of machinery; it focuses heavily on the transfer of knowledge. Keller notes that foreign research and development has been shown to raise domestic TFP substantially in less developed countries (LDCs), greater rates of trade and global openness permitting technology diffusion via FDI.

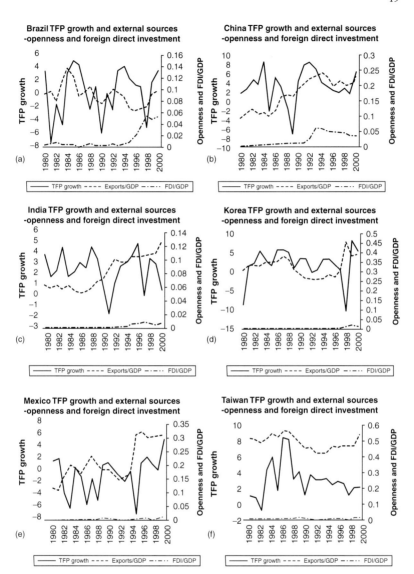

Figure 3.1 External sources: Openness and FDI

Sources: UNIDO, World Productivity Database; United Nations Statistics Division, Commodity Trade Database; UNCTAD, Foreign Direct Investment Database; Republic of Taiwan, National Statistics.

Trade with more technologically advanced countries can, of course, be beneficial to LDCs in that it affords them access to frontier technologies without their having to invest a great deal of time and resources in developing such technologies on their own. But the key is the extent to which such frontier technologies are adapted to the local context. Moreover, it is not only the importing of technologies that can be beneficial to LDCs; in some cases exporting may be advantageous as well. Several studies have noted that there may be 'learning-by-doing' effects that make exporters relatively more productive than their non-exporting counterparts, in particular due to these exporters' interactions with northern consumers. However, since northern consumers usually have different quality standards from those of southern consumers, adaptation to the domestic market is essential. This applies centrally to technology change of the product adaptation variety, to the main focus of entrepreneurs, as well as to the process adaptation type, focused on by most academic economists. Early on Stewart stressed the importance of selecting the appropriate commodity attributes as an important contribution to technology change in the South (Stewart and James, 1982).

One of the impediments in this part of the conceptual arena is the threat of protectionism, especially at a time of overall economic weakness. Currently, while a repetition of the massive 'beggar thy neighbour' policies of the 1930s is not on the horizon, there are disturbing signs of 'under-the-radar' mercantilist measures being implemented, including a rise in anti-dumping measures, 'buy domestic' legislation and the like.

Turning to FDI, Borensztein and colleagues (1998) point out that human development, in the form of education levels (see below), is a prerequisite for a country to take full advantage of these inflows. Similarly, Xu (2000) notes that there is a positive relationship between FDI and TFP, but that this relationship is stronger in middle-income countries (and in countries in the middle of the range in terms of human development indicators, HDIs). Moreover, the positive spillovers from FDI are more pronounced in high-technology than in low-technology sectors. Larraín and colleagues (2001) emphasise the potential benefits from FDI with respect to technological progress. They present the case of Intel, a manufacturer of microprocessors, and its involvement in Costa Rica, a country that is 'very small...when compared with other potential locations for a company of that nature' (p. 197). The presence of Intel in Costa Rica generated large positive spillovers in terms of increased rates of technology diffusion. These positive gains were achieved through two avenues: firstly, Intel funded schools that taught workers technical and vocational skills that were not necessarily

Intel-specific. Secondly, Intel's FDI served as a signalling mechanism: by making such a large and profitable investment in Costa Rica, Intel effectively signalled to others to invest in the country. One of the frequently encountered impediments to technology change is thus the expansive definition of 'strategic sectors', to which FDI is not admitted.

However, FDI can be a double-edged sword: it can be both a source of, and an impediment to, the generation of domestic TFP changes. As Keller (2004) emphasises, multinational companies can stimulate technological learning through labour training, through reduced turnover and through the provision of high-quality intermediate inputs. However, it should also be noted that their real contribution cannot be assessed independently of time and place (Ranis, 1976), in other words it must be related to the particular phase of an LDC's life cycle, as well as to the type (size, resources endowment, etc.) of the LDC in question. In an idealised scenario, the multinational corporation begins as a wholly owned subsidiary, then becomes a joint venture and finally gives way to licensing and management contracts, and so on as the country matures. In this idealised world, a disinvestment/transformation timeframe would be agreed upon *ex ante*, in order to make the eventual transition easier. While the multinational corporation can be particularly helpful to the developing country in the early stages of its growth, in particular during the customary import substitution subphase of its development, in such an ideal world FDI would continue to be supportive when the LDC moved out of this subphase.

However, departures from the above idealised scenario have sometimes prevented this relationship from working well in practice. First, in the absence of any changes to the nature of the initial contract, the relationship between the two parties is likely to become less advantageous for the LDC and more advantageous for the multinational corporation over time. Under most arrangements, the multinational corporation is likely to enjoy a monopoly-like position, and consequently behaves as a 'satisficer'. This means that it may affect technology change adversely, by promoting inappropriate 'luxury goods' and 'luxury processes' and thereby encouraging the tastes and attitudes of local consumers to favour internationally specified rather than appropriate or adaptive domestic goods and to steer local producers towards inappropriate technologies. The multinational corporation may also restrict entry to the export market for would-be local competitors, and prevent their subsidiaries from entering it – which could threaten market-sharing arrangements with other multinational companies (MNCs). Stewart raised early warning signals concerning the double-edged sword feature of FDI and suggested that more attention should be paid to South–South trade and investment contacts.[4] Given the progress of globalisation since she wrote, as well as the emergence of a substantial number of dynamic middle-income countries, her early warnings and suggestions have been fully borne out by recent events.

Keller (2004: p. 769) illuminates another potential departure from the evolutionary ideal between the host country and the corporation. He describes two common avenues of technology transfer: (1) the corporation's subsidiary disseminates technology and information to domestic firms in the host country (and thus assists with the diffusion of possibly inappropriate international technology); or (2) the subsidiary picks up adaptive technologies from local LDC firms (and then 'sources' such technology outward to third parties). Such detrimental patterns may occur because the multinational corporation subsidiary is likely to have more market power than the average domestic firm and may thus be better at sourcing, or because it has been set up with the express purpose of sourcing in the first place.

3.2.1(b)   Foreign patents

Economists and politicians alike have long touted intellectual property (IP) rights, including trademarks, patents, and copyrights, as integral to technological progress and economic development. The authors of the 2001 Human Development Report noted that IP rights are intimately intertwined with technology change and growth because they make it possible for individual innovators to reap an assured return on their initial R&D investment (UNDP, 2001: p. 102). Since the World Trade Organization (WTO) Agreement on Trade-Related Aspects of Intellectual Property Rights (TRIPS), the debate over the implementation of such rights in developing countries has been sharpened, and the potential benefits and impediments to their successful execution have come into clearer focus.

With respect to foreign patents, for instance, it has been emphasised that, in addition to incentivising innovation, patents can serve as a stimulus for the transfer of technology from developed to developing countries. However, just as patents can stimulate technology change, they can also serve as a barrier to the provision of socially valuable goods at a socially appropriate cost. The 2001 Human Development Report (UNDP, 2001) cites, as an example, the development of antiretroviral drugs as indicative of the potential social costs associated with patents. Antiretroviral therapy, which has dramatically cut AIDS deaths in industrial countries, remains an extremely expensive cocktail, which has been produced under US and European patents for some time. Before the introduction of generic versions of these drugs, the cocktail was simply unaffordable by the majority of HIV-positive individuals in the LDCs. Still, while pharmaceutical companies in the developed countries, which have much larger R&D budgets and are thus able to develop a large number of new drugs, are protected financially by IP rights, life-saving medication has generally been too expensive for individuals in the countries that need it the most.

In addition to incentivising risk-taking and to sparking innovation, established IP rights can encourage an increased flow of FDI associated with patents. While some scholars note that this in and of itself may encourage an overreliance on developed countries and thus decrease domestic innovation in LDCs, others note that the flow of ideas and technologies incorporated in foreign patents can definitely be helpful in generating recipient country TFP. As Figure 3.2 indicates, TFP change moves with foreign patents, especially in the case of the three East Asian countries.

Of course, there are legitimate concerns with respect to formalising IP rights in the developing world. The first is a problem of coordination. Acemoglu and Zilibotti (2001) note that, while most developing nations agree that IP rights are necessary, at least in theory, in practice a prisoner's dilemma may exist, particularly in the early stages of development. They note that LDCs acknowledge that IP rights can encourage the flow of ideas and technologies from North to South, and that more formal IP rights in LDCs may even encourage developed countries to devise new technologies that are more appropriate for use in LDC environments. However, each LDC may hesitate to be the first to enforce IP rights while other LDCs take advantage of the new technologies. Acemoglu and Zilibotti point out that the existence of this prisoner's dilemma suggests that there may be a role for a third party, for instance an international institution, to coordinate IP rights in the developing world so as to overcome this coordination failure.

Another, more serious concern surrounding IP rights is that their actual implementation may be at odds with the LDC's public interest. Since individual developed-country innovators face incentives to develop new technologies relevant to their large home markets, where they are guaranteed to earn a profit on their investments (through patents, copyrights and the like), their actions may hurt technology change abroad. For example, in many cases foreign patents inhibit other LDC technology entry, protect their markets against local enterprise, restrict exports or permit firms to charge too high a price for their

54

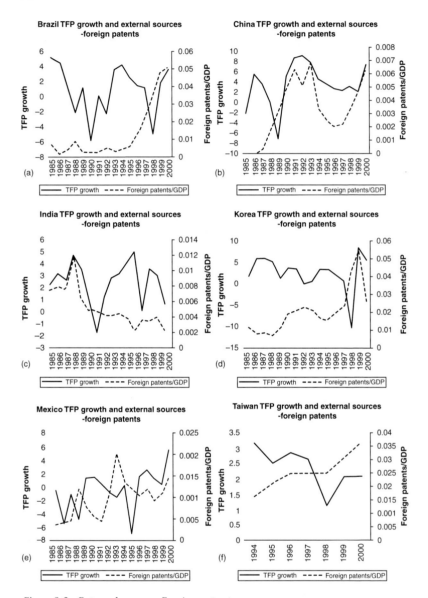

Figure 3.2 External sources: Foreign patents
Sources: World Intellectual Property Organization; UNIDO, World Productivity Database; Republic of Taiwan, National Statistics; United Nations Statistical Division; Taiwan Intellectual Property Office.

product. Ranis (1979: p. 36) notes an example of this phenomenon, in which the granting of patents in the Colombian pharmaceutical industry presented a threat to the development of the local industry, 'not only [by failing] to promote foreign investment, but [also by forcing] the sale of local firms to transnationals'. In this case, while the granting of patents encouraged the flow of ideas and technologies across borders, it also represented an obstacle for domestic Colombian pharmaceutical firms and it hurt Colombian consumers.

Moving from the general to the more specific issue of TRIPS implementation leads us to another concern associated with patents, namely that it has been extremely difficult to enforce the provisions of the TRIPS agreement fairly across LDCs. Different national situations – distinctive cultures and diverse national legislative systems and policies – make it extraordinarily challenging to execute the terms of the agreement even-handedly. The 2001 Human Development Report noted that, while TRIPS may benefit middle-income countries such as Brazil, which are likely to profit from the increased local innovation resulting from IP rights legislation, poorer LDCs that lack formal innovation structures and institutional mechanisms have faced higher costs, without any counterbalancing benefits (UNDP, 2001). As to the future, a differential application of TRIPS to developing countries, depending on their stage of development, would seem to make sense on a permanent basis (currently there is only a time delay granted before full application goes into effect). It is no accident that the more successful LDCs of East Asia were IP 'pirates', until they began to become concerned about their own IP rights being infringed upon by the next wave of emerging economies.

3.2.2   Internal sources and impediments

The existence of an international advanced-country technology frontier clearly dominates the opportunities for technology change in the typical developing country. Yet making appropriate choices on what to adapt, how to adapt it, and what to reject is critical and differentiates the more successful from the less successful countries in the developing world. This, in turn, depends largely on the quality and quantity of relevant domestic activities.

3.2.2(a)   Domestic patents and utility models

Technology transfer, with adaptation, clearly presents a unique opportunity. As new technologies are devised abroad, the adaptation of these new processes or products can decrease capital-labour ratios, make more efficient use of a relatively unskilled labour force, and offer consumers new product attributes that are more closely aligned to their preferences and tastes – all, developments that can lead to a sustained increase in TFP, and hence growth. But the emphasis must be on the extent to which imported technologies are converted into technologies appropriate to the new environment, in other words on the quality of that adaptation process. Echoing Stewart's early work, we are emphasising here the importance of the adaptation of transferred technologies (Stewart, 1977).

The equilibrium state is that the development of most new technologies at the 'frontier' occurs first in those countries or regions where the level of human skill and technical capacity are superior – that is, in the developed countries. It is accepted in theory and practice that LDCs should to some extent rely on these more advanced countries (including, increasingly, some middle-income countries in the South), and thus avoid the cost of the R&D that went into the generation of those technologies. However, as Stewart insisted, the *transplantation* of new technologies is only the first step; it can lead to insufficient or inappropriately biased adaptations, and such adaptations could entail heavy opportunity costs for LDCs. While the factor proportions used to produce a given quality product differ substantially between a typical northern and a southern country, the difference is typically much smaller than the gap in their endowments. With the proper type of adaptation to local conditions, LDCs can reap the benefits of developed countries' investments in the invention process without having to incur relatively large opportunity costs. The success of this effort depends in large part on domestic patents and domestic R&D, both formal and informal.

Pack and Westphal (1986) address essentially the same concern related to the 'tradeability' of technology, noting that technology is only partially tradeable: that is, an individual LDC's capability to make full use of new knowledge and new technologies is, at best, uncertain. They assert that this is because technology is often tacit and the problems of communication and the organisational differences, especially given long distances (institutional and cultural more than geographic), render the implementation of adaptation difficult. Moreover, because technological elements are only partially tradeable, they may require complementary institutional investments. Domestic patents and utility models may be useful at converting tacit into explicit technical knowledge. Foreign patents are likely to induce domestic patents, and domestic patents in turn are likely to induce utility model patents[5] (where these legally exist). As Figure 3.3 shows, the utility model is

57

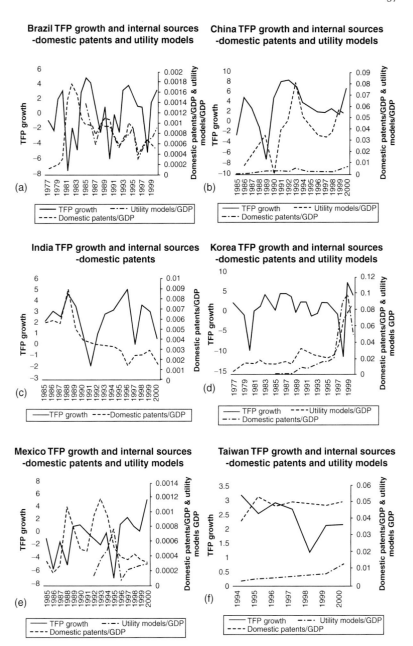

Figure 3.3 Internal sources: Utility models and domestic patents
Sources: WIPO; UNIDO; Republic of Taiwan, National Statistics; UNSD; TIPO.

dominant in Korea and Taiwan and seems to have a high correlation with TFP growth, while, somewhat surprisingly, we may note a close relationship in the case of domestic patents for Brazil and Mexico – perhaps due to these countries' relatively more closed economies. Late comer China is catching up quickly in deploying the utility model. In a given industry, what is frequently observed is a sequencing, from the licensing of foreign patents, to an increase in domestic patents; this is followed by a burst of the utility model, which is especially helpful to medium and small-scale firms.

Where the IP rights regime is weak, individuals and firms face fewer incentives to innovate, because they lack formal mechanisms through which to reap returns on their investment. Due to the fact that patents grant a firm (or an individual) a temporary monopoly position, firms are able to recoup the costs of their initial investments, as well as to earn a profit, by setting a price above their marginal costs. However, if formal IP rights are not put in place, this quasi-monopoly position disappears. In this situation it is not guaranteed that firms will recover the costs of their initial investments, let alone earn a profit from their new technologies. Thus formal IP rights increase the incentives for risk-taking by guaranteeing a financially 'secure' outcome after the initial investment.

3.2.2(b)   *Domestic investment*

Clearly an important domestic source of TFP growth is domestic invest-ment, which is required to 'carry' technology, whether changes in TFP are theoretically viewed as exogenous or endogenous. Using data on gross fixed capital formation[6] as the best measure of the domestic invest-ment rate, as in Figure 3.4, we may note a closer positive relationship between TFP growth and investment rate in the case of Mexico than in some of the other countries depicted in this figure.

The experience of China and India indicates that high investment rates are not necessarily associated with high rates of TFP growth. This may be the result of 'overinvesting' resulting from very high savings rates, coupled with an emphasis – especially in the case of China – on maintaining extremely high growth rates and with the resulting declines in the rate of return to capital and rising capital–output ratios in both countries. Taiwan seems to have maintained stability in TFP growth at much lower levels of the investment rate. There appears to be little rela-tionship between TFP growth and investment in the cases of Korea and Brazil.

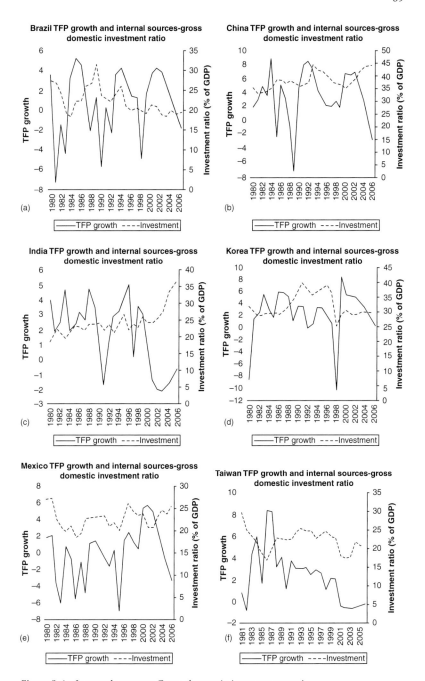

Figure 3.4 Internal sources: Gross domestic investment ratio

3.2.2(c)   *Secondary education choice, S&T personnel and R&D*

'New growth' theorists stress the importance of human development, specifically education, in developing nations, arguing that it improves the *absorptive capacity* of domestic firms. In this context, 'absorptive capacity' refers to the firm's ability to select and adapt foreign technology successfully. They argue that, in order for technologies to be appropriately adapted, workers must possess a basic skill level. These educational requirements of course change over time, and there is increased emphasis on vocational secondary education and, subsequently, S&T-oriented education (see Figure 3.5).[7] There is a contrast between East Asia and Latin America in the realms of S&T personnel and of the role of secondary vocational education, though data on the latter are deficient.

Acemoglu and Zilibotti (2001) add that the skill level of workers in individual developing countries can largely explain relative productivity differences and income gaps between the developed and the developing world. They argue that, even when all countries have access to the same technology, there will still be income gaps and large cross-country differences due to the relatively less skilled LDC labour force. Since most R&D investment takes place in developed countries, the technologies that result from this investment will naturally yield 'North-biased' technologies. Workers who are less conventionally skilled will thus not be able to make effective use of such imported technologies. If the northern bias in favour of skills-intensive technologies continues, LDCs may find themselves increasingly inclined to reject frontier technologies and they would miss an opportunity to adapt these to their own needs and demands. To avoid this result requires general scientific, vocational and technical literacy, and not simple copying of the educational system of the North. By encouraging timely investments in education, particularly with respect to programmes that aim to improve the skill level of the average LDC worker, it becomes possible for LDCs to encourage the appropriate adaptation of imported technologies.

Accordingly, the consensus in the literature is that the universal attainment of primary and, later, secondary education should be a goal for LDCs. Stewart (1977) has insisted that vocational and technical education at the secondary level should be encouraged. Indeed, an important issue is the distinction between education and efforts associated R&D, which are mainly science-based or empirical. The former is defined as 'technology that arises from a change in our basic understanding of the laws governing the environment', and the latter

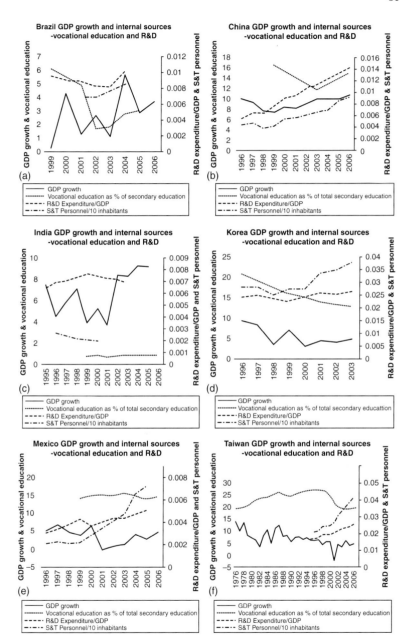

Figure 3.5 Internal sources: S&T personnel, R&D expenditure, vocational education

Sources: UNESCO, UNSD; Republic of Taiwan, National Statistics.

as 'technology that arises after trial-and-error' (Ranis, 1978). Ranis cautions against an overreliance on empirically based technologies, which he cites as a contributory factor to the relative decline of Britain's economic growth and performance in the years after the First World War, following its earlier industrial success. Many new technologies in developing countries arise as the result of 'tinkering' – for example, so-called 'blue collar' R&D in textiles, metalworking, brick-making and beer brewing led to early TFP advances in Japan which did not need to rely on basic scientific advances but made use of the abundant labour supply. Britain was the pioneer in this procedure. Germany, as a follower, facing natural resource scarcity, focused on post-Liebig research labs and engineering schools and outdistanced everyone else in the chemical/ pharmaceutical, iron and steel, and electrical machinery industries by devising new technologies based on a fundamental understanding of science. The US endowment favoured empirically based change and mass as opposed to niche production. As Kuznets (1966) points out, the capacity to use science wisely and the capacity to absorb it as a necessary basis for importing and adapting technology are related to the education system and to the types of interventions, either direct or indirect, practised by governments. An education system that imparts a modicum of scientific understanding to a substantial portion of the population can provide basic building blocks for a discriminating scientific capacity at a relatively early stage in a country's development. Moreover, as the examples of Japan and the United States illustrate, the same country may, further along in its development, itself acquire the capacity to advance the frontiers of science and directly contribute to the frontier. Higher education relevant to more advanced technologies becomes crucial at a later stage.

That new, empirically based technologies in the North can have an extraordinary impact on total factor productivity in the South has been demonstrated time and again. Otsuka and colleagues (1988), for example, refer to the Indian and Japanese cotton-spinning industries and argue that a substantial increase in TFP in Japan in the late nineteenth century occurred as a direct result of the utilisation of an imported technology – the ring – to replace an old one – the mule. In contrast to its Indian counterpart, the Japanese cotton-spinning industry witnessed a 'virtually instantaneous switch from mules to rings' in the space of two years (1887–89), which, in turn, prompted major adaptations in ancillary processes, such as higher speeds of machinery utilisation, the introduction of cotton mixing and the employment of more women to repair broken threads. The authors attribute an overall decline in the capital–labour ratio around the turn of the century to the industry's switch to the ring and to its subsequent labour-using adaptation processes. By contrast, India imported 2 million new mules between 1883 (the date of the first Indian experimentation with rings) and 1900, for cultural reasons failed to include women in the labour force and did not use cotton mixing to decrease its reliance on mule technology. As a consequence, Japanese-owned mills in China, a market previously owned by Indian exporters, expanded their capacity more than eightfold between 1915 and 1928, and the number of Japanese-owned looms increased fifteen times over the same period. Domestic adaptive R&D in Japan was clearly superior to that in India. The Indian colonial managing agency system focused on output quotas instead of profits and thus did not provide the necessary incentives.

Keller (2004) notes that countries with higher levels of expenditure on R&D experience higher rates of productivity growth, because such expenditures are critical for appropriate adaptive responses to international technology. Only 5 per cent of the world's formal R&D is expended by developing countries and the typical LDC spends 0.5 per cent of its GDP in this fashion, compared to the 5 per cent spent by developed countries. The East Asian economies spend between 1.5 and 3.0 per cent of their GDP on official R&D, while the Latin American countries fall below 1 per cent. Firms in LDCs often lack tax or other incentives to invest privately or to take advantage of public sector R&D opportunities. The adequacy of domestic R&D in the context of generating TFP hinges on fiscal incentives and institutional innovations, as well as on education strategies.

The incentives that various firms have to invest in R&D differ depending on the size and market position of the firms in question. For large firms with a position of relative monopoly, the ability may exist, but the incentive to innovate is low; that is, the firm is either maximising profits or coming as close as possible to doing so, and thus has no reason to find a new or efficient means of doing what it has already 'perfected'. More likely, it is 'satisficing' and prefers the stability of the status quo. In successful LDCs, it is in small- and medium-scale firms in relatively competitive industries that most significant R&D activity takes place. By providing access to smaller entrepreneurs on a temporary basis, institutional innovations, including the establishment of R&D institutes, have been very helpful to those firms that cannot afford major organised R&D efforts in the most successful countries; such is the Industrial Technology Research Institute (ITRI) in Taiwan. The more competitive environment faced by these firms usually encourages them to find appropriate adaptive responses. The existence of the utility model patent can also be very helpful in this regard, since much R&D

may be carried out in the form of tinkering (as noted above): blue collar or informal activities on factory floors and in repair shops, including 'reverse engineering', not all of which is captured in the official formal R&D statistics. For example, an LDC may reap a higher payoff from an imported machine if it is tested, used and redesigned by workers on the factory floor, to suit the special needs of the local environment.

The emphasis should thus clearly be on *adaptive* rather than *basic* R&D. Engel sees 'little justification [in developing countries] for basic research except for sustaining a viable teaching effort and keeping your best brains at home' (quoted in Ranis, 1978: p. 22). Most observers agree that the greatest waste of all is second-rate basic research; they advocate instead flexible economic environments, along with science and technical education focused on indigenous improvements and adaptations. However, to neglect basic science-focused R&D entirely may be going too far, particularly in agriculture and health. Without such research on a country or regional basis, Green Revolution technology in agriculture, for example, would not have had the necessary sustaining power and the necessary defence against specific local problems (such as pests and disease). Similarly, in the field of health, few people would argue that a single transnational science can really be equally responsive to the very different conditions around the globe. In almost all industries, some attention to science-based R&D may be helpful, as it is for example in footwear production with regard to different cowhide tanning procedures, or in the textile industry with regard to different humidity requirements. In such areas, minimal scientific literacy is necessary if one is to respond to technological problems, even if an LDC is ill-advised to 'show the flag' in an array of frontier science endeavours.

The benefits of investment in educating and retaining adaptively motivated science and technology personnel domestically – rather than risking losing such individuals to developed nations with strong programmes and more formal education and research structures – are substantial. In the East Asian countries that have experienced success, the building up of S&T personnel was a priority. Japan stands as an example of technical education put to good use; this country is noted for its mastery of reverse engineering, for achieving appropriate adaptation by carefully analysing the structure, function and operation of imported machinery and for changing key elements in line with local factor and institutional endowments. In contrast, other contemporary LDCs, such as in Latin America, typify some of the impediments in this area, for instance through their relative emphasis on academic over vocational education at the secondary level and on the humanities over science and engineering at the tertiary level.

3.3   Summary and some conclusions for policy

Our six-country comparison, in its various dimensions, indicated that, while the world is grey rather than black and white, there are marked differences in the extent to which East Asia, in contrast to Latin America – with South Asia in an intermediate position – took advantage of technological opportunities and reduced some of the obstacles. While most economists agree that R&D is the major source of technological change because it permits adaptation to take place, R&D is clearly subject to perceptible underinvestment, especially in Latin America by comparison with Asia. With increased cheap flows of information and technology now possible across borders, it has become much easier for new technologies to be both imported and exported across the globe. Thus opportunities are mushrooming, but they are not being sufficiently utilised. Some progress has clearly been made: basic research and development has given way to an increased emphasis on adaptive research and development, the need for country-specific R&D being evident. Stewart has rightly maintained from the beginning that R&D is 'the dominant source of innovation today' and that adaptive R&D in particular is critical if LDCs are to develop their own appropriate technologies and avoid overreliance on inappropriate imports from the developed world (Stewart, 1981).

Yet we should recognise that impediments continue to exist to repairing the current LDC underinvestment in R&D, even if we could account for the 'blue collar' R&D, which is not reflected in the available data. Most economists agree that current tax code-embedded R&D programmes tend to benefit larger firms. Moreover, there has been a lack of institutional commitment to R&D among bilateral and multilateral aid agencies. When and where successful R&D programmes do exist, the dissemination of relevant knowledge remains problematic. Complementary human capital investments are required in order to take full advantage of the potential for adaptive technology change. To remedy this, Stewart offered a few suggestions for R&D policy, including the promotion of 'appropriate' technology choices by aid agencies, or the creation of new R&D partnerships, incentivised by tax credits and public grants. In this way, she argues, *basic* (or 'old-style') R&D will no longer be effective and considerable investment in adaptive R&D should be undertaken. In a similar vein, we suggest that government support of R&D institutions that cater to small and medium firms be set on a long-term and gradually declining subsidy basis, in order to ensure focus on private sector 'appropriate adaptation' activity rather than the pursuit of international academic or scientific interests.

Determining appropriate responses to R&D underinvestment and designing effective R&D programmes requires an understanding of where the individual developing country's basic research needs end, and where the caveats against a wasteful scattergun approach begin to take hold. While this is not an easy matter on which to give a decisive answer, the burden of proof must lie with those who would like to initiate advanced university training and basic research, including some obligation to demonstrate a flexible, time-phased relevance to sustained technology change. This may look like the typical hard-headed, narrow economist's prescription. What about the importance of those many possible interconnections, decades apart, that may flow, in some entirely unpredictable way, from what looks like an unconnected intellectual pursuit? Without disparaging these possibilities, we should be offended by the spectacle of open-heart surgery research in countries where malnutrition is prevalent and insist that basic research should not expect to be outside the realm of some flexible, sophisticated version of cost-benefit analysis. Such analysis must try to balance the potential benefits against the possible alternative allocations of scarce financial and – even more importantly, no doubt – human resources. The higher risks of science, due partly to the uncertainty of predicting future two-way interactions between science and technology and partly to the likely inappropriability on a national scale of any such 'returns', render this task unusually difficult. But analysis must still be done; an act of faith does not suffice.

In addition to placing the burden of proof on those who would like to have developing countries pay the 'price of admission' in a given field of basic R&D, it might be possible, although admittedly difficult, to encourage much more specialisation within, and possibly also among, countries on a regional basis. This type of agreement has been reached, for example, in European atomic energy and ballistics research and in African efforts to combat yellow fever and rinderpest regionally – that is, where the required scale and the need to avoid expensive duplication were sufficient to overcome nationalist rivalries. Although the record on similar agreements among developing countries in the field of common market investment allocations, for instance, has not been very encouraging, it has been somewhat better with respect to the use of regional training institutes and research organisations, in other words whenever regionalism was not forced but flowed from the recognition of mutual interest.

If we agree that no developing country can really afford to be either a full-time borrower of science or an across-the-board contributor to it, the same holds for the Hamlet of our piece: domestic human development, as expressed in terms of appropriate education levels. When we speak about a society's national capacity to utilise and modify basic science creatively, we are really referring to a human capacity to make appropriate adaptations to a different environment. Contributions to human knowledge that break new ground and provide scope for major new technological breakthroughs will, with few exceptions, probably remain the province of the North for the time being.

What can we say about the direction that new, science-intensive and engineering-intensive frontier technology is likely to take? The two elements that seem most responsible for determining this direction are the changing resource endowments and the changing public policy. The very different historical behaviour of the natural resource-rich, labour-scarce United States, by comparison with a relatively capital-scarce England and a Germany that felt strapped for natural resources, should be instructive in this respect. Engineering-intensive technology took a different, more capital-intensive path in the wide-open spaces of the United States than in England. And, in Germany, metallurgical science responded to the demands of an iron ore with high phosphorous content; official encouragement of the entire chemical industry was based on the felt need to overcome, by artificial and synthetic short-cuts, the relative unkindness of nature. Japan, after first exploiting its abundant labour resources – and taking an engineering-intensive route analogous to that of the United States – has tended, after the disappearance of its labour surplus, to place more of its eggs in electronics and other high-technology baskets.

While government policies cannot legislate away the basic endowment of a society, they can, if they are flexible and able to overcome national sectional interests, provide important assistance to the transition effort of a developing economy as its resource endowment and institutional capacity change over time. Conversely, if they are dominated by narrow vested interests and/or lacking in historical perspective, such policies can attempt to turn a blind eye to the endowment and lead the system into expensive scientific/technological dead ends and economic stagnation. While there is no rigid unidirectional sequence of the phases that every developing country must follow on the path to mature growth, some attention to the changing roles of science and technology in terms of a changing resource endowment and, especially, of changing human capabilities is essential in all but the most unusual cases.

At the micro- and institution-building levels, the appropriate role of government in the mixed economy context is not unrelated to the appropriability or non-appropriability of the new knowledge acquired. Investment in basic science carries a high risk, in part because of its, at best, indirect and long-term relationship with technology and growth, but also partly because it is generally an international good not even appropriable by a country, let alone by a private party within a country. As we move from basic international science to changes in technology, risks are reduced and private appropriability becomes much more important. As the extent of appropriability rises, so, normally, does the level of private R&D expenditure.

A perceptible trend was for the typical LDC, in the early stages of its independence, to rely on import substitution policies, in an attempt to assert its post-colonial economic independence by beefing up its domestic industry. However, these policies also (and quite often) did harm to local industry by making it less competitive and greatly decreased the incentive to innovate, as firms were protected by tariffs, price controls and foreign exchange rationing. When they are guaranteed unearned profits, producers have less incentive to find new technologies and innovation is stifled. Firms are content to protect their quasi-monopoly position and to adopt a 'satisficing behavior'. While such policies may be necessary in the early stages of an LDC's development, there is always the danger that some bad habits will persist. For example some countries still prohibit the importation of second-hand machinery. Ultimately openness to trade and to the transfer of technology via patents and FDI can provide opportunities in the direction of generating appropriate technology change. Stewart has argued that the objectives of a firm can be changed by influencing the environment in which decision-makers operate. By removing the quasi-monopolist protection that import substitution policies provide to domestic decision-makers, it is possible to influence performance in an innovative direction.

In order to ensure a successful and mutually beneficial relationship between an LDC and the multinational corporation, the latter should ideally be disaggregated into its component parts. Most misunderstandings occur because of the mystique of the powerful, footloose MNC bargaining with the poor, optionless LDC – the latter being pressured to buy what is essentially a 'pig in a poke'. The capital, technology, management and entrepreneurship components of any deal should be spelled out as fully as possible and each component priced out. Screening procedures that exist in virtually every LDC should concentrate more on such disaggregation and full disclosure, thus permitting comparative shopping and something other than 'all or nothing' acceptances or rejections. Fade-out and divestiture agreements can be negotiated much more intelligently *ab initio* – which might, for example, provide for a transition from the wholly owned subsidiary to the joint venture form after ten years, and possibly to further reassessments in the direction of licensing or management contracts thereafter.

We must, of course, contend with the argument that 'it is unlikely that multinational firms will ever be willing to repeat the Japanese experience elsewhere because, from their point of view, they helped create formidable competition to themselves for very meagre returns' (Chudnovsky, 1997: p. 45). Clearly, if offered more at every stage, they will seek more. If, however, there is a clear and anticipated transition from one stage (and one bundle) to another within a particular LDC, competitive pressures among the MNCs should assert themselves, dictating a willingness to accept reasonable rates of return. In this we would be safer in relying on the MNC's long-run profit objective rather than on some public-spirited impulse. Negotiations should recognise that it is better for both parties to plan on living together under changing rules than to attempt to deny the declining value of some major MNC components over time, thus inviting expropriation or other retaliatory actions. The burden of proof would have to be on the side of those like Raymond Vernon, who claimed to see a general tendency for a broadening and deepening relative role for the MNC over time (Vernon, 1972).

LDC screening procedures governing MNC presence could be modified in the direction of greater automaticity, greater predictability and more built-in flexibility over time. Such procedures should reflect a recognition that some of the excesses of the MNC, ranging from transfer pricing to the payment of prematurely high wages, to the inappropriateness of the technology selected, to the underutilisation of patents and to the overutilisation of domestic credit and export prohibition clauses, are clearly related to the overall policy environment of the recipient LDC. The MNC can be effectively forced to put its energies into building better mousetraps and into using adaptive (usually labour-intensive) technologies. In that case the MNC is forced to give up the 'quiet life' of the satisficing monopolist as the transition to a more liberal policy regime is effected. MNCs are quite capable of coming up with appropriate process and product ideas when they are pressured to 'scratch around'.

The importance of indigenous human capabilities in determining the rate of technological change is reflected in the importance attached to vocational education and to scientific personnel, both of which underpin the nature of domestic R&D at different stages of an economy's development. This very capability will serve a developing country well in determining, most importantly, its domestic policies as well its attitude towards foreign patents, towards the multinational company and towards foreign capital, public and private.

The contrast in TFP performance between East Asia and Latin America makes the point rather convincingly. The typical Latin American country, say, Brazil, was larger and better endowed with natural resources and it exhibited a lower labour/land ratio than, say, its East Asian counterpart Taiwan. The existence of a natural resource bonanza induces countries to neglect human capital and the importance of TFP. One manifestation of this natural resource curse is the choice of education strategy – for example Latin America's focus on the academic track at the secondary level, and a disproportionate emphasis on tertiary education, especially in the humanities – in sharp contrast to East Asia's concentration on vocational education at the secondary level and its emphasis on science and technology in a relatively smaller tertiary establishment. Latin America, with its relatively strong unions applying pressure to delay trade liberalisation, felt secure in maintaining its import substitution policies, while East Asia was impelled to shift early on to an internationally competitive human resource-intensive growth path. The consequence was a substantially larger role for TFP – 2.6 per cent in Taiwan compared to 1.0 per cent annually in Brazil between 1966 and 1991 (Young, 1995).

Acknowledgment

The assistance of Sara Lowes is gratefully acknowledged as are the helpful comments on an earlier draft from Valpy FitzGerald, Frances Stewart and Adrian Wood.

Notes

1. For example, see Romer (1990).
2. See also Stewart (1987).
3. UNIDO, World Productivity Database (2007).
4. See Stewart (1972) and especially Stewart (1977: Chapter 7).
5. A low-threshold, short-protection type of patent.
6. From World Development Indicators and the Taiwan Bureau of Statistics.
7. We here substitute highly correlated GDP growth for TFP growth.

References

Acemoglu, D., and F. Zilibotti (2001) 'Productivity Differences'. *The Quarterly Journal of Economics* 116 (2): 563–606.
Behrman, J. (1990) 'The Action of Human Resources and Poverty on One Another'. *Living Standards Measurement Study Working Paper* No. 74 (Washington, DC: World Bank).

Borensztein, E., J. De Gregorio and J.-W. Lee (1998) 'How Does Foreign Direct Investment Affect Economic Growth?' *Journal of International Economics* 45: 115–35.

Chudnovsky, D. (1997) 'Transnational Corporations and Industrialization', United Nations Library on Transnational Corportations, Vol. 11, Geneva: United Nations Conference on Trade and Development.

Keller, W. (2004) 'International Technology Diffusion'. *Journal of Economic Literature* 42 (3): 752–82.

Kuznets, S. (1966) *Modern Economic Growth: Rate, Structure and Spread* (New Haven, CT: Yale University Press).

Larraín, F.B., L.F. López-Calva and A. Rodríguez-Claré (2001) 'Intel: A Case Study of Foreign Direct Investment in Central America'. In F.B. Larraín (ed.) *Economic Development in Latin America, Vol. 1: Growth and Internationalization* (Boston, MA: Harvard University Press).

Otsuka, K., G. Ranis and G. Saxonhouse (1988) *Comparative Technology Choice in Development: The Indian and Japanese Cotton Textile Industries* (Basingstoke: Palgrave Macmillan).

Pack, H., and L. Westphal (1986) 'Industrial Strategy and Technological Change: Theory Versus Reality'. *Journal of Development Economics* 22 (1): 87–128.

Preston, S.H. (1975) 'The Changing Relation between Mortality and Level of Economic Development'. *Population Studies* 29 (2): 231–48.

Ranis, G. (1979) 'Appropriate Technology: Obstacles and Opportunities'. In S. Rosenblatt (ed.) *Technology and Economic Development: A Realistic Perspective* (Boulder, CO: Westview Press).

Ranis, G. (1978) 'Science, Technology, and Development: A Retrospective View'. In W. Beranek and G. Ranis (eds) *Science, Technology, and Economic Development: A Historical and Comparative Study* (New York: Praeger).

Ranis, G. (1976) 'The Multinational Corporation as an Instrument of Development'. In D. Apter and L.W. Goodman (eds) *The Multinational Corporation and Social Change* (New York: Praeger).

Ranis, G., F. Stewart and A. Ramirez (2003) 'Economic Growth and Human Development'. *World Development* 28 (2): 197–219.

Romer, P. (1990) 'Endogenous Technological Change'. *Journal of Political Economy* 98 (5): S71–S102.

Solow, R. (1956) 'A Contribution to the Theory of Economic Growth'. *Quarterly Journal of Economics* 70: 65–94.

Stewart, F. (1987) 'Overview and Conclusions'. In F. Stewart (ed.) *Macro-Policies for Appropriate Technology in Developing Countries* (Boulder, CO: Westview Press).

Stewart, F. (1981) 'Arguments for the Generation of Technology by Less-developed Countries'. *The ANNALS of the American Academy of Political and Social Science* 458: 97–109.

Stewart, F. (1977) *Technology and Underdevelopment* (London: Macmillan).

Stewart, F. (1972) 'Choice of Technique in Developing Countries'. *Journal of Development Studies* 9 (1): 99–121.

Stewart, F., and J. James (eds) (1982) *The Economics of New Technology in Developing Countries* (London; Boulder, CO: Pinter; Westview Press).

UNDP (United Nations Development Programme) (2001) *Human Development Report 2001: Making New Technologies Work for Human Development* (New York: UNDP).

Vernon, R. (1972) *The Economic and Political Consequences of Multinational Enterprise: An Anthology* (Boston, MA: Division of Research, Graduate School of Business Administration, Harvard University).

Xu, B. (2000) 'Multinational Enterprises, Technology Diffusion, and Host Country Productivity Growth'. *Journal of Development Economics* 62 (2): 477–93.

Young, A. (1995) 'The Tyranny of Numbers: Confronting the Statistical Realities of the East Asian Growth Experience'. *Quarterly Journal of Economics* 110 (3): 641–80.

4
Migration and Productivity Patterns in European Regions

Giorgio Barba Navaretti, Gianfranco De Simone, Gianluca Orefice and Angelica Salvi

4.1 Introduction

Migration and offshoring are controversial issues in policy terms: both are seen as threats to domestic employment. Many policy-makers think that placing restrictions on inflows of migrants and on the relocation of production abroad is an effective way of increasing or maintaining domestic employment.

This is a somewhat short-sighted vision, for several reasons. First, the movements of firms and people are interrelated. We know they are driven by similar factors (costs, the size of the market, agglomeration, specialisation of economic activities and the like) and that they interact with each other. For example a large inflow of immigrants, by affecting local labour market conditions, may also affect the incentive to offshore or the attractiveness of the region to foreign investors. Recent contributions have looked at whether migrant flows and foreign direct investment (FDI) are substitutes or complements for a given location (country, province, region) or pair of locations (Aroca and Maloney, 2005; Buch et al., 2005; Kirkegaard, 2005; Kugler and Rapoport, 2005; Docquier and Lodigiani, 2006).

Second, aggregate dynamics often reflect changes at the micro-level. Average values hide movements in the distribution of workers and economic activities which need to be clearly understood and which have important policy implications. Recent papers have shown how firm-level characteristics affect decisions over carrying out international activities and the effect of such activities on performance. Productivity, profitability and size distributions are shaped by changes in market integration induced by trade liberalisation; by changes in the degree of competition in the local market; by the level of aggregation of economic activities; and by the extent of foreign offshoring (Lileeva and Trefler, 2007; Del Gatto et al., 2008; Combes et al., 2009). Equally, understanding how migrants and offshoring affect local labour market conditions entails breaking down the labour force and the standard distinctions between skilled and unskilled workers, or 'white' and 'blue collars', into finer categories, related to the actual tasks performed by workers (Peri and Sparber, 2007; Ottaviano et al., 2010).

Where to produce and whom to hire are interrelated choices at the firm level as well. In any given location, firms may decide to acquire foreign workers either by moving production (or part of it) to a foreign country or by hiring foreign-born workers locally. Barba Navaretti and colleagues (2008) have shown how these are indeed alternative and interrelated choices, partly driven by *ex ante* productivity: high-performance firms are more likely to offshore, whereas lower-performance firms are more likely to hire migrants. Consequently offshoring and migration are also likely to be related to productivity patterns in given locations.

All these studies cast light on how the availability of migrants and opportunities for offshoring are channels through which firms can broaden their set of factors of production and possibly boost productivity. In addition, access to foreign factors of production does not necessarily hinder domestic employment if, by increasing productivity and lowering factor costs, it preserves and enhances competitiveness and growth at the firm level.

The recent economic crisis has often (and we would assert, mistakenly) induced policy-makers to call for a strengthening of the *national* dimension of the economy; migration and the de-localisation of economic activities are obvious targets for criticism here. Policy-makers, however, need to understand the links between factor flows in order to appreciate the full implications of potential policy measures. This is especially important as migration and inward and outward FDI flows have been rising considerably in Europe over the last few years.

The aim of this chapter is to look for empirical regularities linking factor movements to firm-level productivity in regions within the European Union area. By combining several data sets on migration, outward FDI and firm-level productivity, this chapter examines whether factor flows (a) are correlated between each other; (b) are related to average regional productivity at the industry level; and (c) are related to the shape of productivity distributions within industry and regions.

Theoretically, average productivity and productivity dispersion might be affected by migration and offshoring through many different channels. These channels often operate in conflicting directions. For example, according to Barba Navaretti and colleagues (2008), the availability of migrants provides less efficient firms with an opportunity to reduce production costs and to avoid exit even in fairly competitive environments. At the same time, offshoring is a strategy pursued by the most productive firms. Thus a higher share of migrants in a given region might push the productivity cut-off for surviving in the market leftward along the horizontal productivity axis, whereas offshoring might be associated with a rightward shift of the distribution itself.

Labour market effects (and consequently their implications for factor costs) are not clear either. There is a growing controversy over the effects of migrants on local wages: does an increase in the supply of foreign migrants actually reduce local wages? Or does it in fact improve labour productivity, by expanding variety in the supply of skills in the local labour market and by enhancing complementarities with local skills?

Unfortunately, there are serious measurement errors in the data. When we make cross-regional comparisons, we are unable to identify the skill structure of migrants or the industrial composition in terms of employment of migrants and offshoring. We are therefore unable to isolate the specific channels of interaction between factor flows and performance. In this chapter we will therefore take an agnostic approach and see what the data can tell us about the relationship between these variables.

The reminder of the chapter is structured as follows. Section 4.2 describes the relevant stylised facts on immigration and outward FDI for the European regions, and the relevant data. Section 4.3 provides an empirical analysis of the relationship between the regional and the sectoral distribution of TFP, immigration and FDI using firm-level data. Section 4.4 draws conclusions.

4.2 Aggregate stylised facts and data

In this section we document the patterns of immigration and outward and inward FDI for the European regions. First we describe the main data used, then we provide stylised facts, first in the aggregate and then by looking at firm-level data.

4.2.1 Description of the data set

This paper's empirical analysis is based on four main groups of variables aggregated at the NUTS2 regional level for several EU countries: (i) the stock of immigrants; (ii) inward and outward FDI; (iii) firm performance; and (iv) control variables on regional economic indicators.

All the analysis at this stage is carried out as a cross-section; data are therefore stocks or averages for the 2003–06 period.

Data on *immigration* consist of a measure of the stock of immigrants employed in the industrial sector in each region in 2006. This stock is imputed as the sum of the 2001 stock and annual regional flows for the 2002–06 period. While the 2001 regional stock is taken from the Eurostat database, which is based on the 2001 Census, data on immigration flows are only available at the national level and have thus had to be imputed. The imputation rule for regional flows is the following:

$$\text{immigrant inflow}_{r,t,i} = \left(\frac{\text{stock of immigrants}_{2001,r,i}}{\text{stock of immigrants}_{2001,c}} \right) *$$

$$\text{immigrant inflow}_{t,c}$$

where r is each region in the country c, t stands for the year, and i stands for the immigrants' geographic area of origin (European vs. non-European countries). The underlying assumption is that new immigration inflows at country level are distributed across regions following the regional distribution as at 2001. In this chapter we only look at immigrants employed in the industrial sectors.

Outward foreign direct investments are measured as the total number of new greenfield investments from European regions in the sample over the 2003–06 period. The source for this data is the FDI Markets Data set.

Variables on regional economic accounts are taken from the Eurostat database, while variables on the employment level in the region are taken from the Cambridge Econometric data set.

4.2.2   Stylised facts: Aggregate

The first important stylised fact that we note by looking at the aggregate data is that the distributions of migration and FDI stocks are more concentrated than the distribution of broader economic activities. Figure 4.1 reports Lorenz curves of inward FDI, outward FDI and foreign-born labour force across the European regions in our sample. All three are more concentrated than employment in manufacturing. This shows that factor movements tend to concentrate in a few regions with specific characteristics. Figure 4.1 also shows that concentration is particularly high for outward investment.

The second important stylised fact is that the location of factor movements is highly correlated. In Figure 4.2 we report the relationship

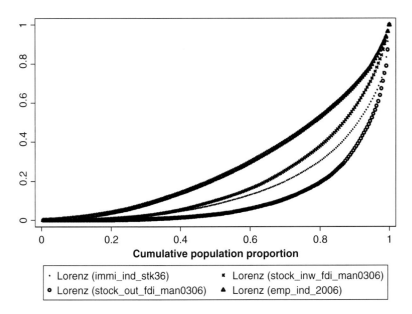

Figure 4.1 Lorenz curves for: (i) Stock of immigrants working in the industrial sector 2003–06; (ii) Stock of inward FDI 2003–06 in manufacturing; (iii) Stock of outward FDI 2003–06 in manufacturing; and (iv) Employment in the industrial sector

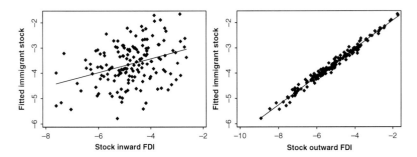

Figure 4.2 Stock of inward (a) and outward (b) FDI 2003–06 in manufacturing per thousand inhabitants vs. fitted values of the estimated stock of immigrants 2003–06, controlling for per capita GDP

Notes: Fitted values from: ln (stock of immigrants 03–06 in industry) $_r = \beta_1$ln (stock of inward FDI 03–06 in manufacturing) $_r + \beta_2$ln (stock of outward FDI 03–06 in manufacturing) $_r + \beta_3$ln (average 03–06 gdp per capita) $_r + \varepsilon_r$.

between the fitted values of migration and the values of inward and outward FDI derived from an OLS regression controlling for GDP per capita. Particularly striking is the strong and very significant correlation between migration and outward FDI (note most observations are on the regression line). But there is also a positive and significant correlation with inward FDI. This confirms that in Figure 4.2 there are unobserved factors, other than GDP per capita, which drive the co-movement of factors of production and with which the latter are somehow interrelated.

To gain a more precise picture of the geographical patterns of FDI and migration across European regions we provide maps of the share of immigrant workers (Figure 4.3a) and outward FDI (Figure 4.3b) across European regions.[1]

4.3   Micro facts

In this section we will relate the intensity of migration and offshoring at the regional level with firm productivity. We use data on manufacturing firms for several European regions, to try to understand how offshoring and migration are related so as to average productivity and the productivity distribution at the regional level.

How do we expect factor mobility to correlate with the productivity of the firms in a given region? In general terms, as factors tend to cluster in high-productivity regions, we should expect a positive correlation

Figure 4.3a   Share of immigrant workers in the industrial sector

Figure 4.3b   Outward FDI in manufacturing per thousand inhabitants
Note: That there is a fairly good overlap between the high migration and high offshoring regions.
Source: GISCO (geographic information system of the European Commission) and Eurostat.

between productivity and migration. Equally, as offshoring involves high fixed costs and is normally carried out by high-productivity firms, it also likely to be positively correlated with high productivity. This link is expected to hold even when one is controlling for GDP per capita.

However, the literature has shown that shocks to the competitive setting in which firms operate or shocks influencing factor costs may affect productivity in several, not always obvious, ways. For example Del Gatto and colleagues (2008) look at the effect of trade openness on the distribution of productivity for French regions and industries. They find that productivity follows a Pareto distribution (this is a stylised fact in most contexts) and that trade openness reduces dispersion, that is, the distance between the most and the least productive firms. Their argument is that increased competition forces the least productive firms to exit the market, thereby increasing the minimum productivity threshold for survival. Changes in market conditions may also affect the overall shape of the productivity distribution of the survivors. For example, Combes and colleagues (2009) argue that in any given location distributions might be affected by both competition and agglomeration effects. While the former might cut distributions from below, the latter might increase the productivity of the most productive firms and shift the distribution rightwards (thus increasing dispersion).

In what follows we will look at the way offshoring and migration interact in affecting productivity outcomes. Of course an analysis of the link between factor movements and firm performance is fraught with problems of endogeneity, as factor endowments affect productivity and vice versa. In addition, theoretical predictions are not clear-cut. Migration might both boost and depress average productivity in a given region. It might boost productivity by increasing the range of skills available in the labour market – which might increase cultural diversity, thus fostering creativity and innovation – and by reducing factor costs, thus favouring a more efficient allocation of resources. But it may also reduce productivity, as it displaces better performing national workers.

Equally, migration might have non-neutral effects on the shape of the distribution. If, for example, migrants are generally unskilled and they are mostly hired by low-productivity firms, then these firms will benefit the most from the presence of immigrants. In this case, regions with a larger share of immigrants can be expected to have a lower mean productivity in the lowest quintile of the industrial productivity distribution. This effect on the lower tail of the distribution will depress average productivity and will have ambiguous effects on dispersion measures. If employing migrant workers reduces the productivity threshold for surviving in the market, then dispersion will increase. If, however, it also raises the average productivity of the least productive firms, then dispersion will decline. In contrast, if migrants are generally skilled individuals, then the effect of immigration is likely to be more concentrated in the upper tail of the distribution.

The consequences of offshoring might also be ambiguous. If, as most of the literature points out, it is only the most productive firms that offshore, then we would expect a higher average productivity for offshoring-intensive regions and stronger effects on the upper tail of the distribution, a phenomenon which thus increases dispersion. However, if the presence of offshorers makes the competitive environment in the region tighter, then the productivity threshold will shift to the right and dispersion will decrease.

At this stage, we take an agnostic approach and simply examine the data to see which patterns emerge. Our results are purely descriptive, as we cannot infer any causal relationship between the variables analysed.

4.3.1   Data description and TFP estimates

Productivity has been computed at the firm level using balance sheet data from the Amadeus data set (Bureau Van Dijk), after assigning to each firm the corresponding two-digit-level regional code (NUTS2).[2] More specifically, we computed the TFP using the Levinsohn-Petrin estimation procedure (see Appendix). Data cover regions from Austria, the Czech Republic, Finland, France, Italy, Latvia, the Netherlands, Norway, Poland, Romania, Spain, Sweden and Slovakia.[3] As a classification of economic activities we adopt the two-digit NACE rev.2 classification,[4] and we restrict the analysis to firms in the manufacturing sectors (i.e. from NACE 10 to 33).

4.3.2   Average productivities at the regional and industry levels

The first step in our analysis is to try to relate average productivity by industry and region to the share of foreign workers as a proportion of total employment and to the number of offshoring projects per thousand inhabitants. In order to do this, we estimate the following regressions with industry fixed effects through OLS:

$$\text{mean TFP}_{r,s} = \beta_1 \text{immi}_r + \beta_2 \text{out FDI}_r + \beta_3 \text{GDP}_r$$
$$+ \beta_4 \text{aggl}_{r,s} + \beta_5 d_r + u_{r,s} \tag{4.1}$$

The dependent variable is the average TFP for each region and industrial sector. The explanatory variables of interest are specified respectively as: (i) the stock of foreign-born immigrants employed in the industrial sector in each region; and (ii) the total number of outward FDIs in industrial sectors in each region over the 2003–06 period. Two region-specific controls have also been added: GDP per capita and an index capturing agglomeration effects in productive activities in the regions. This agglomeration index represents the regional share in each industrial sector and is measured as the number of employees in every region and sector, divided by the total number of employees in every sector. Table 4.1 shows the regression results.

We find that the share of foreign-born workers in total employment by industry is related negatively to average TFP. This might be the outcome of an overall depressing effect of migration on productivity or the outcome of a positive effect on the efficiency of the least productive firms, essentially a leftward shift of the lower tail of the distribution. Offshoring, by contrast, has a positive coefficient, either because it is a more plausible outcome in regions with a higher concentration of efficient firms or because it affects overall productivity positively.

Table 4.1   Mean TFP regression, by region and industry

	Average TFP$_{region, sector}$
log immigration share	−0.018
	(2.98)***
log outward FDI per thousand inhabitants	4.105
	(5.90)***
log per capita GDP	0.158
	(21.98)***
agglomeration index	0.028
	(3.00)***
Controls:	
sector fixed effects	
Observations	3245
R-squared	0.89
F(27, 3218)	1190.53

Notes: Robust t statistics in parentheses; *significant at 10 per cent; **significant at 5 per cent; ***significant at 1 per cent.

In order better to understand what is driving these initial results, we first run quantile regressions, on the empirical equation presented above (4.1). Results of the quantile regressions for the two variables of interest are reported in Figure 4.4 below. These figures relate the level of productivity of the industry/region (horizontal axis) with (i) the coefficient of the relationship between average TFP and foreign workers in the left quadrant, and (ii) the coefficient of the relationship between average TFP and offshoring in the right quadrant.

Note the non-linearity in the relationship between migration and average TFP. The results in the migration regression are driven by the lower-productivity regions (lower quantile), where the coefficient is negative and significant (the shaded area, which represents the confidence interval, never crosses 0). The coefficient turns positive towards the median point of the distribution and then loses significance for the high-productivity regions. In other words, the average negative relationship between migration and TFP is mostly driven by what happens in low-productivity regions.

The relationship between offshoring and TFP is much neater. It is positive and significant (above 0) for the whole range, and it becomes higher the higher the quantile of the distribution. In other words this seems to confirm both the presumption that offshoring is concentrated in high-productivity regions and that it might be particularly effective in boosting productivity in such regions.

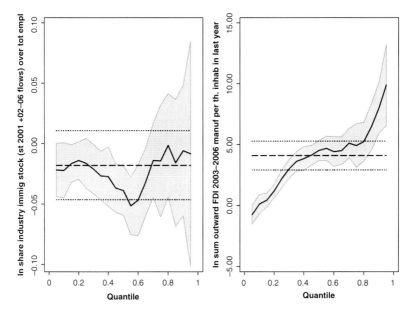

Figure 4.4 Quantile regressions, by region and industry
Notes: Continuous line = quantile estimates; grey area = confidence interval; dashed line = OLS estimate; dotted line = confidence interval for OLS estimates.

4.3.3 Factor movements and productivity distributions

In order to gauge better the relationship between factor movements and productivity, we now look at the shape of the productivity distribution. One way to do so is to look at measures of dispersion, in particular the standard deviation of industry/region distributions. To this end, we run an OLS of the standard deviation of TFP for each region and sector on the same dependent variable used for the first specification (average TFP as dependent variable):

$$\text{std dev TFP}_{r,s} = \beta_1 \text{immi}_r + \beta_2 \text{out FDI}_r + \beta_3 \text{GDP}_r$$
$$+ \beta_4 \text{aggl}_{r,s} + \beta_5 d_r + u_{r,s} \quad (4.2)$$

The results are reported in Table 4.2.

We find that dispersion declines with the stock of foreign workers and increases with offshoring. To understand this outcome better, we need to control for the actual shape of the distribution. Most empirical analyses show that firms' productivity and sizes usually follow a Pareto

Table 4.2   TFP standard deviation regression, by region and industry

	Standard deviation TFP$_{region, sector}$
log immigration share	−0.064
	(14.58)***
log outward FDI per thousand inhabitants	0.465
	(3.04)**
log per capita GDP	0.086
	(21.88)***
agglomeration index	0.061
	(11.62)***
Controls:	
sector dummies	
Observations	2879
R-squared	0.83
F(27, 2852)	706.20

Notes: Robust t statistics in parentheses; *significant at 10 per cent; **significant at 5 per cent; ***significant at 1 per cent.

distribution. In this framework, one reading of these results is as follows: immigration increases the productivity of the least productive firms, therefore shifting the lower tail of the distribution towards the mean and hence strengthening its central tendency. In contrast, offshoring, by increasing the productivity of the best performers, enhances the dispersion and weakens the central tendency.

To see whether this is indeed the case, we carry out a further exercise. We look at the overall productivity distribution across all regions and industries. Industry-specific effects are controlled for because our measure of TFP is computed in deviations from the industry mean. We then compute the quintiles of this distribution. If we then assign a quintile to each firm in our sample, we are able to see how each firm ranks with respect to the overall sample. We then divide regions into high-migration and low-migration ones. Table 4.3 reports the distribution of firms by quintile in high and low migration regions (a) and in high and low offshoring regions (b). For migration, the share of firms is almost equal in the first quintile, higher in high-immigration regions for the second and third quintile and lower in the fourth and fifth. For high-offshoring regions, firms concentrate instead in the fourth and fifth quintile. This confirms our tentative conclusions above, that migration raises the productivity of the least productive firms, also pushing them higher up towards the mean of the distribution. Offshoring, on

Table 4.3a Distribution of number of firms by productivity quintile – high-/low-migration regions

	1st quintile (%)	2nd quintile (%)	3rd quintile (%)	4th quintile (%)	5th quintile (%)
Low-migration regions	24.0	21.2	19.7	18.2	16.9
High-migration regions	23.4	24.4	20.9	17.1	14.2

Note: High-migration regions are those regions where the share of foreign-born workers as a proportion of the total employed in industry is above the mean value of the sample.

Table 4.3b Distribution of number of firms by productivity quintile – high-/low-offshoring regions

	1st quintile (%)	2nd quintile (%)	3rd quintile (%)	4th quintile (%)	5th quintile (%)
Low-offshoring regions	23.8	22.3	20.1	17.9	16.0
High-offshoring regions	19.5	19.1	17.5	24.0	19.9

Note: High-offshoring regions are those regions where the ratio of outward FDI in manufacturing to the total is above the mean value in the sample.

the other hand, is associated with high-productivity firms and probably strengthens them.

To see how the effect of offshoring and migration interact in affecting these distributions, we regress the number of firms in each quintile, industry and region on the usual explanatory variables (Table 4.4). The offshoring and migration variables are interacted with quintile dummies, to capture the effect of factor movements in each specific quintile.

$$n \text{ firms}_{r,s,q} = \beta_1 \text{immi}_r + \beta_2 \text{out FDI}_r + \beta_3 \text{GDP}_r + \beta_4 \text{aggl}_{r,s}$$
$$+ \beta_5 n \text{ firms}_r + \beta_6 d_s + \beta_7 d_q + \beta_7 (\text{immi}^* \text{d\_quintile})_{r,q}$$
$$+ \beta_8 (\text{out FDI}^* \text{d\_quintile})_{r,q} + u_{r,s,q} \qquad (4.3)$$

To account for the fact that the distribution of the number of firms is truncated on the left at zero and that this is a distribution of integer values, we estimate the equation through a Poisson regression.

The results are consistent with the averages reported in Table 4.1. Migration is positively related to the share of firms in the second and

Table 4.4   Number of firms regression, by region and industry

	N. firms _{quintile, region, sector}
log immigration share	−0.224
	(6.46)***
log outward FDI per thousand inhabitants	−0.833
	(0.71)
log per capita GDP	0.264
	(13.74)***
n. firms in region / sector	0.003
	(17.41)***
agglomeration index	0.294
	(13.57)***
quint 2 × log outward FDI	0.484
	(0.30)
quint 3 × log outward FDI	2.689
	(1.74)*
quint 4 × log outward FDI	3.155
	(2.08)**
quint 5 × log outward FDI	2.109
	(1.34)
quint 2 × log immigration share	0.190
	(2.76)***
quint 3 × log immigration share	0.099
	(1.56)
quint 4 × log immigration share	0.049
	(0.81)
quint 5 × log immigration share	0.023
	(0.36)
Controls	
sector dummies	
quintile dummies	
Observations	11934
Wald chi2(40)	39475.31

Notes: Robust t statistics in parentheses; *significant at 10 per cent; **significant at 5 per cent; ***significant at 1 per cent.

third quintile, whereas offshoring is positively related to the share of firms in the fourth quintile.

This outcome is consistent with the final conclusion that migration and offshoring interact and affect not only average productivity across regions, but also the shape of the distribution. Migration enhances the productivity of the least productive firms in the distribution, while offshoring enhances the productivity of the most productive ones.

4.4 Conclusions

This chapter has looked at the interaction between migration and offshoring (measured as the number of outward FDIs) in European regions and at how they are related to productivity distributions in manufacturing at the firm level. These two sources of access to foreign labour are highly correlated: regions with a large population of foreigners also have a large number of offshoring projects. However, migration and offshoring are related to total factor productivities in different ways. A larger share of migrant workers is related to higher efficiency for the least productive firms and to a reduction in both the dispersion and the central tendency of the productivity distribution. Offshoring is related to higher efficiency for the most productive firms and to an increase in the dispersion and a reduction in the central tendency of the productivity distribution.

These results are purely descriptive, as an accurate assessment of the causal effects of factor flows on productivity distributions requires further work, particularly to deal with the endogeneity problems affecting our estimations.

All the same, our findings are in line with the assumption that hiring migrants and offshoring are very different channels through which firms have access to foreign factors of production. Interestingly, whereas foreign workers appear to strengthen the least productive firms, offshoring appears to strengthen the most productive firms. These findings have important policy implications. Restricting migration flows will presumably accelerate the exit of weaker firms from the market, whereas limiting offshoring might hinder the competitiveness of the best-performing firms. Policy-makers should think carefully about these interrelations when designing policies.

A key issue is the composition of migration flows. In our data we are unable to distinguish between skilled and unskilled migrants; however, it is the composition, and not only the size, of these flows that impacts on productivity in host regions. Several studies have shown that the skill structure of migrant flows generates Rybczynski effects and affects the technological choices of firms in the host country (Hanson et al., 2004). Therefore, although the dominant share of migrants is unskilled, in future work we should control for this factor. In particular, we would expect skilled migrants to complement offshoring activities by strengthening the higher tail of the productivity distribution. A sufficiently large increase in the supply of unskilled labour through migration, in contrast, might induce firms to choose simpler labour-intensive technologies. Thus, countries which have introduced targeted migration policies, such as point systems, clearly aim to match the demand for labour in relatively sophisticated tasks and to increase the inflow of highly skilled individuals.

Our findings have implications for policies aimed at promoting the development of industry. In all countries the distribution of firms is skewed towards smaller units. The development and support of small and medium enterprises is invariably a key policy objective in all industrialised economies. Given that size is highly correlated to productivity, our results show that, in the European regions, unskilled migrants are an important factor of production for such firms. Interestingly, policy-makers often support both a restriction in migration flows and the development of small companies, being unaware of the contradiction involved in pursuing these policy agendas simultaneously.

The joint effects of migration and offshoring are of course also important for the higher-spectrum of industry. High-tech sectors employ highly skilled individuals and often need to be recruited on the global labour market. Equally, these companies have international operations across countries; thus a part of their activities is offshored.

However, in non-high-tech sectors, too, companies at the higher end of the productivity distribution have complex international activities, including foreign production. These companies leave behind the capital- and skills-intensive part of their production process in the home country, often employing foreign skilled workers. Regulatory restrictions, both on offshoring and on skilled migration, may therefore severely hinder the competitiveness of these companies.

In conclusion, the main message of this chapter is that policies targeted at regulating migration flows and foreign production are strictly interrelated and can have unexpected effects on industrial development.

Appendix: TFP estimation: The Levinsohn-Petrin (2003) approach

For the estimation of an individual firm's TFP, we used the Levinsohn–Petrin (2003) estimation algorithm. This takes into account the simultaneity bias that usually arises in estimating total factor productivity; and this kind of estimation relies on semi-parametric estimations *à la* Olley-Pakes (1996). The advantage of using the Levinsohn–Petrin approach is that it takes the cost of intermediate inputs as a proxy for unobserved productivity. This has two main implications: (i) it allows us to retain more observations than in the OP estimation, because typically firms report a positive use of inputs; and (ii) as a consequence, the monotonicity condition is more likely to hold for intermediates than for investments. So intermediate inputs m_{it} are expressed as a function of capital stock and productivity ω_{it}:

$$m_{it} = m_t(k_{it}\omega_{it}) \tag{A1}$$

and, if intermediate inputs are strictly increasing, the function can be inverted; in this way we obtain productivity as a function of capital and intermediates:

$$\omega_{it} = s_t(k_{it}m_{it}) \tag{A2}$$

In our estimation intermediate inputs have been approximated by the cost of materials in each firm; capital has been approximated by fixed assets; and labour has been approximated by the number of employees in the firm. As a proxy for the output of firms, we have used the value added of firms. All these data come from the Amadeus database. Each variable has been deflated by using the producer price index at the NACE 2-digit level (from Eurostat) and expressed in log terms. So we may express the Cobb-Douglas production function in logs, obtaining the following linear production function in linear form:

$$y_{it} = \beta_0 + \beta_k k_{it} + \beta_l l_{it} + \beta_m m_{it} + s_t(k_{it}m_{it}) + u_{it}^q \tag{A3}$$

Now we can define the following function:

$$\delta(m_{it}, k_{it}) = \beta_0 + \beta_k k_{it} + s_t(k_{it}, m_{it}) \tag{A4}$$

The estimation proceeds in two steps. In the first, we estimated the following equation – which was intended to give us the consistent coefficients for labour and materials by using a simple OLS model:

$$y_{it} = \beta_l l_{it} + \beta_m m_{it} + \delta(m_{it}, k_{it}) + u_{it}^q \tag{A5}$$

The second stage of the estimation consists in using the estimated $\beta_l \beta_m$, to derive the following second-stage estimating equation:

$$y_{it+1} - \beta_l l_{it+1} - \beta_m m_{it+1} = \beta_0 + \beta_k k_{it+1} + E(\omega_{it+1}|\omega_{it}, \chi_{it+1}) + u_{it+1}^q + \xi_{it+1} \tag{A6}$$

Here $E(\omega_{it+1}|\omega_{it}, \chi_{it+1})$ is the expected productivity at time $t + 1$, given the productivity at time t; χ_{it+1} is a survival indicator variable. By estimating the equation above through the use of Non-Linear Least Squares, we obtained a consistent coefficient for capital. Finally, we derived the TFP as the residual of the equation A2.

Notes

1. Geographical coordinates used to build the map are taken from the Geographical Information System of the European Commission. Missing data are blank in the picture, while the classes used to classify regions are based on the four percentiles of the distribution of the underlying variable.
2. The NUTS (Nomenclature of Territorial Units for Statistics) classification is a hierarchical system – developed and regulated by the European Union – for referencing the economic territory of the EU. The NUTS2 level corresponds to basic regions for the application of regional policies.
3. Belgium, Denmark, Germany and Hungary have been excluded because of a lack of immigration data. The United Kingdom has been excluded in the estimation of TFP because the cost of materials is absent from the Amadeus data set.
4. The Statistical Classification of Economic Activities in the European Community, commonly referred to as NACE, is a European industry standard classification system consisting of a 6-digit code.

References

Aroca, P., and W.F. Maloney (2005) 'Migration, Trade, and Foreign Direct Investment in Mexico'. *World Bank Economic Review* 19 (3): 449–72.

Barba, Navaretti G., G. Bertola and A. Sembenelli (2008) 'Offshoring and Immigrant Employment: Firm Level Theory and Evidence'. *CEPR Discussion Paper* No. 6743 (London: Centre for Economic Policy Research).

Buch, C.M., J. Kleinert, A. Lipponer and F. Toubal (2005) 'Determinants and Effects of Foreign Direct Investment: Evidence from German Firm-level Data'. *Economic Policy* 20 (41): 52–110.

Combes, P.P., G. Duranton, L. Gobillon, D. Puga and S. Roux (2009) 'The Productivity Advantages of Large Cities: Distinguishing Agglomeration from Firm Selection'. *CEPR Discussion Paper* No. 7191 (London: Centre for Economic Policy Research).

Del Gatto, M., I.P. Ottaviano and M. Pagnini (2008) 'Openess to Trade and Industry Cost Dispersion: Evidence from a Panel of Italian Firms'. *Journal of Regional Science* 48 (1): 97–129.

Docquier, F., and E. Lodigiani (2006) 'Skilled Migration and Business Networks'. *Discussion Paper* 2006-36 (Louvain: Department des Sciences Economiques de l'Universite Catholique de Louvain).

Hanson, G., M. Slaughter and N. Gandal (2004) 'Technology, Trade, and Adjustment to Immigration in Israel'. *European Economic Review* 48: 403–28.

Kirkegaard, J.F. (2005) 'Outsourcing and Skill Imports: Foreign High-Skilled Workers on H-1B and L-1 Visas in the United States'. *Institute for International*

Economics Working Paper No. 05-15 (Washington, D.C.: Institute for International Economics).

Kugler, M., and H. Rapoport (2005) 'Skilled Emigration, Business Network and Foreign Direct Investment'. *CESifo Working Paper* No. 1455 (Munich: CESifo).

Levinsohn, J., and A. Petrin (2003) 'Estimationg Production Functions Using Inputs to Control for Unobservables'. *Review of Economic Studies* 70 (2): 317–41.

Lileeva, A., and D. Trefler (2007) 'Improved Access to Foreign Markets Raises Plant-level Productivity...for Some Plants'. *NBER Working Paper* No. 13297 (Cambridge, MA: National Bureau of Economic Research).

Olley, S., and A. Pakes (1996) 'The Dynamics of Productivity in the Telecommunications Equipment Industry'. *Econometrica* 64 (6): 1263–97.

Ottaviano, G., G. Peri and G.C. Wright (2010) 'Immigration, Offshoring and American Jobs'. *Centro Studi Luca d'Agliano Working Papers* No. 2 (Milan/Turin: University of Milan/ Fondazione Luigi Einaudi).

Peri, G., and C. Sparber (2007) 'Task Specialization, Comparative Advantages and the Effects of Immigration on Wages'. *NBER Working Paper* No. 13389 (Cambridge, MA: National Bureau of Economic Research).

5

Revisiting *Technology and Underdevelopment*: Climate Change, Politics and the 'D' of Solar Energy Technology in Contemporary India

Barbara Harriss-White with Sunali Rohra and Nigel Singh

We are at sea without navigation instruments.[1]

5.1 Introduction

In *Technology and Underdevelopment*, the far-sighted and far-reaching book she published in 1977, Frances Stewart explored technological transfers which were inappropriate for their new factor endowments. She analysed the implications of technological dependence for income distribution and employment in developing countries. In this chapter, which is in two related parts, we first revisit *Technology and Underdevelopment* in the light of subsequent research on – and criticism of – innovation systems. We argue a case for embedding the analysis of technological packages or systems in policy, and for the analysis of policy in the politics of markets. In the second part, we develop the first stage of such a political analysis of markets, pertaining to the 'D' of technology, in order (i) to attempt to explain the retarded development of apparently appropriate solar energy technology in India and (ii) to evaluate the relative weight of the explanatory factors emphasised in *Technology and Underdevelopment* and of those of later approaches.

5.2 Technology and underdevelopment

Technology and Underdevelopment starts from the inappropriateness of much technology in developing countries (DCs) (Stewart, 1977:

pp. xi–xiii). Two questions arise: (i) is the right technology not available to decision-makers? or (ii) are wrong choices being made by them? Stewart answers 'no' to the first and 'yes' and 'no' to the second. First, there is usually more than one technology available. Capital-intensive, second-hand, 'obsolete', traditional DC technologies and new ones may co-exist inside the set of 'world technology' (pp. 22–25). Even a range of efficient technologies may co-exist, particularly if the problem of choice is redefined from being one about a specific product to being one about specific kinds of human needs (pp. 170–73, 196–204). So a prior problem to that of choice is, she argues, one of information.

Second, even informed choices may be wrong, because the selection mechanism is the product of existing technological arrangements (p. 92) and cannot be used *ex ante* to change them. In *Technology and Underdevelopment*, 'D' is the development of technological goods and services sold from advanced countries (ACs) to DCs on terms favourable to ACs. 'Choice of technique' ought to be the choice not to be technologically and politically dependent (pp. 168–77). However, what happens in practice is that pressure from 'complementary processes' (p. 276) – one of which is the development of a local alliance of interests in AC technology – reproduces an AC environment for investment, factors and products, and results in a modern ('F') sector with high incomes but limited control over the relative prices set by AC technology. This sector then develops what is now called a 'lock-in' or a 'path-dependence'. Its technological dynamism serves to increase the gulf between the 'F' sector and the needs of the mass of people (the 'L' sector) in poor countries, over time, in ways which become increasingly unavoidable (pp. 83–90). Were technology appropriate for labour surplus economies to be made available, it would 'threaten the efficiency of th(at) existing system' (p. 278).

Stewart's answer to the second question involves a paradox. The choice of the right technique requires the right technology, and the right technology requires economic changes that are likely to occur after, rather than before, this technology emerges. As a result, although technology may be inappropriate for the factor endowment and inappropriate for domestic mass needs, it may be appropriate for elite demand if it substitutes for imports; and it may also be appropriate for export markets.[2]

No sooner had *Technology and Underdevelopment* appeared than its argument was engulfed by structural adjustment, liberalisation and globalisation. How has it stood the test of time? Our discussion will focus on three aspects of the book: institutions, energy, and politics and policy.

5.2.1 Institutions

One of *Technology and Underdevelopment*'s insights is that 'technology is a package and each technique is designed to be operated within a particular *technological system*' (p. 276, our italics). The elements of the system – 'associated processes' (p. 276), or 'linkages' (pp. 81–83) – pervade the book. They include information/knowledge (pp. 2–3); the organisation of production – which affects capacity utilisation and management as well as upstream and downstream linkages between techniques (pp. 4, 61–66, 194); and the distribution of incomes – which shapes markets for the products of technology and determines the opportunity cost of labour, which in turn affects technological productivity (pp. 66–74). They also include infrastructure for communications, banking and insurance (p. 81); local scientific and engineering capabilities; legal and administrative institutions; managerial capacities; and, last but not least, an appropriately skilled labour force (pp. 8, 74), with social services and associated infrastructure (p. 7).

We are a long way from Zvi Griliches' classic and parsimonious analytical framework for innovations in technology, which privileges relative prices and costs (Griliches, 1957). But, while in the territory of institutions, *Technology and Underdevelopment* is also far from the contemporary literature examining the institutional barriers to DC access to AC/global cutting-edge, F-sector technologies – because, unlike *Technology and Underdevelopment*, this literature mostly takes for granted (and thus neglects) the labour requirements and employment multipliers of such technologies, together with their poverty-reducing potential (see for example Correa, 2000; Basheer, 2005; Barton, 2007).

Stewart's insight into the packaged nature of technology not only focused on the currently unfashionable concern for employment but also fully anticipated the analytical framework for 'innovations systems', now conventionally used both to evaluate and to promote (or policy-engineer) the institutional system required to nurture new technology.[3] In her concept of 'technological system' and in 'innovation systems' there are sets of overlapping ideas which are getting at something important – the institutional ecosystem, *other* than relative prices and information, which needs to be in place for the 'D' of R&D to happen.

Innovation systems (IS) came into being to address the paradox of the invisible hand identified by Stewart: the price of new technology does not drop unless supply rises faster than demand, but demand will not rise while the price exceeds that of established alternatives. Its insight is that the institutional ecosystem affects both the social legitimacy of the process and the social returns to it, and thus adoption, diffusion and relative prices. IS posits an interrelated set of 'actors', 'networks' and 'institutions', which may encourage or constrain the process (Jacobsson and Johnson, 2000; Schneider et al., 2008). Prime movers are technological, political and financial; networks for information are particularly important; and institutions include hard and soft infrastructure, cultural norms and organisations. There are 'policy implications' involved in all three, and the approach stresses the interactions needed for choices which maximise allocative efficiency.

As an evaluative tool, IS lacks a theory enabling the identification of key actors, networks and institutions at the material level at which the system actually operates, hence it is unable to specify the dynamics of those interactions which generate allocatively efficient outcomes.[4] 'Actor' is a term developed to replace 'agent' in a critique of the dualism of agency and structure, but this dualism has not been transcended in IS because 'structure' is represented by 'institutions'.[5] In IS, labour is not regarded as an actor. (There is scant concern for the jobs which condition social legitimacy.) 'Networks' reduce varied and incommensurable power relations to quantifiable and comparable nodes and flows. The joint concept of 'actor–network' indicates the possibility of emergent individual and collective agency. However, in practical applications of IS, the analytical categories of actor, network and institution all prove to be substitutable.

In response to criticism, IS has been extended to cater for the need to specify outcomes, the need for detail, and the need for quantifiable indicators, so that innovations systems may be rigorously compared (Hekkert et al., 2007). Indicators comprise market outcomes, including entrepreneurial activity, market formation and resource mobilisation; and social outcomes, including knowledge and its control. The IS approach has normative ambition, in that missing features may be 'engineered'. Yet the 'government', which is so central to Stewart's system, is notable by its absence.

While Stewart has pioneered a concept of policy as a technology,[6] she cautioned that the existing system forecloses options in technical choice. At best, a technological system will be subject to 'institutional co-evolution' (among which she placed greatest confidence in institutions of South–South trade).[7] The institutions identified as the technological system in *Technology and Underdevelopment* have withstood the challenge from IS.

5.2.2   Energy

> How does mankind live?...By sunshine...The starting point of economics should be the first and second laws of thermodynamics.[8]

Technology is not purely a social product. It also depends on materials and energy. The incapacity of the biophysical system of the planet to cope with the by-products of development is the most important social problem of the twenty-first century. So how energy was treated in *Technology and Underdevelopment* affects its contemporary relevance. Stewart handled energy in several ways: as a resource, as an input, as fuel (known as 'blood' to Kenyan maize-grinders; Stewart, 1977: pp. 2, 7, 24, 221–22, 246); as the basis for labelling techniques (e.g. hand/water/diesel; p. 229); as a capital goods sector producing an intermediate good (p. 152) – both sector and good being subject to great technical vitality and dynamism and being characterised by lumpily substitutable techniques (p. 146); and as a source of obsolescence (p. 12). She used energy as an example of inappropriate technology, as opposed to 'sources of energy like sun and wind which are abundantly available in third world countries' (p. 60); but she did not pursue further this insight, which is central to the second part of this chapter.

In the thirty-three years since *Technology and Underdevelopment* was published, global warming has become the biggest threat to development and vice versa. We conceive of the threat of global warming in several dimensions: physical, economic, political, ontological, even 'existential'.[9] To Stewart's final clarion call (p. 278) – 'what is needed above all is local technical innovation directed to local needs' – one has to add that what is needed above all is technical innovation which minimises greenhouse gases and maximises the physical efficiency of materials, energy and the creation of jobs. The AC technology which has introduced the distortions of the 'F' sector into DCs is now disastrously inappropriate for ACs as well.

Stewart argues consistently that alternative technology has to be 'introduced as a system if it is to be efficient' (p. 110). She recognised that a 'macro level change' (as would be implied by changed structures of subsidies designed to reduce fossil-fuel-based energy, or by a generalised energy and materials-minimising and employment-maximising economy worldwide) would involve an 'alternative political economy' with a 'different distribution of benefits' (p. 277). Quite early on in *Technology and Underdevelopment*, she concludes that the *'answer is to be found in the realm of politics rather than economics and technology'* (p. 112 – our italics).

5.2.3 Politics and policy

Carbon Dioxide Equivalent (CO2e) is being added to the atmosphere at the historically unprecedented rate of 2 per cent per annum. So the treatment of politics in *Technology and Underdevelopment* is of central importance not only to Stewart's own argument, but also to the relevance of her argument to current circumstances.

She defines a political economy as a distribution of control over resources (p. 73). While not wholly determined by techniques and technology, it is strongly associated with them (p. 110). At its heart, technical choice privileges 'different types of decision makers' (pp. 73, 276). These include the government, which can have social as well as economic objectives (pp. 22–24). Governments, however, are more often 'representatives of a particular political economy rather than its arbiters' (p. 272), which implies that the agency of the legislative and executive arms of the state is confined. The technological 'selection mechanism' (pp. 92, 278) involves firms which vary in scale and in access to finance, together with policy-makers who also decide the sequencing and scope of physical infrastructure (pp. 22–24). Finally, there is political will (p. 278).

5.2.4 Comments on technology and underdevelopment

First, Stewart argues – and her fieldwork shows – that technical change does not occur by one 'decision', but by many decisions in a process. Yet, although the book is about decision, agency, employment and poverty reduction, their corollary, social change, is conspicuous by its absence.

Second, Stewart's analysis is ambivalent about the relation between selection, choice and their opposite, dependency. 'Political will' is her way out of this corner. Not long after the book's appearance, Schaffer deconstructed political will as an escape hatch for planning elites to invoke when intentions and projects fail (Schaffer, 1984). It is a political–academic 'will-o-the-wisp' instructively replaced by 'political interest', by which we mean society's capacities to organise, make and implement decisions through the contested social relations which dynamise production (and reproduction).[10]

Third, state and government are conflated as representatives of a political economy rather than as arbiters of social change. They are a constraint on decision-making for 'L'. In an important paper, Mushtaq Khan has addressed the view of the state as constraint, laying out what states must do and what transformative states succeed in doing: create and protect property rights; develop agriculture, industry and services; and manage the costs of, and the opposition to, these two projects (Khan, 2004). They must create incentives and gather revenue for the promotion and protection of industrialisation; enforce rules and resource the inevitable political stability transfers; buy off the opposition from victims; and create and manage new political institutions. Not only is this a very tall order, but its dynamic force is contestation. In *Technology and Underdevelopment*, 'L' and 'F' sectors are distinguished, but 'L' does not actively oppose 'F',[11] labour does not oppose capital, different types of capital do not oppose each other,[12] nor are socially regulated fractions of capital recognised as being at loggerheads.

Fourth, Stewart discusses capitalism using the terms 'economy', 'markets', 'firms' and 'labour'. Capitalist development is rarely mentioned, and only in passing. By denying it a role and by not examining its institutions, dynamism and politics, Stewart disables her own normative case for systemically appropriate technology.

Fifth, regulation is taken as given in *Technology and Underdevelopment*, yet it determines innovation adoption and is continually contested. If the fruits of applied research 'R' are novel, they will precede regulation, while the 'D' of technology must be regulated in the interests of the reproduction of any society.

Sixth, while it neglects regulation, *Technology and Underdevelopment* does not restrict policy to the decision on technology. It expands the concept of technology to include management, law and administration, thereby expanding the scientific scope of policy as well. But its treatment of policy as technology de-politicises policy. Many scholars have now shown how a de-politicised conception of policy is at the heart of aid-driven development, busily creating fields of bureaucratic-cum-technical interest which, while they may fail in terms of their explicit objectives, succeed in their own perpetuation – and in so doing stifle other kinds of politics.[13] Policy for energy and climate change is no exception.[14]

5.2.5   The Politics of technical change

In the absence of AC technologies known to exist and to be urgently needed in order to discover what is retarding 'D', alternative ways of thinking about the politics of technical change are useful. Here David Dickson's contemporary histories of UK, US and DC science and technology politics, published around the same time as *Technology and Underdevelopment* (1974, 1988), are relevant.[15] Dickson's concern is closely aligned with Stewart's: the conditions under which environmentally safe technology, which is appropriate for public needs, might be developed.[16] Like Stewart, Dickson moves between the macro and the micro, the AC and the DC; but his analysis, unlike Stewart's, is grounded in the 'political conflicts and ambiguities underlying almost all technological decisions' (Dickson, 1988: p. 303). His meticulously detailed historical method reveals a politically driven process in which, despite Friedmanite criticism of any public funding for science, state expenditure has protected basic science, while, in spite of decentralised state control, states have targeted funding increasingly towards fields with military and industrial applications (computing, biotechnology, materials, and so on; pp. 2, 39, 44, 72–77).

Dickson explains how the 'government' becomes no mere representative but an arbiter of the dynamic political economy of science and technology. Since this political process is the backcloth on which the current traffic of technological 'D' moves, it needs a summary here. The process involves simultaneous feedback relations between 'science' (universities and public labs), the 'state' and 'industry'. Demands from labour and environmental movements for science and technology to be socially relevant prove 'a cacophony, making decision making difficult' (p. 53). They have been subdued by deliberate exclusion from decision processes and by increasing secrecy (p. 54).

The first set of feedback relations between science and the state becomes mediated by industry and party politics. University establishments which may be supposed to embody divided political loyalties (p. 106) have moved towards a position hostile to 'state interference' and easily captured by private funders. Dickson strives, but fails, to refute the hypothesis that scientific evidence is subordinated to commercial interests. And policy-based evidence parades as evidence-based policy (pp. 22–25, chapter 6).

The second set of feedback relations involves science and industry. Increasingly, science and business become politically unified and opposed to control by the state (pp. 86–95). 'Corporate science' funds university research, supplementing public funds and privately appropriating the 'D' phase of public research, where ownership is key to political control and regulation. It is then a short step for industry to expand control from 'D' to publicly funded 'R' (pp. 66–95).[17]

The last set of feedbacks relates industry to the state. Privately appropriated technology becomes an instrument of foreign policy. Skilled labour is invited in one direction, and technology is allowed to be exported if it reduces production costs and can be closely controlled – for exported technology has the potential to be used to compete with and erode the carefully constructed metropolitan 'competitive' advantage (chapter 4). In Stewart's terms, the 'government' and the 'firms' are now politically fused.[18] Policy-making then comes under the aegis of economics, which develops it as an exemplary field for cost–benefit analysis (p. 286). In Stewart's terms, 'decision-making' and 'political will' become fused.

'The value of science as a policy instrument is both limited and dangerous' (p. 299), since there is no neat division between facts and values and the facts of science are open to more than a single interpretation. The paradox Dickson explains is that, with the rule of experts and science instated in public policy, scientific autonomy and the state are undermined as the expression of the public interest. In terms of Stewart's framework, structure ('government') and agency ('decision-making' and 'firms') are fused.

It is not the inefficiencies of regulation that provoke this Polanyian swing of the pendulum towards 'market society'.[19] Rather it is the paucity of resources devoted to the public interest that disincentivises innovative investment and that capitalist industry therefore has to control (p. 302).[20] Moreover, the unprecedented diffusion worldwide of a paradigm that Leys (2001) has called 'market driven politics' does not generate policy coherence.[21] One of the reasons for policy incoherence is that conflicts within 'industry' weaken it in relation to the state and to civil society.[22] Elsewhere we have argued that this incoherence also emanates systematically from the transformation of some core functions of the bureaucracy – advisory, regulative and disciplinary – into fields of accumulation through the logic and the disciplines of commodification (Harriss-White, 2008).[23] Commodities are not only invented with new technology, they are also transformed from non-commodity forms. The process has engulfed agriculture, the commons, the home, the building blocks of life and the public sphere, including the policy process. Capital's inability to halt the process of commodification is undermining its own regulative needs.[24] Domestic market politics is also part of the structure of the global deals at stake in 2009. Scaled-up, there is international market-driven politics; scaled-down, there is national and local market-driven politics, the precise balance of forces being context specific.

This necessarily compressed account remains the market-political context for the development of low-emission technology in ACs and for its transfer to DCs, as called for by the Stern Review of the Economics of Climate Change (2006). Renewable energy (RE), in which the energy transfers in production are too small to deplete the resource (Helm,

2004: p. 348), is an 'F' sector technology that is a 'prior' to the rest of the new technological and industrial revolution. While RE research is not a key constraint, the problem lies in its 'D' in high-emitting ACs, in its diffusion to developing countries and in the politics of its 'D' there. RE remains a twenty-first-century example of the paradigm of the technological dependence criticised by Stewart in 1977, but its development is inappropriately slow almost everywhere.

So the second part of this chapter initiates an analysis of renewable energy focusing on 'D', on solar technology, on the politics of markets, on the institutions Stewart identified in her expanded conception of a technological system, and on India.

India makes a valuable contrast to the US/UK because: (a) while it is a democracy, it is still a developing country; (b) it has an energy policy statement that is politically coherent;[25] and (c) its energy economy is so much more state-controlled that to use an analytical frame privileging markets might be regarded as perverse. But, as Polanyi wrote, it is *laissez-faire* that is planned, while planning is not (Polanyi, 1944: p. 14) – so this context for an exploration of the scope of a political analysis of markets in technology development is justified.

Market politics must therefore cover direct state economic control and participation, the indirect parametric regulation of private competition, as well as the politics of industrial organisation through which economic power is structured in markets, the collective action without which competition cannot take place and the key social institutions in which markets are embedded (White, 1993).

5.3 'India'

'India' is a complex symbol in the international climate change policy debates. Along with the US, China, Brazil and South Africa, India is key to the limited Copenhagen climate 'deal' made by non-signatories to the first round of the Kyoto treaty. In the analysis of the fall-out of the failure to create a second global round – which includes the renewal of climate change denial – domestic politics have been neglected. While ACs see India as a threat in flow terms, 'India' (that is, the state, the media and the policy 'commentariat') sees the problem in terms of CO_2 stocks, and itself as a victim of the pollution of ACs (Panagariya, 2009: pp. 40–44). India argues strongly for an international technology transfer to DCs. It does this at a time when its growth has produced inequality rather than eradicating poverty, when its contemporary 'technological package' has produced jobless growth rather than mass employment, and when its consumption patterns produce CO_2 at the top end of the income distribution at levels approaching those of North America (20.6 tonnes per person per annum), departing rapidly from the eventual 'CO_2-stabilising' world average of 2 tonnes.[26]

In 2010, over half of India's 27,000 villages, (and 487 million people), are still off-grid and depend on state-distributed and subsidised kerosene, on animal and human energy, candles and biomass, including cow dung and charcoal. India's demand for primary energy is expected to leap from 400 million toe[27] to 1.2 billion toe by 2030, by which date the per capita consumption of electricity is expected to have tripled from its current 660 kilowatt-hours per capita (kWh/cap), which represents 7 per cent of the Organisation for Economic Co-operation and Development (OECD) average, to 2,000 kWh.[28] Currently 75 per cent of this electricity is generated from coal and lignite, relatively and absolutely the dirtiest sources. They are justified as the resources of preference both because of huge reserves under state monopoly control and also because of the legitimacy and immediacy of the objective of poverty eradication (GOI, 2006).

Yet solar energy technologies have the estimated physical potential to provide for up to 94 per cent of India's additional electricity needs by 2031–32. India plans to add 640 gigawatts (GW). The upper-end estimated potential of solar energy is estimated at 600 GW, according to the Indian Renewable Energy Development Agency, not to mention wind, upgraded biomass and small hydro, which exceed 100 GW (McKinsey, 2008). In addition, solar energy can leapfrog grid extension. Its employment multiplier is greater than other forms of renewable energy (Kammen et al., 2004).[29] It can contribute significantly to national energy security. Its cost (Rs 20–25 per unit in 2009) is thought to be comparable to, or less than, that of electricity from coal- and oil-fired generating stations *once the latter's externalities and current subsidies are factored in* (WISE, 2008).[30] This potential was recognised in India during the brief period in the late 1970s when, reeling from the second oil price shock, many OECD governments, together with China, encouraged publicly funded science to explore alternative energy (Dickson, 1988; Martinez-Alier and Schlupmann, 1990: p. 18; Schneider et al., 2008). The elements of an Indian 'technological package' or innovation system were engineered in the 1970s and 1980s, on a time-par with Germany and well before the impetus that Rajiv Gandhi gave to the unfolding process of liberalisation. But these elements were not sufficient to give a significant boost to alternative energy.

Solar energy at present supplies only 0.75 per cent of India's electricity.[31] Just 5 per cent of the Ministry of New and Renewable Energy's (MNRE) budget is devoted to solar under the eleventh Five Year Plan (GOI, 2008b). Meanwhile fossil-fuel-based electricity generation continues to benefit from a very large set of public support measures and subsidies – averaging 150 per cent of the capital costs of projects between 1993 and 2003 (WISE, 2008: pp. 73–80).[32] It is both in the national and in the global public interest that India develop solar and other renewable energy. There are, however, powerful sectional interests on the other side.

In mid-2008, the Indian prime minister pledged 'all our scientific, technical and managerial talents with financial sources to develop solar energy'.[33] Just six months later, India's Integrated Energy Policy was formally accepted by the Indian government, with RE in its entirety planned to account for no more than 5–6 per cent of the energy mix by 2031–32. In August 2009, the Indian government changed this target to 25 per cent for solar alone, but only provided it is aid-funded.[34] Moreover, while the National Solar Mission was launched in 2007, a new 'Jawaharlal Nehru National Solar Mission' was launched in November 2009.[35] Why this instability? Why have 'sources of energy like sun and wind[,] which are abundantly available in third world countries' (Stewart, 1977: p. 60), been so dramatically retarded in a technologically competent society like India's? Is the right technology not available to decision-makers, or are wrong choices being made by them?

To answer Stewart's questions, the institutional architecture for solar energy was researched, in an application of the extended framework for the politics of the technology system and of its markets, which has been developed here (Harriss-White et al., 2009). The research is summarised in the Appendix. In what follows we outline the implications of this architecture for the political and social relationships at stake in the 'D' of solar energy.

5.3.1 State control

The 1970s technology system for RE privileges institutions, which (like the energy sector as a whole) are under public ownership and control in order to encourage research, to disseminate technology and to protect infant industries at all scales, ranging from the assembly and export of grid-connectable applications (the main present orientation) to the supply of rural off-grid appliances. The solar technology system is part of the remit of the State Electricity Boards; it is scattered through several ministries and many state bodies; and it is marked by their proliferation, by an acceleration of central government policy initiatives, by a surge in discursive support, by underfunding (particularly for capital subsidies) and by discretionary policy at state level (e.g. long-term solar energy purchase contracts). This structure of intervention has led to widely differing state trajectories. RE as a whole is marginalised. Furthermore, within RE, public sector wind has been favoured over solar energy, even though India has problems with intermittency.

5.3.2   State regulation

Only recently have the drivers of solar development shifted towards private capital. Markets require not only a legal–regulative framework and finance, they require infrastructure, sites, information, supply chains and entrepreneurs. Private and state firms are regulated through the Electricity Act of 2003, which invests the central state with authority to specify policy, tariffs, grid transmission standards and dispute resolution but leaves it without mandatory powers of enforcement. Regulative discretion for the private sector includes tax exemptions and guaranteed rates of return for exporting firms. International intellectual property (IP) rights are reported *not* to have prevented the development of private solar technology. This happens through licensing and joint ventures.

India's regulative institutions operate a two-track approach – manifest both in state participation and direct control, and in private sector regulation, and visible in other areas of policy such as food. This arrangement results in domestic technology policy and institutions which are operationally incoherent at different political scales. While the domestic duplication/copying/reverse engineering of innovations made elsewhere is advocated, so too is the (free) international transfer of technologies, to be funded by ACs (Singh, 2009: p. 11).[36] While India's international politics supports the transfer of ownership of intellectual property rights (IPRs), national politics supports licensing and imports. While 'R' is designed to be in state hands, it is now being *de facto* privatised.[37] 'D' is a field of competition between an array of public and private agents operating at various scales, from the district to the nation, all marginalised by conventional energy corporations. Hybrid institutions of state control and private regulation and a diverse ecological policy generate high coordination costs between state and market interaction – as when feed-in tariffs have to be negotiated at state level only if they are triggered by private suppliers, who have to make investments in advance.

5.3.3 Industrial organisation

The markets for manufacturing and retailing off-grid appliances are polarised between the niche interests of industrial oligopolists on the one hand, and a mass of small specialists, many in the informal economy, on the other. Markets are so constrained that some major companies depend on local NGOs in unstable hybrid delivery systems to reach the bottom of the pyramid. By contrast, grid-compatible technology is a sector with three state corporations, nine private solar cell manufacturers, eighteen photovoltaic (PV) companies, a 'handful' initiating thin-film applications, plus small firms manufacturing components and bespoke applications.[38] Intermediate goods and raw materials (ingots, wafers, thin-film silica, and so on) are imported, many from Japan, and 70 per cent of what is manufactured is exported, mostly to Europe. Informal contacts enable Indian entrepreneurs to find ways of acquiring the most protected element – process technology – in the face of the indifference of their own finance capital.

5.3.4 Organisation of finance

The centre and the states struggle to maintain their selective and significant subsidies and support measures on coal, gas, oil, hydro-electricity and nuclear power. States reel under subsidy burdens for agricultural electricity, itself the result of party political competition. The state electricity boards themselves are saturated with locked-in subsidies. As a result – and reinforced by the pressures of neoliberal politics – the resources required to subsidise RE are not forthcoming. The private banking sector is averse to risk and has a feeble record for RE by comparison with state funding agencies. The immediate lumpy capital costs dominating loan use for RE are severe disincentives. Only one solar plant has been funded through private equity and through the capital markets. Yet, despite state finance agencies being supplied with funds from the private sector which are then lent onwards at higher interest, the supply of solar finance is overwhelmed by demand. International development banks, UN agencies and NGO-development agency hybrids have started to finance solar applications.

5.3.5 Private collective action

There is no constituency for RE in the Indian trade union movement.[39] Even the political activity generated by industrial associations falls far short of the invasion of the policy process by business interests, as in the OECD heartland. There are only three solar business associations (listed in the Appendix). They are engaged in improving public knowledge and in reducing the social distance between research and business. The four major general industrial lobbies (listed in the Appendix) have acknowledged RE only very recently; are developing a field of information rather than one of investment or of policy; and they do not speak with one voice. Collective action is an element of political contingency.

5.3.6   Social embedding

An informed policy elite is essential to supply the political leverage needed to release the limiting constraints on 'D'. But solar energy is part of a political culture that has given low priority and status to RE and its ministries and agencies. It is part of a social culture that has prevented easy contact between publicly funded science, entrepreneurs and society. India has had RE research institutions in place for two decades, with little impact on solar energy or society. Only twelve university departments are research-active in RE, and the skills vacuum is so intense that some Indian firms plan joint research ventures abroad. With the exception of the World Institute for Sustainable Energy (WISE) in Pune, and the Energy Research Institute (TERI) in New Delhi, the think tanks, some with industrial funding, have also placed solar energy development on their margins. Environmental movements are fully occupied with the agenda of forest problems, genetically modified seeds, urban air pollution, toxic waste and industrial accidents, and RE has no constituency. The media have focused on greenhouse gas stocks rather than flows, on environmental justice and – if at all – on solar energy as a means of adaptation rather than mitigation. Despite endorsement from the prime minister, civil society is generally ignorant about solar energy and its possibilities, and it is left to a very small number of institutions with different interests to strive to establish its legitimacy.

5.4   Conclusions

In this chapter we have tested an approach to the understanding of technology and development which is complementary to that of *Technology and Underdevelopment* while building on some of Stewart's conceptual tools. It situates technical change in the politics of markets, which is in turn embedded in state policies and social institutions. The results will be discussed in three sections: the light shed on the theorising of technological change; the analytical substance of our work; and its implications for policy.

5.4.1 Theoretical and methodological conclusions

Stewart conceived of technology as having many elements – a package – and included many institutions among the factors making a technological system in which the package develops. They are listed in Section 5.2.1 above. While the parsimony of the institutional toolkit of the conventional 'innovations systems' approach may appeal, the case of solar energy in India confirms the importance of the expanded list, in particular Stewart's inclusion of infrastructure for communications, banking and insurance; scientific and engineering capabilities; legal and administrative institutions (here: IPRs and licences); managerial capacities; and an appropriately skilled labour force. 'Banking' needs expansion to include institutions for finance, aid, subsidies and support measures.

These are *general* requirements often missing from the analysis of the existing or theoretically desirable 'innovation systems' for a specific product.

The case of solar energy also reinforces the theoretical argument for a political approach to technical change, and our evaluation of long-stalled and inappropriately slow technological change introduces a political dynamic to the idea of the technological system. Understanding this dynamic requires expanding the concept of the 'political' into the market and conceiving of the choice of technique as an element in the development of capitalist markets. Capital must expand, and in so doing it strategises to introduce new technology, reduce labour costs, transform state-protected sectors into fields of profit, and persuade the state to support a process which threatens the state itself. The state must then fight back and also select those risks it will bear, or capitulate.

Key institutions are those of state control/'participation'; state regulation facilitating change; the (self- and state-regulated) organisation of market structures which affect resistance to disruptive change; the collective action which is a necessary prior to market competition; and the wider social forces in which capitalist markets are always embedded.[40] To understand these institutions and the politics of the interests they reflect needs information which is voluminous and elusive, much of it not publicly available, some competitively secret. A first scratch at the surface involves laying out its 'architecture': the institutional elements through which the political dynamic is construed. This has been one of the main purposes of this chapter.

5.4.2   Substantive conclusions

The research reported in this chapter has revealed a different balance of political forces from those described by Dickson and summarised earlier. Starting with the hypothesis that technological change is conflictual, Dickson built an analysis of politically fused/hegemonised institutions and agency. Stewart, with a similar institutional toolkit, modelled the state as representing a particular political economy. But in India's solar sector, science is not fused with capital – there is hardly any relationship between the two. Science is subordinate to the state and, while there certainly is rule by experts in the Planning Commission, RE policy is not made by RE experts. Nor is there any sign of the general mobilisation of science demanded by the prime minister. The state's RE technology system, with just twelve underfunded research departments active in RE research, is inappropriate for capital. Yet the state is ceding agency to it. There is as yet a very tenuous feedback relation between capital and the state. Finally, civil society is weak not because it has been disabled, as in Dickson's scenario, but because it has not yet been mobilised.

The Indian state embodies the interests of a range of technology systems. In RE, the state created the institutions designed to develop RE, but it did not endow them with the power to challenge state-owned incumbent technology. Although no established energy institutions have been threatened, and RE was at the time not envisaged as the essential precondition to a materials revolution, RE has been treated as though it were a threat. What our analysis shows is how the politics of the technological system for RE has *by itself* been sufficient to disable 'D'.

In *Technology and Underdevelopment*, Stewart asked whether the right technology is not available or whether the wrong choices are being made. The answers here are 'no but' and 'yes but'. RE – even solar – is not one technology but a set of them, each one with components making a 'package'. The right technologies are available and are not obstructed by patent law so much as by the structure of domestic subsidies, the reluctance of banks, price instabilities and the coordination failures of the technological package built to facilitate them. The wrong choices are locked into India's energy system through the non-transparent, life-cycle and life-time requirements of fossil-fuel technologies dominating public support and infrastructure. The wrong choices are also the product of public finances locked into subsidy burdens in other sectors. India is not unusual in this respect. It is unusual in its public support for renewable energy.

While the solar technological package was initiated precociously early, its subsequent development has marginalised and dis-incentivised solar energy. The paradox of precocity and failure needs to be explained by the politics of markets in an energy sector still dominated by state ownership and much more comprehensively state-regulated for development in the public interest than food is.

5.4.2(a)   *State institutions and politics*

States can work without markets, but markets cannot work without states, even if in accommodating private and public interests states may create techno-political systems which retard or prevent the development of markets. While the state is now creating, by increments, a technological package for private capital, it is slow to redefine the public good as the good of private solar business. Despite the prime minister's discursive encouragement, and despite continual expansion of solar goals alongside rapidly receding dates for them, public institutions are not fast-tracking solar technology development. Regulation is suffused with discretion and hard to enforce. Indeed, some regulative policy is *designed* to be incoherent, as for example when states compete to negotiate feed-in tariffs which are triggered only when business initiates them. This institutional architecture, in which evolutionary reform gives rise to complexity without destroying redundant institutions along the way, not only generates inconsistency but also serves to stall the 'D' of technical change. The state is incapacitated from operating in the public interest, which would prioritise the rapid development of solar energy technology.

There is also a social and cultural distance between state, science and market institutions, combined with low status for RE, which cannot be altered just by policy technology and institutional design alone.

5.4.2(b)   *Market institutions and politics*

Though it protects its own solar industry, the US has not been able to prevent RE being developed elsewhere, notably in Japan and Germany.[41] This 'F' sector technology is not prevented from flowing to a technologically capable country like India – indeed the Obama administration is now selectively encouraging business partnerships – but it flows at a price. Licences are not a constraint, but their cost rations them to the apex of the RE sector and reinforces inequality in the sector's organisation. In the face of incoherent domestic policies for solar energy, and with the sector dominated by state enterprises and by a private oligopoly, together with a large number of small specialist firms, India is developing technology for export. In practice it needs to develop this technology for the domestic market.[42]

Despite a well-developed banking sector and a huge corps of innovative engineers, markets for money and labour do not support the sector. Apex industrial lobbies are at the stage of informing rather than representing the interests of manufacturers. Labour is inactive politically and given lowest policy priority as a factor of production. Trade associations and hybrid institutions of collective action struggle to establish the legitimacy of solar energy. The sector is poorly recognised – and not backed – by civil society. Neither science nor the media have developed public education with respect to solar energy. Environmental movements have many objectives other than the promotion of solar technology, and RE is a niche specialism in environmental think tanks.

Calls for 'political will' face these complex manifestations of political interests. The global response to climate change requires a radical and rapid shift in technology, what Stewart called 'macro level change'. But RE, the forerunner of this change, cannot generate macro-level change through the technological system constructed by the political interests analysed here. In India, one of the strategically most important nations in the climate change response, the existing institutional architecture for solar energy, while constantly evolving, is hostile to the 'new technological paradigms', to the development of which the Indian government itself is discursively committed. We have confirmed that what Stewart terms an 'alternative political economy' cannot be engineered through incremental change to a technological system that has developed internal structural and social inconsistencies through incremental change.[43] There are no precedents in a neoliberal era for the institutional destruction needed to fast-track the technological elements of the new energy revolution, which must precede the revolution in materials.

5.4.3   Policy-relevant findings

First, this research suggests that India's *international political initiatives* may be mis-prioritised with respect to technology transfer. IPRs are no barrier to the expansion of advanced capabilities in the solar energy sector. In the contradictory regulative framework in which India calls for an international funding body to remove a barrier that does not exist, India may be acting as trustee for the interests of less technologically proficient DCs.[44] And/or it may be looking far beyond imitative adaptation, to a time when IPRs in new thin-film technology may be protected by their developers in a manner radically different from their current licensing practice. The international attention on IPRs is distracting attention from more serious policy problems.

Second, equity in public support would mean both/either addressing the costs of the negative externalities of fossil fuel and nuclear energy and removing their subsidies and support and/or providing new forms of energy, in particular solar, with comparable or greater public support measures, as befits such socially valuable infant industries. In the neoliberal order, RE is being required to develop without the kind and level of protection hitherto given worldwide to socially useful energy technologies. Not to support RE is an extraordinary historical anomaly, not simply in India's response but in the global response to climate change. Prime among the problems here and well outside the public framing of the 'D' of RE, it is in the immediate public interest in this era of apparently liberalised competition to know the degree of *underestimation of the cost to society (and of the pressures on public finance) of conventional fossil-fuel-based, hydro- and nuclear power.* No complete calculations of energy subsidies and support measures net of tax have ever been made. This is the problem needing international funding. This is a *general* policy implication – drawn from literature not confined to India.[45]

Third, while this chapter has revealed the combination of institutional complexity and low status in solar energy's technological system as a formidable obstacle to its development, *the limiting constraint on solar energy is financial* – particularly for commercial pilot projects. Like renewables generally, solar energy has heavy up-front capital costs and relatively low running costs. While the costs of on-grid technology have been declining worldwide and those of many off-grid applications are profitable without subsidy, India's banks are so far from being entrepreneurial for the RE sector, interest on loans is so high, that solar finance has been the preserve of public banks for public sector initiatives or international development banks and aid agencies. This surely has to be changed, but change depends on the second policy implication outlined above. Obvious priorities are off-grid solar technology and loans to grid-interactive solar energy developers, whether private or public.

Finally, the institutional life of solar energy has been not so much a process of technical choice as a painfully drawn-out *process of resistance*, both to indifference and to developments opposed to solar energy – a resistance mounted by entrepreneurs in private and public sectors who are marginalised by their own elites. This conclusion is well supported by the sheaves of policy statements – 'official transcripts' – in which plans for solar development are pushed to the margins. Official transcripts of the government of India on Copenhagen include the Integrated Energy Policy (GOI, 2006) and the National Action Plan on Climate Change (GOI, 2008a). *Resistance* has been theorised as a property of subaltern classes, expressed both openly and through 'hidden transcripts' – the private 'offstage' dialogue about practices and purposes (Scott, 1990). The latter awaits research. That the 'D' of solar energy so far has been an act of elite resistance is not so far-fetched a conclusion when one is faced with mass denial about coal and lignite as *not* being the natural order, as *not* being the arrangement making 'pro-poor development' possible, and about 'cleaner coal' as *not* being the paramount technological imperative. These are all carefully constructed 'foregone conclusions' and 'policy imperatives' (Schaffer, 1984).

Multiple institutional failures in India's technological/innovation system for RE have yet to be tested for reflecting the success of the politics of resistance by the established energy sectors in public ownership.[46] However, using the expanded framework developed here we have shown how the political architecture and interests are changing; and it would be a mark of greatly needed progress if, unlike *Technology and Underdevelopment*, our substantive analysis were *not* to stand the test of time.

Acknowledgment

We are grateful to participants – in particular to Adrian Wood – at *Overcoming Persistent Inequality and Poverty: A Conference in Honour of Frances Stewart*, held in Oxford, 17–18 September 2009, and to the editors – in particular to Judith Heyer – for their constructive comments. We are also grateful to the several international and Indian research scientists and 21 prominent public and private sector stakeholders in India who were kind enough to help Rohra and Singh with their research projects. Harriss-White thanks Rome-1 University, La Sapienza, for a visiting fellowship which enabled revisions to the conference paper to be made.

Appendix

Table 5.A.1 India's technology system and market architecture for solar energy

		1970s	1980s	1990s	2000s	Proposed
State participation/ control	central	1976 Department of Nonconventional Energy Indian Institutes of Technology (IIT) and Indian Institutes of Science (IISc) (public research)	1980 National solar PV energy programme 1982 Solar Energy Centres 1987 Indian RE Development Agency	1992 Ministry of New and Renewable Energy	2002 off-grid appliance subsidies 2004 Renewable Power Obligations (non-mandatory) 2006 Technology Incubators 2007 Export Incentive Package 2007 National Solar Mission 2008 On-grid (feed-in) policy 2009 J. Nehru Solar Mission	
	states	State Electricity Boards State Power and Grid Corporations	National Solar PV Energy Programme nodal agencies	1994 Network: Aditya outlets – off-grid appliances	Special Export Zones Feed-in tariffs (selective) 2007 Special Incentives Package Scheme	Joint ventures for research International IP transfer to private sector

Table 5.A.1 (Continued)

		1970s	1980s	1990s	2000s	Proposed
						Solar parks, and solar energy infrastructure in technology parks and industrial townships
State regulation of private markets		1970 Patent Act – products		1999 Patent Act for process/TRIPS compliance 1999 Central (Electricity) Act (tariffs/terms + conditions of trading and transmission/ standards/ dispute resolution)	2002+ RE under SEZs/tech parks 2008 IPRs in universities 2009 National Incentive Package scheme	
Industrial organisation	Off-grid			Many appliances public and private oligopoly/some private-NGO hybrids for bottom of pyramid markets; mass of small specialist manufacturers and retail outlets		

Category				
On-grid				Thermal and PV – ingots/wafers imported from Japan/ USA/Germany Three public corporations, nine private solar cell manufacturers, 18 PV firms 12 firms licensed to manufacture for export Thin film amorphous silica imported by 'handful' of firms
Finance	1987 Indian RE Development Agency			Global-regional and national public finance to state agencies IFC few private equity ventures Foreign aid Retail: NGOs, NGO-private hybrids, foreign aid
Private collective action	1976 Solar Energy Society of India for Public R&D and education Federation of Indian Chambers of Commerce and Industry (FICCI)	1988 National Association of Software and Services Companies (NASSCOM)	1992 Confederation of Indian Industry (CII)	Institutional hybrids Solar Equipment Materials International – research and private sector links Energy efficiency but not RE

Table 5.A.1 (Continued)

	1970s	1980s	1990s	2000s	Proposed
	Association of Chambers of Commerce and Industry of India (ASSOCHAM)			Indian Semi-conductor Association – public knowledge 2009 US-India Solar Energy Partnership 2009 FICCI conference/Ministry of Environment 2009 ASSOCHAM: RE conference 2008 CII starts work on RE No trade union activity on RE 2009 New Trade Union Initiative (NTUI) + >100 environmental organisations create climate change memorandum	
Social embeddedness	science RE low status Little specialist education				

environmental movements	RE marginalised
think tanks	Energy Research Institute feasibility studies for private sector. RE in only four of 218 publications in 2007–08.
	Centre for Science and Environment – little on renewables.
	World Institute for Sustainable Energy (WISE) develops Centre for Solar Energy
media	Focus on wind/stocks/justice not on RE

Sources: CII (2007); NASSCOM (2009); Rohra (2009); SEMI (2009); TERI (2009).

Notes

1. Sir Crispin Tickell, the distinguished retired civil servant who persuaded Margaret Thatcher, when prime minister, of the significance of global warming, speaking at the London School of Economics, 5 June 2009.
2. When capital-intensive techniques are introduced into labour-intensive economies the alternatives are the creation of a dual economy (right decisions for the wrong sector – the 'F' sector leaving the rest (L) to develop inefficiently without appropriate science and technology (pp. 72–3)) or development white elephants and 'generalised rust' (wrong decisions).
3. Another not incompatible subfield created by sociologists involves the idea of a 'market ecosystem' – and consists of the institutions and technologies of the value chain, its tacit knowledge, networks and collective action (Saxenian, 1994).
4. Indeed the idea that it is intuitively obvious has been used by Callon (1991: p. 152) to argue that such networks can be understood as a 'black box' whose behaviour is known – 'heavy with norms' – and then drawn on as resources by other networks, in which case they are said to be 'punctualised' (Goodman, 1999: p. 27). Entire complex technologies or technological packages may thus be taken for granted until extreme events which test or destroy them thereby reveal their components.
5. From actor network theory emerging from Crozier and Friedberg's (1977) critique of structuralism and pioneered by Latour (1987, 1994), in his studies of the power relations of science.
6. For which she was honoured as one of the world's top 50 outstanding technological leaders in 2003 by *Scientific American*.
7. Her attention to collective action and groups was to emerge later, cf. Heyer et al. (2002).
8. Juan Martinez-Alier, quoting Soddy discussing Marx's neglect of energy (1990: p. 135).
9. Dieter Helm, speaking at the London School of Economics, 5 June 2009.
10. This understanding of political economy is close to Bernstein (2010, chapter 2, p. 6). Political economy was the original name for economics and its definition is evidently still subject to debate. Martinez-Alier (1995) for instance, defines it as that branch of economics focussing on distributional conflicts.
11. Nor does L provide necessary goods and services to F.
12. Falkner (2007) analyses in some detail the implications of dynamic conflicts over environmental policies and technologies between companies and sectors in the 'F' economy.
13. Ferguson (1991) and Escobar (1995) – critiqued in turn for their overdetermination and exaggerated focus on one particular development discourse, see Fernandez (2008).
14. The 'mediation by science' of climate change is one of Giddens' four reasons for its uniqueness as a policy problem or 'issue'. The others are its abstract nature, its invisibility and its relevance to the future not the present (Giddens, 2009). But its de-politicisation is a device for procrastination and the prevention of change. It has been balm to the elected, unelected and retired politicians responsible for reacting to the clamour for political will,

many of whom also publicly ask for it, for instance Tony Blair, Lord Giddens and Lord Mandelson speaking at the London School of Economics, 5 June 2009; Al Gore speaking in Oxford, 7 July 2009.

15. So is the study of discursive framing and the various trajectories of scientism in policy processes but space prevents this. It was laid out in Schaffer (1984) and is well reviewed in Greenhalgh (2008: Preface and chapter 1).

16. Dickson's solution is a democratic process of technology development which would work to a logic in which markets operate within parameters set politically in the public interest.

17. For the first time in history, cutting-edge military technology develops independently of direct, formal state control (Willett, 2002).

18. In the US case, through mechanisms such as tax incentives, protective patent and regulatory reform (justified to create domestic 'international competitiveness') and controls over the export of knowledge, by the mid 1980s a class of corporate, financial and military interests was taking over the US research agenda (pp. 49, 89, 185). Their political instruments include multilateral private funding of centres of excellence, open-ended private funding with the donor controlling patentable outputs, private donations matched by congressionally approved funds, spin-offs and consultancies by publicly funded technologists to industry. R and D are re-conceptualised as investments (pp. 33, 53).

19. On the contours of the contemporary Polanyian swing, see Stewart (2009); Harriss-White (2009).

20. See NFU (2005) for a contemporary manifestation from British capital.

21. Helm (2004) and Prins and Rayner (2007) use eclectic approaches to British energy policy analysis and conclude that it is incoherent.

22. See Falkner (2007) and Buck (2007: p. 70, footnote 25) for the institutional variety involved in climate change response. In a political analysis of the UK energy sector up to 2006, Harriss-White and Harriss (2007) showed that the politics of energy markets prevents the development of renewable energy through both party politics and non-party politics, the latter taking both democratically open and concealed forms.

23. See also Leys (2007: chapter 3).

24. So much so that in energy, as of 2007, the British state was not able to define (and regulate in) the public interest, the long-term interest, nor was it able to mediate between the conflicting interests whose existence it was discursively hell-bent on denying (Harriss-White and Harriss, 2007).

25. GOI (2006). With its emphasis on coal it is environmentally reactionary.

26. See Billett's content analysis of Indian media (Billett, 2009). The UK/EU's average is 9 tonnes; India's currently is 1.2 tonnes (UNDP, 2007).

27. toe = tonnes of oil equivalent.

28. Installed generation is planned to expand from 160 to 800 GW by 2031–2. See GOI (2008a).

29. In India, 25–40 direct jobs per MW (ten in production, 33 in installation, three to four in systems wholesaling and supply and one to two in research) (Weiss, 2009).

30. Large hydro is also heavily subsidised. Externalities have never been costed.

31. 1.2 GW out of a total generating capacity of 160 GW in 2008 (McKinsey, 2008).

32. Fossil fuel energy is also taxed; but it is the structure of subsidies not the taxes which determines the competitive advantage of the energy sources.
33. 'In this strategy, the sun occupies centre stage, as it should, being literally the original source of all energy. We will pool all our scientific, technical and managerial talents with financial sources to develop solar energy as a source of abundant energy to power our economy and transform the lives of our people and change the face of India' (Dr Manmohan Singh, launching India's National Action Plan on Climate Change, June 2008).
34. M. Rahman, 'India Sets Out Ambitious Solar Power Plan to be Paid for by Rich Nations'. *The Guardian*, 4 August 2009.
35. This has an upwardly revised solar target of 20,000 megawatts (MW) by the end of the thirteenth Five Year Plan in 2022, a 17-fold expansion on 2008, together with a single window investment facility (GOI, 2009).
36. See also M. Rahman, 'India Sets Out Ambitious Solar Power Plan to be Paid for by Rich Nations'. *The Guardian*, 4 August 2009.
37. The ease of import exacerbates disincentives for the domestic R being encouraged in the Indian Institutes of Science.
38. In 2009.
39. There is also remarkably little technology literature which considers employment, not only in India.
40. In India's dominant informal economy these form a social structure which tends to stabilise accumulation (see Harriss-White, 2003).
41. In the OECD as a whole, including the US, R & D for RE grew between 1978 and 1983 but atrophied thereafter. In the UK it declined in real terms between 1994 and 2003. Over the OECD, public funding for civil nuclear energy is currently 20 times greater than for RE (Jacobsson and Johnson, 2000; Schneider et al., 2008).
42. The oft-used comparator of pharmaceuticals – which developed capabilities through reverse engineering in the era before India's accession to the World Trade Organization (WTO) such that after the Agreement on Trade-Related Aspects of Intellectual Property Rights (TRIPS) its apex could develop indigenous R & D (Kale and Little, 2007) – is inappropriate on two grounds: (i) the post-TRIPS regulative context, and (ii) limited patent constraints.
43. Again, India is not unique in this. A similar process is currently 'complexifying' the reform to the incrementally evolved publicly-funded international agricultural research system under the Consultative Group on International Agricultural Research (CGIAR).
44. The phrase is Barton's (2007); see Singh (2009).
45. WISE (2008) scoured the literature worldwide finding limited evidence, which nevertheless indicated extensive subsidies on energy from fossil fuel.
46. See Lakhotia (2009) on the business interests benefiting from India's nuclear deal though he was unable to discover whether they actively thwart RE. See Chatterjee (2009) on coal politics.

References

Barton, J. (2007) *Intellectual Property and Access to Clean Technologies in Developing Countries – An Analysis of Solar Photovoltaic, Biofuel and Wind Technologies* (Geneva: International Centre for Trade and Sustainable Development).

Basheer, S. (2005) 'India's Tryst with TRIPS: The Patents (Amendment) Act 2005'. *Indian Journal of Law and Technology* 1: 15–46.

Bernstein, H. (2010) *The Dynamics of Agrarian Change*. Brill

Billett, S. (2009) 'Dividing Climate Change: Global Warming in the Indian Mass Media'. *Climatic Change* 99 (1–2): 1–16.

Buck, D. (2007) 'The Ecological Question: Can Capitalism Prevail?' In L. Panitch and C. Leys (eds) *Coming to Terms with Nature* (New York: Monthly Review Press).

Callon, M. (1991) 'Techno-economic Networks and Irreversibility'. In J. Law (ed.) *A Sociology of Monsters: Essays on Power, Technology and Domination* (London: Routledge).

Chatterjee, E. (2009) 'Power Politics: Rent-seeking, Climate Change and the Indian Electricity Sector'. MSc Thesis, University of Oxford.

CII (Confederation of Indian Industry) (2007) *White Paper on Strategy for 11th Plan and Beyond* (New Delhi: CII/CEA).

Correa, C. (2000) *Intellectual Property Rights, the WTO and Developing Countries – The TRIPS Agreement and Policy Options* (London, New York: Zed Books).

Crozier, M., and E. Friedberg (1977) *L'Acteur et le Système* (Paris: Editions du Seuil).

Dickson, D. (1974) *Alternative Technology and the Politics of Technical Change* (London: Fontana Collins).

Dickson, D. (1984/1988) *The New Politics of Science* (Chicago, IL: University of Chicago Press).

Escobar, A. (1995) *Encountering Development: The Making and Unmaking of the Third World* (Princeton, NJ: Princeton University Press).

Falkner, R. (2007) 'A Neo-pluralist Perspective on Business Power in Global Environmental Governance'. *Paper presented at the British International Studies Association* Annual Conference, Cambridge, UK, 17–19 December.

Ferguson, J. (1991) *The Anti-Politics Machine: Development, Depoliticisation and Bureaucratic Power in Lesotho* (Minneapolis, MN: University of Minnesota Press).

Fernandez, B. (2008) 'Engendering Poverty Policy in India: Towards a New Feminist Theoretical Framework'. DPhil Thesis, University of Oxford.

Giddens, A. (2009) *The Politics of Climate Change* (Cambridge: Polity).

Goodman, D. (1999) 'Agro-food Studies in the "Age of Ecology": Nature, Corporeality, Bio-politics'. *European Journal for Rural Sociology* 39 (1): 17–36.

GOI (Government of India) (2006) *Integrated Energy Policy* (New Delhi: Ministry of Power).

GOI (Government of India) (2008a) National Action Plan on Climate Change. Prime Minister's Council on Climate Change. Online: http://pmindia.nic.in/climate_change.htm (accessed 11 November 2010).

GOI (Government of India) (2008b) *Eleventh Five Year Plan* (New Delhi: Planning Commission).

GOI (Government of India) (2009) Jawaharlal Nehru National Solar Mission:Towards Building SOLAR INDIA. Online: http://mnre.gov.in/pdf/mission-document-JNNSM.pdf (accessed 11 November 2010).

Greenhalgh, S. (2008) *Just One Child: Science and Policy in Deng's China* (Berkeley, CA: University of California Press).

Griliches, Z. (1957) *Technology, Education and Productivity: Early Papers with Notes to Subsequent Literature* (New York: Basil Blackwell).

Harriss-White, B. (2009) 'Three Invisible Hands'. *Journal of International Development* 21: 776–80.

Harriss-White, B. (2008) 'Market Politics and Climate Change'. *Development* 51 (3): 350–58.

Harriss-White, B. (2003) *India Working* (Cambridge: Cambridge University Press).

Harriss-White, B., and E. Harriss (2007) 'Unsustainable Capitalism: The Politics of Renewable Energy in the UK'. In L. Panitch and C. Leys (eds) *Coming to Terms with Nature* (New York: Monthly Review Press).

Harriss-White, B., S. Rohra and N. Singh (2009) 'The Political Architecture of India's Technology System for Solar Energy'. *Economic and Political Weekly* 44 (47): 49–60.

Hekkert, M.P., R.A.A. Suurs, S.O. Negro, S. Kuhlmann and R.E.H.M. Smits (2007) 'Functions of Innovation Systems: A New Approach for Analysing Technological Change'. *Technological Forecasting and Social Change* 74 (4): 413–32.

Helm, D. (2004) *Energy, the State and the Market: British Energy Policy since 1979* (Oxford: Oxford University Press).

Heyer J., F. Stewart and R. Thorp (eds) (2002) *Group Behaviour and Development: Is the Market Destroying Co-operation?* (Oxford: Oxford University Press).

Jacobsson, S., and A. Johnson (2000) 'The Diffusion of Renewable Energy Technology: An Analytical Framework and Key Issues for Research'. *Energy Policy* 28: 625–40.

Kale, D., and S. Little (2007) 'From Imitation to Innovation: The Evolution of R&D Capabilities and Learning Processes in the Indian Pharmaceutical Industry'. *Technology Analysis and Strategic Management* 19 (5): 589–609.

Kammen, D., K. Kapadia and M. Fripp (2004) 'Putting Renewable Energy to Work: How Many Jobs Can the Clean Energy Industry Generate?' *RAEL Report* (Berkeley, CA: University of California).

Khan, M. (2004) 'State Failure in Developing Countries and Institutional Reform Strategies'. In B. Tungodden, N. Stern and I. Kolstad (eds) *Toward Pro-Poor Policies: Aid, Institutions, and Globalization* (Washington, D.C.: World Bank and Oxford University Press).

Lakhotia, K. (2009) 'Nuclear Politics in India'. MSc Thesis, University of Oxford.

Latour, B. (1987) *Science in Action* (Cambridge, MA: Harvard University Press).

Latour, B. (1994) 'On Technical Mediation – Philosophy, Sociology, Genealogy'. *Common Knowledge* 3 (2): 29–64.

Leys, C. (2001) *Market Driven Politics* (London: Verso).

Leys, C. (2007) *Total Capitalism* (New Delhi: Three Essays Press).

Mallett, A., and R. Haum (2009) 'PV Case Study' for UK-India Collaboration to Identify the Barriers to the Transfer of Low Carbon Technology: Phase Two. Sussex Energy Group (SPRU, University of Sussex), The Energy Research Institute (New Delhi), Institute of Development Studies (University of Sussex).

Martinez-Alier, J., and K. Schlupmann (1990) *Ecological Economics: Energy, Environment and Society* (Oxford: Basil Blackwell).

Martinez-Alier, J. (1995) 'Political Ecology, Distribution Conflicts and Economic Incommensurability'. *New Left Review* 1 (211): 70–88.

McKinsey (2008) 'Electric Power and Natural Gas'. McKinsey Quarterly Winter Bulletin No. 4, McKinsey India.

NASSCOM (National Association of Software and Services Companies) (2009) *Annual Report* 2008–9 (NASSCOM).

NFU (National Farmers' Union) (2005) *Climate Change and Agriculture* (London: National Farmers' Union).

Panagariya, A. (2009) 'Climate Change and India: Implications and Policy Options'. Paper prepared for the NCAER-Brookings India Policy Forum 2009, New Delhi, 14–15 July.

Polanyi, K. (1944) *The Great Transformation: The Political and Economic Origins of Our Time* (Boston: Beacon Press).

Prins, G., and S. Rayner (2007) 'The Wrong Trousers. Radically Rethinking Climate Policy'. *Joint Discussion Paper* (Oxford, London: James Martin Institute for Science and Civilization, University of Oxford; the MacKinder Centre for the Study of Long-Wave Events, London School of Economics).

Rohra, S. (2009) 'Solar Energy: Why and How to Develop and Diffuse it in India?' MSc Thesis, University of Oxford.

Saxenian, A.-L. (1994) *Regional Advantage: Culture and Competition in Silicon Valley and Route 128* (Cambridge, MA: Harvard University Press).

Schaffer, B. (1984) 'Towards Responsibility'. In E. Clay and B. Schaffer (eds) *Room for Manoeuvre* (London: Heinemann).

Schneider, P., J. Meadway, M. Harris and R. Halkett (2008) *An Initial Exploration of the NESTA Functional Model of Innovation Systems with Regard to Wind Power in the UK* (London: NESTA).

Scott, J. (1990) *Domination and the Arts of Resistance: Hidden Transcripts* (Newhaven, CT: Yale University Press).

Semi Conductor Equipment and Materials International (SEMI) (2009) PV Group White Paper – the Solar PV Landscape in India; an Industry Perpsective. Online: http://www.pvgroup.org/NewsArchive/ctr_029194 (accessed 11 November 2010).

Singh, N. (2009) 'Solar Photovoltaic Production in India and the Supply of Intellectual Property Rights'. MSc Thesis, University of Oxford.

Stewart, F. (1977) *Technology and Underdevelopment* (London: Macmillan).

Stewart, F. (2009) 'Relaxing the Shackles: The Invisible Pendulum'. *Journal of International Development* 21: 765–71.

TERI (The Energy Resource Institute) (2009) *Annual Report, 2007–8* (New Delhi: TERI).

Thompson, P. (1988) *The Nature of Work* (2nd ed.) (London: Macmillan).

UNDP (United Nations Development Programme) (2007) *Fighting Climate Change: Human Solidarity in a Divided World – Human Development Report* (New York: UNDP).

Weiss, B. (2009) 'Jobs More Important Than Price per Watt to Key Policy Makers', The Grid, SEMI. Online: http://www.pvgroup.org/NewsArchive/CTR_031030 (accessed 11 November 2010).

White, G. (1993) 'The Political Analysis of Markets'. *Bulletin Institute of Development Studies* 24 (3): 1–11.

Willett, S. (2002) 'Weapons at the Turn of the Millennium'. In B. Harriss-White (ed.) *Globalisation and Insecurity* (Basingstoke: Palgrave Macmillan).

WISE (World Institute for Sustainable Energy) (2008) *Power Drain: Hidden Subsidies to Conventional Power in India* (Pune: World Institute of Sustainable Energy).

Part III

Human Development, Income Distribution and Poverty

6
Advancing Human Development: Values, Groups, Power and Conflict

Séverine Deneulin

6.1 Introduction

In one of my first doctoral supervision meetings with Frances Stewart, I found a recurring comment pencilled throughout my abstract philosophical discussions on the capability approach: 'What does this mean for the real world?' During subsequent doctoral supervisions, she often emphasised three points. First, humans are not free individual agents who decide and act on the basis of their own reasoning. They are profoundly social and embedded into layers of complex social relationships. Human actions are never disconnected from the wider networks of social relations and institutions in which people are historically situated. In other words, human existence entails belonging, and this provides the condition for the exercise of freedom and agency. Another point that she was always quick to make was that policy decisions were the result of differences in power between groups, whether political parties, social movements, international organisations, civil society organisations, global corporations, companies or business associations. One final point that she emphasised, linked to the latter, was conflict. When one makes an individual decision about one's life, there are often conflicting claims, which are equally valuable. This is even more so when collective decisions are made. Collective decision-making is fraught with conflict which cannot always be resolved in a straightforward way, through reasoning.

This chapter explores these three points further, and focuses on an analysis of the dynamics of value formation and its influence on policy. It begins by discussing how values shape development policies and how the human development and capability approach conceives of the role of values in policy-making. The third section reviews some literature from psychology, sociology and philosophy which offers further insights into value formation and the policy influence of values. The fourth section puts forward some analytical tools that help us better understand the dynamics of value change and its policy impact. In particular, it discusses the role of groups as drivers of value change and the power that different groups command. It argues that policy change is often the result of conflict between groups which embed different value frameworks. The fifth section applies these analytical tools to the case of development policy-making in Costa Rica. The chapter concludes by discussing the implications of taking into account groups, power and conflict in the formation of values for advancing human development.

6.2   Values in human development

Policies and values are inextricably linked. For example, American slavery was abolished because some people endorsed the value of equal dignity among all human beings, whatever the colour of their skin. Women were granted equal political, civil, economic and social rights with men because they refused to endorse the value of women's subordination to men and adopted instead the value of equality. Labour rights were introduced because workers campaigned for society to recognise the value of labour and the dignity of workers. Undoubtedly certain economic, social and political preconditions were necessary for slavery to be abolished and for labour and women's rights to be guaranteed; nonetheless, anti-slavery and women's and labour movements, together with their values regarding equality and dignity, played a significant role in shifting policy and in enshrining these values into law. A better understanding of why people endorse certain values and not others, and of the processes that lead to value change, is therefore crucial for advancing human development and for providing the conditions for human flourishing.

After decades of neglect due to the dominance of positivist economics on development economics, there has been a recent interest in taking values seriously in development. In that regard, the works of Amartya Sen and the capability approach have played a significant role in bringing the ethical dimensions of economics to the fore and, as a consequence, in bringing ethics and the question of values to the heart of development economics and development studies.[1] This renewed interest in values extends to development policy circles.

In November 2008, the UK Department for International Development (DFID), in collaboration with the UK Foreign Office and the Ministry of

Defence, organised a seminar entitled 'Values 2020: How Will Changing Values and Beliefs in the UK and Key Regions Influence Development and Foreign Policy in Practice?'.[2] The motivation for the seminar was a growing awareness that policies were not likely to succeed if they did not respond to people's values. For example, trying to make a country implement environmental policies while the majority of its population does not value care for the environment is bound to fail; such a policy will work only if people's values are made to include protection of the environment as a central value. In the same way, democratisation policy will be a challenge unless people uphold values traditionally associated with democracy – such as tolerance, equality, fairness, respect for others and the rule of law. A clear understanding of people's values and of how they change is thus essential for policies to succeed.

The 'Values 2020' seminar discussions led to some interesting conclusions for the arguments of this chapter. Values were widely regarded as relating to how people should live and behave. It was recognised that values are not static, but constantly respond to influences and economic and social processes. These latter were termed 'drivers of values'. The seminar identified several: global capitalism (materialism and a conception of the good life as linked to material wealth); environmentalism (a shift away from consumerism); class and inequality (one's position in the economy); religion and secularism; ethnicity and identity (how one identifies oneself as belonging to a specific group); immigration and the diaspora (immigration may change the dominant values of a society, and may also change the values of the immigrants' countries of origin); and urbanisation (cities change people's values).

In addition to recognising that values are shaped by political, economic and social processes and in turn influence them, the seminar noted that values are heterogeneous within societies, albeit they have some degree of homogeneity. Speaking of British values or Muslim values in the aggregate, as if every British or Muslim person held the same values, masks a huge variety of views among the British or the Muslim population. Yet there is some relative homogeneity of values within a society, so that one can state that there are values which characterise British society, which are different from those which characterise, say, Nigeria or Japan.

That a policy needs to respond to people's values in order to succeed – the initial concern of the seminar discussed above – has been one of the core arguments of the human development and capability approach. In his version of the capability approach, Amartya Sen has left open the question of precisely what values development policy should be based upon – the approach only affirms that policies have to be judged within the space of capabilities or freedoms.[3] It falls short of specifying 'valuable' capabilities beyond saying that policy ought to promote the 'capabilities of persons to lead the kind of lives they value – and have reason to value' (Sen, 1999a: p. 18). However, while the approach does not specifically define valuable capabilities, it states that the 'capabilities people have reason to choose and value' are, or should be, in line with the values implicit in the universal human rights declaration (Sen, 2004).

In her version of the capability approach, Martha Nussbaum has put the case for policies to promote an open-ended list of central human capabilities (Nussbaum, 2000). She entitles the second chapter of *Women and Human Development* 'In Defense of Universal Values'. She argues that certain 'very general values' such as 'the dignity of the person, the integrity of the body, basic political rights and liberties, basic economic opportunities and so forth' (Nussbaum, 2000: p. 41) should be the universal norm for assessing women's lives – and development – worldwide. Her central human capabilities reflect these values.

The secondary literature on the capability approach extends Sen's and Nussbaum's analysis of values. Qizilbash (2002) reviews the different conceptualisations of advantage in development (primary goods, incomes, resources, capabilities, needs, etc.), and observes that all these share common values such as concern with human beings and the quality of human lives, universality (every human being should be able to live a good human life) and 'component pluralism' (a good human life cannot be reduced to one dimension). Qizilbash distinguishes capabilities from values. Capabilities are the objects of values – for example the 'capability to play' is a specific instantiation of the value of 'enjoyment', or the 'capability to gain employment' is an instantiation of the value of 'accomplishment'. Alkire (2002) similarly makes a careful distinction between values and capabilities, and separates the exercise of valuing from capabilities. Values are what allows people to prioritise their capabilities. They are what enables people to judge what is important in their lives and what dimension of human wellbeing it is more worthwhile to pursue in given contexts.

However, despite the centrality of values, the capability literature does not say much about the values which come into play during the valuation exercise. Alkire (2002) does not examine the reasons why people value certain dimensions of wellbeing and not others. In other words, she does not analyse the values, or value frameworks, which her respondents use in their value judgments. In the opening page of *Valuing Freedoms*, she writes that one of the beneficiaries of an Oxfam project in rural Pakistan 'values the income the rose project produces' and values the fact that her clothing smells nicely of roses, together with the inner peace that she derives from using roses in religious ceremonies. Other respondents value the greater confidence that working in the rose project has given them.

Thus, while emphasising the importance of values in development, what the capability approach actually stresses is not so much values in themselves as the act of valuing, which it closely associates with the act of reasoning. Democracy is the place *par excellence* where the act of reasoning takes place. According to Sen, democratic practice is a crucial mechanism for constructing people's values and for determining policy decisions (Sen, 1999a, 1999b). For example the practice of democracy might construct the value of solidarity, which will then serve as a criterion for the democratic exercise of reasoning about what policy priorities should be established. This may lead to policy decisions which extend public health services or improve the quality of state-provided education. Conversely, democratic practice may construct other values, such as that of individual choice. This may lead to policy decisions which privatise public utilities and allow for greater private sector involvement in the health and education sectors.

Despite stressing the importance of people's values for development and policy (in terms of values which shape the reasoning process and the outcomes), the capability approach falls short of offering a detailed analysis of what the values themselves are, how they are formed and how they change. What values are used as criteria in value judgments? Why is it that certain countries use the value of 'individual choice' as a criterion for policy decisions, while others use the value of 'solidarity'? How is it that at a certain point in time a country may have made decisions according to the criterion of solidarity but has now changed this for individual choice? An examination of some literature from the areas of psychology, sociology and philosophy may help answer these questions.

6.3   Values in the wider social sciences

Social psychology provides a more precise conceptualisation of values than the human development and capability approach. Values 'are concepts or beliefs, pertain to desirable end-states or behaviours, transcend specific situations, guide selection or evaluation of behaviour and events, and are ordered by relative importance' (Schwartz, 1992: p. 6).[4]

From this definition, one can attribute two core characteristics to values: they refer to what is believed to be good (it is assumed here that something is desirable because it is thought to be good); and they guide human action. Research in social psychology has tried to identify which values guide people's behaviours and has found that there are some which guide people's actions universally, and that societies and individuals prioritise and express these universal values differently. On the basis of evidence from twenty countries, Schwartz (1992) singles out ten values which are universal but prioritised differently across societies and among individuals: (1) self-direction (creativity, freedom, independence, curiosity, choosing one's goals); (2) stimulation (seeking an exciting life, taking risks, seeking novelty); (3) hedonism (pleasure and enjoyment in life); (4) achievement (seeking success, ambition and influence); (5) power (authority, wealth, social recognition); (6) security (social order, harmony, family security, national security); (7) conformity (obedience, self-discipline, politeness, honouring parents); (8) tradition (respect for symbols and practices that represent the shared experience of groups); (9) universalism (social justice, equality, peace, beauty, protecting the environment); and (10) benevolence (honesty, helpfulness, forgiveness, loyalty, responsibility).[5]

One can object that the link between values and behaviour is not as straightforward as the above definition suggests. One might value honesty but behave in dishonest ways, for instance by failing to pay a train fare because one knows that it is very unlikely that the ticket will be checked. Research in social psychology has widely documented the so-called 'value–action gap'. On the basis of experimental research and a review of the literature, Verplanken and Holland (2002) have concluded that there is a strong link between value and behaviour but that a value is more likely to influence behaviour if it is central to the conception of self (one might say that one values honesty but one may not identify oneself as an honest person); if the specific case calls for the value of honesty (being honest in paying one's train fare is not the same as being honest with one's spouse); and if there are no other values which come into consideration (one might lie to one's children about the terminal disease of one's spouse in order to protect them).

Whereas psychology is more concerned with the individual than with society, the discipline of sociology emphasises the role of social norms in the translation of values into behaviours. As in social psychology, values 'define what is considered important, worthwhile and desirable'

(Giddens, 2004: p. 22), but sociology adds to this the important concept of social norms, which are 'the rules of behaviour which reflect or embody a culture's values' (ibid.: p. 22). Giddens gives, as contrasting examples, the values of achievement and hospitality. In some cultures, there are strong social norms which put pressure on people to be professionally high achievers. Failing to be professionally successful might inflict on the person a sense of guilt, social disapproval or personal failure. Other cultures may have strong social norms regarding the values of hospitality and redistribution. Failing to honour guests adequately may result in a similar sense of guilt, social disapproval or personal failure.

Structuration theory has shown (Giddens, 1984) that there is a two-way relationship between structures and social norms on the one hand, and individual agency on the other. Individuals act within the constraints of certain social norms and structures, but these norms and structures are themselves changed by people's individual actions.[6] For example, the way in which Western societies value the institution of marriage has undergone radical changes over the last fifty years through the actions of individuals, such as feminist writers. A society's values, and its corresponding enforcement of social norms, are thus not unchangeable. As the next section will illustrate, some individuals (and the groups they form) are agents of change and have the power to alter a society's core social norms and the values which the latter represent. But why are values different across cultures, and why do they change? Some literature from political philosophy may give us some further insights.

Like sociologists, some political philosophers have stressed the links between values and social practices (Raz, 1999, 2003) – what sociologists called social norms. For example, values such as 'solidarity' or 'freedom' would be meaningless without the shared social practices which sustain them (taxation, distribution of benefits, freedom of expression, freedom of association, etc.). Values are what the philosopher Charles Taylor calls 'irreducibly social goods' (Taylor, 1995: pp. 127–45). They inhere in social relationships, whether in specific groups, such as the values which are sustained by the social practices of small communities – family, trade union or women's institute group – or wider communities; examples of the latter would be the values which are sustained by the social practices of a religious community, or those bound by a common history or language.

There are many groups from which people derive their values. One of the first groups into which humans are born is the family, which is itself moulded by many other groups. The child grows up endorsing the values embedded in the social practices which surround him or her – even the language one learns is a social practice which contains certain values, for example with regard to gender relations or attitudes (such as respect for the elders and people in authority). The social practices of the family may themselves be influenced by other groups (such as religious ones) and by their view of what constitutes a 'family'. The child may also endorse the values of the education system, which contains its own distinctive set of practices and values. In addition to schools, the media are also an important influence on people's values.

Unlike sociology, which limits itself to analysing the social influences on people's values, philosophy addresses ethical questions regarding the 'goodness' of values, and whether some expressions of values are better than others, for instance whether it is better to give priority to the value of 'achievement' over that of 'solidarity', or whether it is, say, more desirable to express the value of 'achievement' through competition than through good craftsmanship. In other words, philosophy examines the moral claims which underpin a society's core values and social norms.

There are many different ethical theories leading to different conclusions, or to different answers to the question 'What should one do?' or 'How should one live?'. The same ethical theory may also have different interpretations. Hence what is perceived as 'good' is constantly debated among individuals and changes over time, as do the values and social practices which support any particular conception of the 'good'. For example, laws against the unfair treatment of women represent a social practice which has changed over time because society has come to understand equality in different ways following a change in the conception of what a 'good life' (for women) should be about.

These insights from psychology, sociology and philosophy – that values are connected to what people perceive as good, that there are universal values which societies and individuals prioritise differently, and that people draw their values from the various groups to which they belong – help us answer some questions that the human development and capability approach has left unanswered. They also help us understand better how values are formed and change. The next section examines further the dynamics of value change within the context of human development policy.

6.4 Policy and the dynamics of value change

Analysing the dynamics of value formation and change is central to advancing human development, for some values are more conducive to providing the conditions for human flourishing than others[7] – assuming here an objectivist interpretation of human wellbeing. This section analyses two core ingredients in the interaction between, and dynamics of, value change and policy: groups as 'drivers of values' (what structuration theory refers to as the 'agency/structure' dynamics); and the power that these groups command in society, which often leads to situations of conflict.

6.4.1 Groups as 'drivers of values'

In a study of group behaviour and development, Stewart (2002) examined the dynamic interaction between the macro-environment, groups and development thinking. She argued that the mode of functioning of groups, whether groups tended to operate on a 'power/control', 'quasi-market' or 'cooperative' basis (Heyer et al., 2002), was greatly influenced by their social environment. Although she did not explore the extent to which groups in turn affected the macro-environment, her analysis gives us some insights.

She alludes to the importance of 'claims groups'[8] in challenging prevailing social norms and the social order and the distribution of assets in society; such were the trade unions in nineteenth-century Europe, or the suffragette movement. Other groups whose influence in shaping the macro-environment Stewart (2002) highlights are international financial institutions. She also notes that these groups have often met with opposition, and that the resulting social environment and its characteristic norms and distribution of assets and benefits are often the outcome of power struggles between groups.

Stewart advances a similar argument in an article on 'Groups and Capabilities' (Stewart, 2005), where she emphasises the importance of groups in human development – not only in directly promoting human freedoms through collective action (such as credit union groups offering better economic opportunities to the marginalised), but also in shaping what people value. In that respect, she notes that some groups shape people's values in ways that might not be conducive to human development; such as for example those groups that make people value respect for 'national' security over respect for human life, as is the case in some nationalist groups.

These groups can be seen as 'drivers of values' or agents of value change. To recall, the DFID seminar discussed in Section 6.2 included among these drivers of values the global capitalist economic system, environmentalism, class, religion, ethnicity, and urbanisation. But beyond these drivers of values there are certain powerful groups. Global capitalism is a system sustained by groups of people such as multinational companies, international financial institutions and, most fundamentally, academic groups which practise a certain type of economic theory.[9] Similarly, environmentalism is driven by environmental groups, by 'claims groups' which confront others, which prioritise different values, such as economic profits, over environmental care. Urbanisation changes people's values when they migrate to the cities, because cities are dominated by groups that uphold different values (or a different prioritisation of values) from those of the dominant groups in rural areas.

This analysis of groups as agents of value change has remained absent from the human development and capability approach literature so far. There is a lot of talk about democracy as an important space where people reason on the basis of their values and where values are constructed, but there is little on the many groups which inhabit the democratic space and which construct people's values too, groups like religious communities, the education system, global corporations or the media. When Alkire (2002) mentioned that women in a Pakistani village valued the rose project because they could use the roses in religious ceremonies, she implicitly made the claim that religion was a significant source of values in people's lives. The human development and capability approach would be enriched by a more substantial analysis of the relational spaces which shape people's values and of the groups which dominate them.

In a critique of the individualism of the capability approach, Evans (2002) cites the empires of Coca-Cola and MTV as shaping people's values and the realm of what they consider to be 'valuable'. Sandel (2005) discusses how market practices and commercial pressures may corrupt civic institutions.[10] When commercial advertising is used to finance education, it risks introducing a consumer attitude among students. Similarly for the health sector: seeing medication as a market product to boost companies' profits damages people's perception of healthcare as a public good. When the logic of markets and marketing is introduced into democratic institutions, their underlying civic values might be under threat. As Sandel puts it:

> When government leans too heavily on the borrowed appeal of cartoon characters and cutting-edge ads, it may boost its approval ratings but squander the dignity and authority of the public realm. And without a public realm in good repair, democratic citizens have little hope of directing the market forces and commercial pressures that quicken by the day and shape our lives in untold ways.
>
> (Sandel, 2005: p. 80)

Thus a value-based approach to development, which the human development and capability approach is, needs to include an analysis of the groups or communities which foster or nurture certain kinds of values. But another point must be taken into consideration: that value change is often the result of conflict between groups.

6.4.2   Power and conflict

Changing the prevailing values in a given society is often confrontational, for it entails direct opposition to the dominant groups which promote, and have an interest in promoting, these values. Power – and its frequent consequence, conflict, whether overt or hidden – lies at the core of agency and structural change (Giddens, 1984; Lukes, 2005). The French Revolution and American Civil Rights movement are good examples of this.[11]

Eighteenth-century France was characterised by a well-ordered society, divided between the aristocracy and landless peasants. The prevailing values of French society at the time were respect for authority and respect for tradition. These values were mainly promoted by two powerful groups, which had an interest in maintaining that prioritisation of values: the king and his entourage of aristocratic landlords on the one hand, and, on the other, the Catholic Church, which had a strong association with the monarchy and aristocracy. The change towards a social order in which the values of 'solidarity, fraternity and liberty' prevailed was accompanied by massive power struggles and conflicts. We should note here that a correspondence between a group's values and and its interests is not always necessary. The elite groups might indeed have an interest in prioritising the value of achievement over those of solidarity and of willingness to redistribute; hence they would attribute poverty to a lack of effort on the part of poor people instead of regarding it as the result of structural inequality and injustice for which the elite groups are responsible. But in some instances people in impoverished conditions might uphold values which make them respect the related social norms against their own interests, irrespective of the power of the elite. The widespread practice of dowry in Southeast Asia and its devastating consequences on poor family's lives is a good example of this fact. Indeed, poor people often continue to prioritise the values of 'tradition' and 'honour', despite the negative impacts of these values on their wellbeing.

The civil rights movement in the United States is another illustration of the conflicts which often accompany value – and policy – changes in society. The idea of a 'good society' as one in which blacks and whites were segregated according to a God-given social order was questioned by groups of blacks (and sometimes whites). This entailed conflict between different groups with competing visions of the good society, and hence competing value systems or frameworks. The values upon which policies were based in the United States in the 1970s were the direct outcome of that power struggle between conflicting groups with competing value frameworks or value prioritisations.

Other countries, which have known similar conflicts between groups with competing visions of the good society and values, have experienced less fortunate human development outcomes. Guatemala and El Salvador were both engulfed in conflicts between groups of landowners and landless farmers during the 1970s and 1980s, each trying to impose their own values and their vision of the 'good society'. After nearly two decades of neoliberal policies in El Salvador during which the policy scene was dominated by the landed elite and business class, the leader of the group which campaigned for land rights in the 1980s has recently come peacefully to power through democratic elections – a result signalling a likely change in the dominant values which underpin policy-making in El Salvador. Guatemala, in contrast, remains dominated by the whites and *mestizos*, a situation which leaves nearly half of its population marginalised and in conditions of acute poverty.

Often enough, the promotion of human freedoms is not a peaceful enterprise. In a paper which provides a sociological reading of the capability approach, Feldman and Gellert (2006) write:

> The welfare states, which perhaps come closer to providing for the capability(ies) that Sen and Nussbaum advocate, did not emerge in the abstract world in which people decided to 'assign responsibilities' to institutions that promoted social welfare programmes (Nussbaum, 2004: p. 15). Rather, welfare states were historically produced in Western Europe and North America in the early decades of the twentieth century through struggle and negotiation by working-class and women's movements.
>
> (Feldman and Gellert, 2006: p. 429)

But value changes need not always be the result of violent conflict and power struggles. Conflict may be hidden. This is especially the case for value changes triggered by capitalism and global markets. In the *Challenge of Affluence*, Avner Offer (2006) provides a history of the changes brought about by a mass consumption society. He argues that affluence is driven by novelty or, in other words, that a consumerist capitalist system has made a priority of the value of 'stimulation' (using Schwartz's classification), leading people to want new things all the time. This constant search for novelty, made possible by expanding consumer choices, nurtures impatience, and impatience, Offer concludes, undermines human wellbeing (among other things, through increased addiction, levels of depression, family breakdown and stress).

Consumerism is also changing people's values in developing countries. Research conducted by the Wellbeing in Developing Countries Group funded by the UK Economic Social and Research Council (WeD, 2007) reported that poor households in rural areas in Thailand favoured humility over attaining status through job achievement or consumption of goods, while households in urban areas favoured gaining status and adopting a highly consumerist lifestyle. This conflict of values was very apparent when urban migrants came back to their villages.

To sum up, the human development and capability approach needs to provide, in addition to an evaluative framework for states of affairs, an analysis of the dynamics of value formation, of the different groups which shape these values, of the degree of power they command, and of their consequent influence on policy. The next section shows how such an analysis might explain human development achievements, taking recent history in Costa Rica as an example.

6.5   Values and policies in Costa Rica

Costa Rica has long stood out as an exception in Central America, where its neighbours perform less well in terms of human development. The country has achieved high levels of human wellbeing, with education and health indicators nearing those of industrialised nations (Mesa-Lago, 2000). The policies that made these achievements possible did not emerge from a normative vacuum, but rested on certain values that were the outcome of a particular configuration of groups and of the power these commanded. The present section discusses Costa Rica's history in the light of the above analysis of the dynamics of value change, group interaction and policies.[12]

6.5.1   Phase 1: Compulsory education

A first set of policies that played a crucial role in Costa Rica's development path was introduced at the end of the nineteenth century. In 1886, the Costa Rican Constitution declared primary education free and compulsory for both sexes, and sanctions were imposed on parents who did not comply. The impact of the policy was dramatic and illiteracy fell sharply; it was reduced by more than half in both urban and rural areas.

The government's decision to introduce universal primary education was the result of an interaction between groups and the values they held. The dominant political group at the time was the bourgeoisie. Costa Rica had experienced a coffee boom, which led to the emergence of a politically prominent coffee elite. That group endorsed the values of liberal capitalism and saw education as necessary to building a skilled workforce that would lead the country to a higher path of economic development (Ameringer, 1982). Unlike other Central American countries, the Costa Rican elite did not endorse values of domination and power over the workforce, because the population was ethnically homogenous – the indigenous population at the time of colonisation was numerically low, which meant that European settlers had to cultivate the land themselves (Wilson, 1998) and, because the labour force was scarce, wages could not be kept low. We can observe here the importance of the macro-environment in shaping the kinds of values that groups will endorse. The values endorsed by the Costa Rican bourgeoisie radically differed from those of, say, the Guatemalan bourgeoisie, because of the different macro-environment of these two countries in terms of the indigenous population.

Another feature of the Costa Rican bourgeoisie was its strong commitment to the values of secularism: here it was following the lead of the French bourgeoisie during the Enlightenment. Having introduced universal state-sponsored primary education, the government also banned religious schools and closed down the church-run university (which reopened as a state university in 1948). The bourgeoisie saw education as a means of pursuing freedom and reason, central values of the Enlightenment, and feared that an education based on religion might conflict with these values (Ameringer, 1982). There was some conflict here with the Catholic Church, but not to the same extent as might have happened elsewhere in Central America. This was because the Church in Costa Rica was not linked to the colonisation enterprise as it was in neighbouring countries, where a strong alliance between the military, the Church and the elite exploited the indigenous population. The power configuration in Costa Rica thus allowed for the liberal and secular values of the bourgeoisie to prevail at that time and to be embodied in concrete educational policies.

6.5.2   Phase 2: Social security

The values of liberal capitalism were tested after the First World War. The country experienced economic and social collapse due to a sharp fall in coffee prices, Costa Rica's main export. *Laissez-faire* policies failed to re-establish economic and social stability. A political party, the Reformist Party, was created in the 1920s around the values of social democracy, which prompted the government to introduce a range of social policies never used before, such as school meals. The party was created by a Catholic priest trained in Belgium, where he had encountered the Catholic Church's 'social doctrine'.[13] The social doctrine comprised a set of values developed in late nineteenth-century Europe by priests who were close to the workers' struggle during industrialisation. They were officially promoted by Pope Leon XIII in his 1891 encyclical, *Rerum novarum*, which condemned unbridled capitalism and called for social protection and recognition of workers' rights.

We can see here again how a certain community, the Church, created certain values and how this process interacted with the macro-environment. The Costa Rican terrain was receptive to the values expressed in the social doctrine; in this respect Costa Rica was unlike the neighbouring countries, where the local Church was more resistant to such an interpretation of the Gospel because of the Church's direct alliance with the elite. Because of the relatively egalitarian nature of Costa Rican society, the translation of the new social values into policy did not require a violent conflict, as would later be the case in other Central American countries.

This path of social reform in Costa Rica took another turn with the election of Rafael Calderón Guardia as president in 1940. Calderón introduced a social security scheme which incorporated social insurance and social welfare programmes for the poorest. He also introduced other social guarantees, for instance the eight-hour working day, the minimum wage, protection against arbitrary dismissal and the right of workers to organise (Ameringer, 1982; Wilson, 1998).

As in the previous cases we have looked at, the introduction of these policies reflects the values of some groups and their respective power. Once again, an influential group was the Catholic Church and its social doctrine. Calderón was a paediatrician; he trained as a doctor in Belgium, and there he saw the impact of the Church's social doctrine on social action: Belgian Cardinal Joseph Cardijn introduced the 'see-judge-act' methodology for social action, and many Christian political groups sprang from it.

Another influential group behind the introduction of the social security scheme was the Communist Party, which had become politically strong in Costa Rica by the late 1930s. Calderón encountered opposition from the elite, whose members were reluctant to make such generous social rights available. But he was able to bypass this opposition by forming a coalition between the Communist Party and the Catholic Church, as both endorsed the values of solidarity and protection for the workers. However, one should note here that this power configuration between groups – the alliance between Catholics and Communists against the elite – was shaped by the macro-environment. This power configuration in Costa Rica would have been totally different a decade later, during the Cold War, when no such alliance would have been possible. Communists and Catholics would then be in conflict over the value of atheism instead of united around the value of solidarity.

6.5.3   Phase 3: Expansion of the welfare state

A third decisive period in Costa Rica's development story was that of the post-war decades. In 1949 President José Figueres introduced compulsory secondary education, making both primary and secondary education free and state-financed. Food and clothing for poor students were provided by the state, and adult education programmes were organised for those left out by the educational system. Figueres also introduced a law that allocated 6 per cent of GDP each year to public expenditure in education. He nationalised the banking system, abolished the army and imposed a wealth tax. These measures allowed the state to plan economic development, and they also led to a political weakening of the coffee elite. By weakening the power of the coffee elite and by strengthening the role of the state in the economy, Figueres determined the subsequent conditions for the economic and social development of the country (Ameringer, 1982; Mesa-Lago, 2000).

His party, the Partido Liberación Nacional (PLN), won the most votes throughout the post-war period. Among the policies implemented were education policies, which further improved child and adult education and increased rural educational coverage, and an expansion of the health system. A special health programme, involving a network of health centres and mobile clinics, was established for those living in rural areas. This emphasis on primary healthcare led to a significant improvement in health (Garnier et al., 1997). These policies were based on the core value of solidarity – that no-one should be in want – and on the belief that the state was the best keeper of this value.

The reason why these values prevailed in post-war Costa Rica has again to do with the power configuration of different groups, the values they held, and their interaction with the macro-environment. José Figueres was influenced by socialist intellectual groups. Ameringer (1978) reports that, when studying engineering in the United States,

Figueres spent time in libraries reading the socialist theories of Charles Fourier and Saint-Simon. But, unlike in other Central American countries, the power configuration of Costa Rica enabled socialist ideas to prevail. There was no strong alliance between the elite and the military – a power configuration which led to the overthrow of socialist regimes in other Latin American countries in the post-war period. At the same time, the creation, by Figueres, of the PLN and its underlying social democratic values shaped the values that Costa Rican citizens held, engendering a virtuous circle of policy-value construction-policy.

Alongside political parties, trade unions have been another important group for nurturing social democratic values. Sánchez-Ancochea (2005) emphasises that, in addition to the PLN, the trade unions of public sector employees were crucial in expanding the welfare state in Costa Rica. Once again, the macro-environment in Costa Rica during the post-war era, facilitated as it was by earlier developments, was conducive to a harmonious power configuration between trade unions and socially oriented political parties and to the nurturing of social democratic values within Costa Rican society, unlike in other Central American neighbouring countries, where the elite and military groups (together with the United States) banned trade unions and overthrew socially oriented political parties.

6.5.4   Phase 4: Neoliberalism

This social democratic model underwent a profound crisis in 1980–82 due to the oil price rise and the subsequent rise in interest rates. The Costa Rican economy no longer benefited from low-interest loans from international banks to finance its welfare institutions. Its external debt increased sharply, GDP per capita fell, unemployment doubled, inflation soared, real wages contracted and poverty increased. Drastic structural adjustment policies were needed to deal with the crisis. The World Bank and the United States Agency for International Development (USAID) pressed the Costa Rican government to reduce its protectionism and to increase the share of the private sector in the economy (Clark, 2001).

The crisis of the 1980s introduced a structural change in the macro-environment which in turn led to a different power configuration of groups within Costa Rica, and hence to a different value prioritisation – the values of achievement and freedom took precedence over the values of solidarity. This change in macro-environment also led to a change in values within each dominant group. While the PLN had been characterised by social democratic values during the post-war period, the economic crisis brought an ideological change inside the PLN's own ranks. The PLN became a party which supported greater private sector participation in the economy and the liberalisation of markets. The banks which had been nationalised in the late 1940s were privatised in 2002. The pension and health systems have also been progressively privatised since the 1990s.

Section 6.3 argued that values are linked to what people believe to be 'good'. Value prioritisation changes because people come to understand 'how to live well together' differently. While the post-war era was characterised by a consensus that a strong welfare state was the best guarantee for 'living well', the economic crisis of the 1980s challenged that vision. Given soaring interest rates, state intervention and the expansion of welfare institutions could no longer be financed through borrowing. Continuing to uphold the values of state-sponsored solidarity was now perceived as an obstacle to 'living well'. Instead, in a process facilitated by certain economic theories and by the groups which followed them, the dominant political group in Costa Rica, the PLN, changed its conception of what was 'good', that is, certain members of the party started to believe that the prioritisation of the values of achievement and freedom – the major values inherent in market liberalism – would bring about a better society than one centred around the value of state-sponsored solidarity.

Rovira Más (2004) talks of a 'new style of development'. The consensus that development is about expansion of the welfare state is being slowly replaced by a consensus that development is about market freedom. He argues that this new style is the result of historic struggles between groups. Among them, he highlights the group of economists trained in neoclassical economics, the international financial institutions, and the Costa Rican political parties which have chosen to endorse the dominant values held by these groups. However, there are also groups which are resisting the policies implemented by these dominant groups. The most striking example was the popular protests throughout Costa Rica in 2000, which were carried out by a coalition of trade unions, student organisations and many popular organisations and were intended to prevent the privatisation of the telecommunication company, which they saw as a symbol of Costa Rica's social democratic heritage.

Today that heritage remains strong. For example, in 1994 an independent body was created to monitor progress on human development. The *Estado de la Nación* (*State of the Nation*) publishes yearly politically independent accounts of Costa Rica's social and economic achievements, of the health of its democracy and of the protection of its environment.

The latest *Estado de la Nación* (2008) notes that Costa Rica remains a social exception in Central America but that inequality, as measured by the Gini coefficient, is rapidly rising. Also, the rate of social investment has still not regained its 1980 peak in real terms. Since 2000, FODESAF (Fondo de Desarrollo Social y Asignaciones), a key welfare institution, has lost 28 per cent of its real income and 30 per cent of its spending capacity. Which policy, based on whose values, will dominate in the next decade will depend on the power configuration of dominant groups and on the macro-environment in which they operate. The 2008 financial crisis might generate new dynamics of change and question people's current prioritisation of values.

6.6 Conclusion

In her analysis of groups in the capability approach, Stewart (2005) concluded that:

> Given their importance in determining whether people lead good lives (i.e. adopt valuable capabilities) it is important to support groups that encourage valuable capabilities as against those that do the opposite. The implication of this is that priority should be given to researching group capabilities from a conceptual, empirical and policy perspective.
>
> Stewart (2005: p. 199)

This is what the present chapter has tried to do: offer an analysis of the dynamics of value change and of its impact on policy, within the context of the human development and capability approach. This requires paying careful attention to the groups from which individuals draw their values and to the respective power they command. It also entails acknowledging the reality of conflict as a positive force for social change.

Today consumerism, or a capitalist economic order based on mass consumption, is no doubt one of the major drivers of values shaping policies in the world. But this does not automatically lead to the fatalistic conclusion that nothing can be done about the power of unfettered global markets in shaping people's lives and what they value. Other groups can shape in other directions what people value. I have named religious groups as important groups which nurture certain values and which can counteract the dominant values carried by a global capitalist system. Trade unions, environmental groups and political pressure groups are other groups where other values may be formed.

Advancing human development rests on a certain class of values. So far, writings on the human development and capability approach have neglected the importance of nurturing the kinds of values which are conducive to human development and to a more just social order. This chapter has emphasised the importance of the formative role of groups in shaping people's values in certain ways. The Human Development and Capability Association (HDCA), the Human Development Report Office and universities that teach human development in their curriculum can act as such formative groups – or communities – shaping people around the values that are necessary for promoting social justice and human flourishing. Whether these groups can challenge the power of others, which promote values at odds with human flourishing – such as those related to consumerism and materialism – is a matter of perseverance and hope.

Acknowledgments

I thank Judith Heyer, Nick Townsend and Peter Davis for helpful comments on an earlier draft.

Notes

1. See Sen (1987) and Alkire and Deneulin (2009) for a summary of the capability literature.
2. The event was organised by the Overseas Development Institute. A seminar report, not for public circulation, was drafted by Bhavna Sharma of ODI.
3. 'In the capability-based assessment of justice, individual claims are not to be assessed in terms of the resources or primary goods the persons respectively hold, but by the freedoms they actually enjoy to choose the lives that they have reason to value' (Sen, 1992: p. 81).
4. See Rohan (2000) for the various definitions of values in social psychology.
5. The value of spirituality (meaning and harmony through the transcendence of everyday reality) is a value which was found in some countries but not all the 20 countries studied by Schwartz.
6. As Marx famously claimed, 'Men [sic] make their own history but not in circumstances of their own choosing'.
7. For example, Kasser and Kanner (2004) document the negative impact of materialistic values on people's wellbeing.
8. Heyer et al. (2002) attributed three functions to groups: (1) overcoming market failures; (2) advancing claims to power and/or resources; and (3) altering distributions of benefits in society (pro-bono functions).
9. For the ways in which studying economics shapes the values of economics students, see Frank et al. (1993).
10. He also discussed this theme in his Reith Lectures on BBC radio in June 2009. The lectures can be heard at www.bbc.co.uk/radio4/reith/.

11. For an analysis of such 'dynamics of contention' and the mechanisms through which groups are successful in changing the existing social order, including a detailed analysis of the French Revolution and the American Civil Rights movement, see McAdam, Tarrow and Tilly (2001).
12. This section is drawn from material in Deneulin (2005, 2006).
13. Internal conflicts led to the dissolution of the Reform Party in the late 1920s (Ameringer, 1982).

References

Alkire, S. (2002) *Valuing Freedoms* (Oxford: Oxford University Press).
Alkire, S., and S. Deneulin (2009) 'The Human Development and Capability Approach'. In S. Deneulin with L. Shahani (eds) *An Introduction to the Human Development and Capability Approach* (London: Earthscan).
Ameringer, C. (1978) *Don Pepe: A Political Biography of José Figueres of Costa Rica* (Albuquerque: University of New Mexico Press).
Ameringer, C. (1982) *Democracy in Costa Rica* (New York: Praeger Publishers).
Clark, Mary A. (2001) *Gradual Economic Reform in Latin America* (New York: SUNY Press).
Deneulin, S. (2006) *The Capability Approach and the Praxis of Development* (Basingstoke: Palgrave Macmillan).
Deneulin, S. (2005) 'Development as Freedom and the Costa Rican Human Development Story'. *Oxford Development Studies* 33 (3/4): 493–510.
Estado de la Nación (2008) *Estado de la Nación en Desarrollo Humano Sostenible* (San José: UNDP Costa Rica). Available at www.estadonacion.or.cr. (accessed 11 November 2010).
Evans, P. (2002) 'Collective Capabilities, Culture and Amartya Sen's Development as Freedom'. *Studies in Comparative International Development* 37 (2): 54–60.
Feldman, S., and P. Gellert (2006) 'The Seductive Quality of Central Human Capabilities: Sociological Insights into Nussbaum and Sen's Disagreement'. *Economy and Society* 35 (3): 423–53.
Frank, R., T. Gilovich and D. Regan (1993) 'Does Studying Economics Inhibit Cooperation?' *Journal of Economic Perspectives* 7 (2): 159–71.
Garnier, L., R. Grynspan, R. Hidalgo, G. Monge and J. Trejos (1997) 'Costa Rica: Social Development and Heterodox Adjustment'. In R. Jolly and S. Mehrotra (eds) *Development with a Human Face* (Oxford: Clarendon Press).
Giddens, A. (2004) *Sociology*, 4th ed. (Cambridge: Polity).
Giddens, A. (1984) *The Constitution of Society* (Oxford: Basil Blackwell).
Heyer, J., F. Stewart and R. Thorp (eds) (2002) *Group Behaviour and Development* (Oxford: Oxford University Press).
Kasser, T., and A.D. Kanner (eds) (2004) *Psychology and Consumer Culture: The Struggle for a Good Life in a Materialistic World* (Washington, DC: American Psychological Association).
Lukes, S. (2005) *Power: A Radical View*, 2nd ed. (Basingstoke: Palgrave Macmillan).
McAdam, D., S. Tarrow and C. Tilly (2001) *Dynamics of Contention* (Cambridge: Cambridge University Press).

Mesa-Lago, C. (2000) 'Achieving and Sustaining Social Development with Limited Resources: The Experience of Costa Rica'. In D. Ghai (ed.) *Social Development and Public Policy: A Study of Some Successful Experiences* (London: Macmillan).

Nussbaum, M. (2004), 'Beyond the Social Contract: Capabilities and Global Justice'. *Oxford Development Studies* 32 (1): 3–18.

Nussbaum, M. (2000) *Women and Human Development* (Cambridge: Cambridge University Press).

Offer, A. (2006) *The Challenge of Affluence* (Oxford: Oxford University Press).

Qizilbash, M. (2002) 'Development, Common Foes and Shared Values'. *Review of Political Economy* 14 (4): 463–80.

Raz, J. (2003) *The Practice of Value* (Oxford: Oxford University Press).

Raz, J. (1999) *Engaging Reason: On the Theory of Value and Action* (Oxford: Oxford University Press).

Rohan, M.J. (2000) 'A Rose by Any Name? The Values Construct'. *Personality and Social Psychology Review* 4 (3): 255–77.

Rovira Más, J. (2004) 'El Nuevo Estilo Nacional de Desarrollo de Costa Rica 1984–2003'. In M. Flórez-Estrada and G. Hernández (eds) *¿Debe Costa Rica Aprobarlo? TLC con Estados Unidos* (San José: Universidad de Costa Rica).

Sánchez-Ancochea, D. (2005) 'Domestic Capital, Civil Servants and the State: Costa Rica and the Dominican Republic under Globalisation'. *Journal of Latin American Studies* 37 (4): 693–726.

Sandel, M. (2005) *Public Philosophy: Essays on Morality in Politics* (Cambridge, MA: Harvard University Press).

Schwartz, S.H. (1992) 'Universals in the Content and Structure of Values: Theoretical Advances and Empirical Tests in 20 Countries'. *Advances in Experimental Psychology* 25: 1–65.

Sen, A. (2004), 'Elements of a Theory of Human Rights'. *Philosophy and Public Affairs* 32 (4): 315–56.

Sen, A. (1999a) *Development as Freedom* (New York: Knopf).

Sen, A. (1999b) 'Democracy as Universal Value'. *Journal of Democracy* 10 (3): 3–17.

Sen, A. (1992) *Inequality Reexamined* (Oxford: Clarendon Press).

Sen, A. (1987) *On Ethics and Economics* (Oxford: Basil Blackwell).

Stewart, F. (2005) 'Groups and Capabilities'. *Journal of Human Development* 6 (2): 185–204.

Stewart, F. (2002) 'Dynamic Interactions Between the Macro-Environment, Development Thinking and Group Behaviour'. In J. Heyer, F. Stewart and R. Thorp (eds) *Group Behaviour and Development* (Oxford: Oxford University Press).

Taylor, C. (1995) *Philosophical Arguments* (Cambridge, MA: Harvard University Press).

Verplanken, B., and R. Holland (2002) 'Motivated Decision-Making: Effects of Activation and Self-Centrality of Values on Choices and Behavior'. *Journal of Personality and Social Psychology* 82 (3): 434–47.

WeD (2007) 'Wellbeing in International Development: Country Report Thailand', Online: http://www.welldev.org.uk/conference2007/final-papers/country/Thailandfinal.pdf (accessed July 2009).

Wilson, B.M. (1998) *Costa Rica: Politics, Economics and Democracy* (London: Lynne Rienner).

7
Welfare Regimes and Economic Development: Bridging the Conceptual Gap

Thandika Mkandawire

7.1 Introduction

When in 1999 I proposed to the board of the United Nations Research Institute for Social Development (UNRISD) a research agenda on 'Social Policy in a Development Context', Frances Stewart was then a member of the board. A question was raised as to why context was in the singular form. I argued that we wanted to examine the role of social policy where economic development was *intentionally* on the agenda. We also wanted to examine how social policy could be a transformative or developmental tool without compromising its intrinsic value. Stewart was one of the strongest supporters of this new programme, which a chairman of the board was later to label the institute's 'flagship' research programme. The research agenda itself was inspired by the Copenhagen Social Summit held in 1995, whose resolution insisted that social development and economic development are not separable but mutually constitutive and that, although the situations of developing countries and developed countries differ, social issues in each revolve around the same fundamental matters of economic welfare, equity and social justice. One implication of this is that conversations between the literatures on social development and economic development strategies in developing countries on the one hand, and those on welfare regimes and social policy in developed countries on the other can contribute to the construction of a single analytical framework for the shared agenda of human development.

Almost immediately after the beginning of the UNRISD research programme we were struck by the gap between the theoretical work on welfare states in the Organisation for Economic Co-operation and

Development (OECD) countries and the literature on social policy in developing countries. Over the years, and especially in the 1980s, two literatures flourished: one relating to social policy in developed countries (Rimlinger, 1971; Wilensky, 1975; Titmuss et al., 1987; Gilbert and Gilbert, 1989; Esping-Andersen, 1990) and one on 'developmental states' (Amsden, 1985; Morton, 1990; Wade, 1991; Evans, 1992). There was remarkably little interaction between these two literatures. In more recent years a literature on 'developmental welfare states' has emerged (Yeun-wen, 1997; Goodman et al., 1998; Holliday, 2000; Midgley and Tang, 2001; Huber, 2002; Gough et al., 2004; Kuhnle and Hort, 2004; Mkandawire, 2004; Kwon, 2005; Karshenas and Moghadam, 2007; Riesco, 2007; Yeun-wen and Finer, 2007). Its relationship with the foundational literature on welfare states remains cautious and guarded and, where it is at all informed by this literature, it marginalises the 'developmental state' literature.

I argue that the bifurcation of social policy research relating to developing and developed countries has widened the gap between the theoretical advances in the study of welfare states in developed countries and the more empirical and descriptive work on social policies in developing countries and has undermined cross-fertilisation and mutual learning. The importance of the literature focused mainly on OECD countries to developing countries does not lie so much in the taxonomic outcomes of its research endeavours as in the relevance to human development of the issues it addresses, its underscoring of the synergies between different aspects of social and economic policy, and its recognition of varieties of ways of managing capitalist economies. The learning is, of course, not one way. Indeed we have seen how social policy experiments in developing countries have found emulators in developed countries, leading to fears of 'Latin Americanisation'.[1]

Cross-fertilisation presupposes the fecundity and openness of each of the literatures involved in the exchange. I suggest that the problem is not entirely due to the neglect, by welfare state theorists in the North, of the experiences of developing countries, but also to weaknesses in the conceptual understanding of social policy in the developing country context.

Social policy is defined here as a collective intervention to affect social welfare, social institutions and social relations directly. It is concerned with the redistributive effects of economic policy, the protection of people from the vagaries of the market and the changing circumstances of age, the enhancement of the productive potential of members of society, and the reconciliation of the burden of reproduction with that of other social tasks. Successful societies have given social policy all these objectives, although the weighting of tasks has varied between countries and, within each country, from period to period. Welfare regimes refer to the normative weight attached to these tasks and to the ways in which these elements of social policy are aligned and clustered to establish some coherence among them.

The present chapter starts with some comments on the undertheorisation of social policy in the development process. It then goes on to look at some of the reasons for mutual neglect in the two literatures. These are discussed under the following headings: OECD bias; developing country bias; the linear view of history; the static comparative approach; and wage labour bias and segmentation. This investigation is followed by a discussion of the disconnection between social policy and development strategy in the developing country literature. There is a final section on the crisis of the welfare state and where that leaves us today.

7.2 Undertheorisation of social policy in the development process

While the literature on welfare regimes is reasonably well developed for the developed countries, social policy in developing countries is remarkably undertheorised. There is no clear theory of how social policy acts on development-enhancing factors so as to induce growth, nor is there agreement on the patterns of growth that are most appropriate to meeting the spectrum of social goals that are now on both national and international agendas (Mkandawire, 2001). There is little in social policy studies in developing countries as heuristically potent as Titmuss's and Esping-Andersen's work on welfare regimes (Titmuss et al., 1987; Esping-Andersen, 1990). Despite the recent slew of studies on welfare regimes in developing countries, Isabel Mares and Matthew Carnes conclude in a recent survey that 'our grasp of the variation in the design and economic consequences of social policies in developing economies is sketchy and preliminary' (Mares and Carnes, 2009: p. 94). One consequence of this undertheorisation is that writing on social policy in developing countries has tended towards 'thick description, thin explanation' (Mackintosh and Tibandebage, 2004: p. 145). Even the most ambitious statement of social policy in developing countries – the 'basic needs strategy' – did not evolve into a comprehensive and coherent theory of the relationship between development and social policy. It remained a 'category comprising several different approaches and specific measures that reflect considerable differences regarding emphases and priorities' (Martinussen, 1997: p. 298). Today, many social policy initiatives such as the Millennium Development Goals (MDG) exhibit the weakness of their theoretical underpinnings and take the form of a shopping list with no suggestions for optimal sequencing or interlinkages.

7.3   Reasons for mutual neglect

The undertheorisation of social policy in developing countries can be attributed to several closely related factors underlying the two litera- tures. The first factor is the 'bias' of each of these literatures, to which we now turn.

7.3.1   The OECD bias

Those working at the cutting edge of welfare state theories in the OECD countries have seldom paid attention to the experiences of social policy in developing countries, often finding their normative premises unacceptable (Midgley, 1995) or finding that the paucity of data was not conducive to the inclusion of developing countries in the taxonomic empirical studies that were *à la mode*. Social poli- cies in the developing countries were rendered invisible by what one might call 'normative dissonance'. Their normative basis (nationalism or developmentalism, for instance) was not salient in the welfare ideolo- gies of the developed countries, especially as articulated in the post-war period (Midgley and Tang, 2001). The 'developmental states', for exam- ple, were seen to have had strong 'productivist' features that included 'growth-oriented states and subordination of all aspects of state pol- icy, including social policy, to economic/industrial objectives' (Holliday, 2000: p. 709). Whenever 'catching up' among the 'late industrialisers' is carried out in a hothouse fashion, social policy becomes a much more important instrument and objective than was the case with the earlier industrialisers. For some, the fact that this harnessing of social policy to economic development instrumentalises social policy under- cuts the intrinsic value of social policy's pursuits. This is the polar opposite of the objectives of those for whom 'decommodification' has been a central concern (Esping-Andersen, 1990). These views sit uneasily with the concerns of development, with its focus on the 'mobilisa- tion' of human resources (Room, 2002). The tendency was to disparage social policies in developmental states as 'top-down', 'instrumentalist' or 'productivist', as if that automatically deprived them of the sta- tus of social policy. However, instrumentalisation does not necessarily erode the intrinsic value of human development, especially when one considers the bi-directional relationship between means and ends. In developing countries an important premise for the achievement of the most desired social goals is significant improvements in levels of material production. We should also note that, while there are differences in the extent to which issues of reproduction, redistribution, production and protection feature in different welfare systems, no economy incorporates only one element in its polices. There is usually a mix of all these, different weights being attached to each of them.

Another source of 'normative dissonance' has been the top-down nature of the introduction of social policies, and their paternalism, in contrast to the putatively 'voice'-driven welfare states of the OECD countries.[2] In addition, there is the fact that social policies were introduced or carried out by countries with unsavoury authoritarian developmental regimes. These characteristics led to a position that did not accommodate the extension of welfare state notions to developing countries, since the latter were not driven by issues of equity and social justice. There was simply no willingness to accept that key elements of social policy might be explicable along the same lines for societies with different political regimes.

As for the empirical relevance of social policy in developing countries, it could be argued that the 'OECD bias' has made the experiences of developing countries unnecessarily opaque, because, in addition to the often evoked paucity of statistical data, the social policy instruments used in developing countries have not always been drawn from the familiar arsenal of social policy in developed countries.[3] Far-reaching interventions that might not have been thought of as social policy have included land reform and security of tenure through the 'decommodification' of land; food subsidies; affirmative action programmes; active labour market policies; the Indian Rural Employment Guarantee scheme;[4] 'pan-territorial pricing' whereby government covers transport costs from remote areas; and commodity stabilisation programmes. The neglect of this 'social protection by other means', as Mishra terms it (Mishra, 2004), has produced a measurement bias which, in the extreme, has led to the misreading of the East Asian variant of developmental states as a 'social-policy-free zone' (Chang, 2004: p. 251).

7.3.2 The developing countries bias

In its turn, the literature on developing countries has paid little attention to the welfare regimes literature of developed countries. One cause of the neglect of the experiences of welfare states has been the dominant understanding of the relationship between growth and accumulation. Social policy, like economic growth, always relates to how economic surplus is produced, how it is distributed and how it is allocated between consumption and its further production. In the development theories that were dominant in the 1950s and the 1960s, there was 'the partitioning of national output into "consumption" and "investment", with a welfare function defined on consumption and the achievement of growth related to investment suggesting a conflict between welfare and future welfare' (Sen, 1997: p. 9).[5] The widespread view was that economic growth was maximised by high levels of investment, which meant keeping mass consumption down. To ensure that the surplus was reinvested, it was important to ensure that the functional distribution of income favoured those with the highest propensity to save and/or invest.[6] The 'leftist' version of this tendency favoured the capture of the economic surplus by the state through the nationalisation of the means of production, through taxation of luxury consumption and land rents, and so on, while demanding that labour make 'sacrifices' to further the construction of socialism or nation-building (Mahalanobis, 1953; Baran, 1957; Dobb, 1969). On the 'right', the model involved keeping down the demands of labour through repression or through the 'nationalisation' of labour for delivery to private capital at low cost (Gregor, 1979). Aspirations for comprehensive social policy were part of the dreaded 'revolutions of rising expectations' that had to be kept in check (Huntington, 1968). As one leading textbook on development stated in the mid-sixties, there was 'the cruel choice between rapid (self-sustained) expansion and democratic processes' (Bhagwati, 1966: p. 204). Amartya Sen gave these 'blood, sweat and tears' approaches to development the acronym BLAST (Sen, 1997). There were few dissenting voices. One was that of Arthur Lewis, who rejected the trade-off between political rights and development on the grounds that development meant the widening of the 'range of human choices' (Lewis, 1955). This was a point that would later be central to Amartya Sen's capabilities approach. On social policy, the dissenters argued that trade-offs between growth and welfare only existed if one ignored the fact that labour is, crudely stated, 'a produced and reproduced means of production' and that its quality depended on the inputs expended on its reproduction. As Lewis put it:

> Neither is there any excuse for not developing a proper range of social services – medical services, unemployment pay, pensions and the like – in the absence of which the industrial worker is forced to keep one foot in the village so that he can return to it in case of need.

The effect would be a healthier labour force, more settled, and more anxious for improvement on the job.

(Lewis, 1955: pp. 193–94)

Similarly, Gunnar Myrdal insisted: 'The productivity of higher consumption levels stands for me as a major motivation for the direction of development policy in underdeveloped countries. Higher consumption levels are a condition for a more rapid and stable growth' (Myrdal, 1984: p. 154).

Furthermore, structuralists argued that redistribution, by favouring groups with high propensities to consume, would stimulate demand and therefore growth in economies characterised by underutilised capacity.

These more positive views never really caught on very widely at the time and where they did, they later had to contend with the spectacular performance of the authoritarian 'development states' of East Asia on the one hand, and with the poor performance of the largest democracy – India – and many populist regimes that had introduced extensive social policies on the other. Notions of 'democratic developmentalism' (White, 1998) and of 'developmental welfare states' only acquired greater attention late in the last millennium with a steady flow of literature on welfare regimes in developing countries (Yeun-wen, 1997; Kwon, 1999; Aspalter, 2002; Figueira and Figueira, 2002; Huber, 2002; Gough, 2004; Hall and Midgley, 2004; Mkandawire, 2004; Pierson, 2004; Huat, 2005; Haggard and Kaufman, 2008). They also had to contend with the dismal economic performance of many socially progressive regimes in developing countries.

Finally, theories of development that dominated the 1970s, especially the Dependency School, with its revolutionary voluntarism and pessimism about the effectiveness of local politics, were generally dismissive of any ameliorative measures by 'dependent states', considering them to be 'bourgeois reformism', 'redistributive populism' or 'petty bourgeois socialism'. As such, it was argued, they did not deserve analytical attention, let alone support (Staniland, 1985). Interestingly, the new neoliberal theories of the 1990s and early 2000s, which focus on the internal causes of economic performance, have also tended to dismiss social policy measures as evidence of 'policy capture' or clientelism and neopatrimonialism (Gibson and Hoffman, 2002).

7.3.3 The linear view of history

Another factor underlying mutual neglect between the literature on welfare regimes in developed countries and the literature on social policy in developing countries was a linear view of development, in which the developed countries and the welfare states, especially the Scandinavian ones, were presented as being in a 'state of culmination' (Therborn, 1987), whose key ingredients could not be part of the process itself. Social policy was treated as something to be engaged in only after reaching a certain development threshold. In the extreme, the normative bases of the means of development would be different from those of the ends of development, as countries would have to traverse the 'vale of tears' of inequality and social exclusion, and possibly also of authoritarian rule, before putting into practice the broad political and social agenda.

Two arguments have been advanced for this linear view. The first stressed the functional relationship between the expansion of the welfare state and economic growth (Wilensky, 1975). In this view, the state grows to meet the needs of the growing economy. The 'logic of industrialism' suggested that all countries were bound to move in the same direction because, as industrialisation proceeded, it inevitably led to demographic shifts, dislocation and all that constituted the 'social question'. This view was often supported by empirical evidence, drawn from cross-sectional studies, which showed a positive relationship between social expenditure, the degree of social security coverage and the level of per capita income. The linear view appears today in the analysis that suggests that East Asian countries are now 'growing out of the development state' and entering the 'welfare state' stages (Peng and Wong, 2004). The second argument, closely related to the functionalist argument, was the *affordability* argument, which stated that welfare measures were a luxury poor countries simply could not afford. A recent example is the World Bank arguing against pension schemes on the grounds that they are unaffordable in Africa (Holzmann et al., 2005).

The linear view can be challenged along the same lines as those used by Gerschenkron (1962) arguing against Rostovian 'stages of growth' theories (Rostow, 1960). Gerschenkron claimed that one of the advantages of 'late industrialisation' is that access to experiences and knowledge accumulated by the forerunners makes development a purposeful process of 'catching up'. 'Latecomers' can telescope development, leapfrogging some stages and adopting certain measures at much earlier stages of their development than the pioneers. In the sphere of social policy, 'late industrialisers' have tended to adopt certain welfare measures at much earlier phases than the 'pioneers', and with more comprehensive levels of coverage (Pierson, 2004; Vartiainen, 2004). Experiences with social policies in advanced welfare countries have provided important lessons for today's latecomers in terms of their effects, both intended and unintended. Obviously, neither the rationale for adopting these policies nor the actual practice will be exact replicas of those of the pioneers at some earlier stage. For one thing, many instrumental benefits of social policies may have emerged only *ex post* for the pioneer countries, while for late industrialisers they are acquired *ex ante*, which makes it possible deliberately to exploit the lessons at much earlier stages of development than a linear view would suggest.

Finally, politics matters in determining patterns and sizes of welfare expenditures and the timing of their introduction. This has been used to explain the simultaneous existence of different welfare regimes in developed countries, as identified by Titmuss and later theorised by Esping-Andersen (Esping-Andersen, 1990). Even among poor countries there are sharp differences in welfare efforts within the same income group. Similarly, the *affordability* argument can be addressed by bearing in mind that social security was introduced earlier and at much lower levels of development in the latecomers than among the pioneers of industrialisation. Many welfare policies in the welfare states of Europe were introduced at levels of per capita income that are comparable to per capita incomes of Latin American developing countries. Indeed today's developing countries spend more on social transfers, including pensions, than the advanced OECD countries spent historically at a similar age structure and at similar income levels (Lindert, 2004).

7.3.4 A static comparative approach

A further factor that has made the literature on welfare states unattractive to LDCs has been its static comparative approach and its preoccupation with issues of distribution and protection, while it was taking high levels of development as a given. Such an approach takes as given precisely those issues that are the central preoccupations of developing countries – economic growth and structural change. This approach has led to the view that the welfare state is in some sense non-productive and not concerned with issues of dynamic efficiency. Some of this effect can be blamed on the 'Nordic bias' of the literature, which has tended to privilege the redistributive and protective aspects of social policy (Room, 2002; Hudson and Kuhner, 2009). It should, however, be borne in mind that attribution of the neglect of production to a 'Nordic bias' does not do justice to the practices of actually existing 'welfare regimes'. The academic literature has misrepresented these regimes by privileging protection. It has missed out something that has been crucial in the sustainability of their welfare efforts – the augmentation of their productive capacity. The consequence is that 'the relationship between the welfare state and efficiency is under-theorised and under-studied, both theoretically and empirically' (Palme, 2007: p. 4).

For social democracies in which full employment was a major premise of the welfare regime, production was always a central concern (Goodin, 2001; Kuhnle and Hort, 2004; Kangas and Palme, 2005). After all, the expression 'productive welfare state' dates from the 1930s and came from Sweden. Not surprisingly, it was Gunnar Myrdal more than anyone else who insisted on the productive role of 'social investment'. Jenny Andersson argues emphatically that 'a core notion in the ideology of Swedish social democracy was the articulation of "growth" and "security" as coherent and mutually supportive ideological objectives' (Andersson, 2006: p. 118).[7] In any case, this 'Nordic bias' has now been addressed through the notion of 'production regimes', which highlights the 'elective affinities' and synergies among policies in production and welfare systems (Hall and Soskice, 2001; Huber and Stephens, 2001; Manow, 2001; Iversen, 2005).

Both the linear and the comparative static view of welfare regimes have led to a blindness in actual social policy practices and thinking among 'late industrialisers'. Thus the focus on social security aspects of the Bismarckian welfare state, with its corporatist features for securing industrial peace, obscures its 'welfare developmentalist' features, which included the mobilisation of savings and the training regimes associated with it, which are its main attraction to other late industrialisers (Rimlinger, 1971). In many ways, the Bismarckian state belongs to the 'developmentalist' tradition and its weaknesses and strengths can be traced to this aspect of its policies. Among nineteenth-century practitioners and proponents of industrialisation there was always the view that social policy was part of the story of 'catching up'. Thus, as Levi-Faur notes, 'List was able to offer an analysis that connected government education policies and the notion of human capital with the desired outcome of economic development' (cited in Selwyn, 2009).

Versions of the Bismarckian welfare state were adopted by many late industrialisers in Europe, Latin America, Asia and Africa. Japanese planners, inspired by the German Historical School, concluded that, 'without a social policy to protect and train the labour force, capital would not be able to sustain the cycle of reproduction' (Gao, 1997: p. 58). In the East Asian case, social policy was embedded in the development policy of states whose fear of massive unemployment led to a focus on generating full employment and improving the skill base, which resulted in a prioritisation of education and, to some extent, of healthcare, rather than to income maintenance schemes (Deyo, 1992).

The *CEPALISTA* (a name derived from the acronomy of the United Nations Commision for Latin America and the Caribbean) developmentalism in Latin America, which formalised import substitution strategies, was associated with social policies based on universalist principles (Molyneux, 2006). While there was recognition that, in the initial phases, the model would be based on a highly segmented welfare state, the expectation within this model was that, with economic growth and structural change (or development), this segmentation, together with economic dualism, would end. Leading champions of import substitution often brought in the distributive role of social policy to argue that this would increase effective demand and allow for the deepening of the import substitution process (Riesco, 2007). Such demand would favour more labour-intensive techniques, which would generate more employment. In the event the logic of the model, combined with the constellation of political interests and the alignment of social forces, produced highly segmented welfare regimes that remained durable.

In Africa, the 'nationalist–developmentalist' ideologies informing new states also tended to introduce extensive social policies, partly to correct colonial injustice (land reform, affirmative action, and extension of hitherto racially exclusive social rights to indigenous people) and partly for 'nation-building' purposes (free education, rural health services, regional policies etc.; Adesina, 2007). As a mark of their belonging to the comity of nations, they also adopted a number of international conventions that had a significant impact on social policy practices. Others, guided by variants of 'socialisms' that flourished in Africa, went further and sought to introduce highly redistributive and socially inclusive policies (Young, 1982).

In policy circles these ideas were later to feature in the 'basic needs strategies' that would simultaneously and purposefully address issues of growth and equity. The World Bank also produced its own variant of 'redistribution with growth' strategies (Chenery et al., 1974).

7.3.5 Wage labour bias and segmentation

One criticism raised against the welfare regime literature is that it deals with economies which are too different to produce models that can be relevant to developing countries. For some the central preoccupations of developing countries are so different that a livelihoods framework is deemed more appropriate than a language of social policy which privileges state provision (Devereux and Cook, 2000). Perhaps the single most important distinction is the prevalence of formal wage labour in the developed countries in contrast with the developing countries, where economic dualism is such that large sections of the population fall outside the formal wage labour economy (Kabeer, 2004). On the basis of this observation it is argued that the introduction of labour market-based welfare policies in developing countries is inappropriate (a) because it only benefits those in the formal wage labour market and (b) because it is administratively impossible to extend at all widely in the absence of formal employment (Rudra, 2002). This argument has become part of 'neoliberal populism' (Weyland, 1999) and has been appropriated by international institutions to justify the dismantling of incipient welfare regimes and to pursue targeted social policy putatively in favour of the 'deserving poor' and of insistence on 'flexible labour markets' shifting the burden of social protection from capitalists to the state.

Historically, the foundation of many of today's most successful universalistic welfare states was 'stratified universalism', or exclusive voluntary provision of social services to members of certain groups. In their Bismarckian origins, entitlements to social protection were associated with the employment situation, market performance and skills. Many late industrialisers have tended to accept similar links between social policy and wage labour. Thus, in Germany and Japan, universal social rights to a minimum level of subsistence were not initially extended to all members of the community. These states came into existence by granting privileges to groups whose cooperation in economic modernisation and nation-building was deemed indispensable by political and economic elites (Manow, 2001). These initially exclusive rights were to form the basis of the universalistic welfare state that eventually emerged in Germany. Similarly, in East Asia the welfare state, in the initial phase, was composed predominantly of insurance systems for industrial workers. In Japan, early health insurance targeted the 'elite labour force ... which were crucial for the country's industrial–military complex and economic development' (Peng, 2005: p. 75). The Japanese welfare state became more universal later on. The real issue is not whether welfare states are segmented in their initial phases or at any points in their long history, but what the pace of the extension of the welfare benefits is. The failure to take a dynamic view of segmentation has often led to the erosion of incipient welfare states in developing countries and to a reversal in historical terms, as systems of 'selective inclusion' such as those associated with import substitution industrialisation are replaced by a system of 'generalised exclusion' in the context of an outward-oriented model of development (Bayón et al., 2000: p. 103).

7.4 The economic and social policy disconnection

One feature of the literature on the welfare state in OECD countries was that it was predicated, on the one hand, on a close association with Keynesian macroeconomic thinking about demand management and economic policy as the distinctive mode of economic intervention, and, on the other hand, on the social policy regimes of the time. It is this association that justified the soubriquet 'social Keynesianism' or 'Keynesian welfare state' to denote the elective affinity between economic and social policies of the time (Weir and Skocpol, 1983). For developing countries, theorising of social policy has largely failed to connect to dominant development strategies or to be fully thought through in the light of such strategies. In the case of import substitution strategies there was a rejection of the relevance of Keynesian economics to the supply-side concerns of developing countries on the one hand, with – especially in Latin America – acceptance of versions of Keynesian underconsumption theses on the demand side on the other. One consequence of this situation was that often only the 'welfarist' elements of the 'Keynesian welfare state' were adopted, which led to a failure to connect social policy to the production side. This failure showed up in the low levels of investment in human capital and redistribution in Latin American economies, at least when these were compared to East Asian economies. Even in East Asian economies, many social policies and their relation to growth remained only implicit (Deyo, 1992), the idea of 'developmental welfare states' being a more recent codification of the relationship.

Matters were not made better by the reticence of many economists on matters of social policy, although, even when some economists made quite explicit overtures to social policy, the response from social policy analysts tended to be muted or dismissive. One such overture came from economic historians, who made the point that, in the process of 'catch-up', a country must have what Abramovitz and others (Abramovitz 1986, 1995) refer to as 'social capability'. This includes a number of things upon which social policy has an important bearing – human capital, social institutions, social cohesion and social adaptability and flexibility. Significant progress has also been made with the wide acceptance, by economists, of human development indicators as indicators of social wellbeing. This in itself should facilitate dialogue. Furthermore, there is now considerable recognition of the bi-directional causality between economic growth and many indicators of social well-being. Thus Ranis and colleagues (2000) refer to the 'HD [human development] improvement function', which is a kind of production function that relates welfare efforts to outcomes and vice versa. This 'production function' has close a affinity to the notions of a welfare regime that is not only measured by efforts such as levels of spending, but includes norms that attach weight to these efforts and the complementary institutions, which translate welfare efforts into welfare outcomes. Finally, there are the endogenous growth theories, which recognise that 'human capital' (proxied by levels of secondary school education or infant mortality), social inclusion (proxied by income distribution and the like) and political stability are important determinants of economic growth. Endogenous growth theorists usually confine themselves to an assertion of the importance of these social conditions for development. Rarely do they pursue the further question: what did, or what should, public policy do to produce the favourable 'initial conditions' or 'exogenous factors' to enhance human capital? However, endogenous growth theories open up channels of communication and can serve as a basis for developing an analytical framework that captures the multifunctional roles of social policy and defines their interconnections as welfare regimes in the process of development.

7.5 The crisis of the welfare state and structural adjustment

With the ascendancy of neoliberalism, there was an assault on the social policies that constituted the welfare state and on the Keynesian economic policies that came with them. Neoliberals claimed that the overexpansion of the government had led to economic sclerosis, as the welfare state 'resulted in institutions and structures that today constitute an obstacle to economic efficiency and economic growth because of their lack of flexibility and their one-sided concerns for income safety and distribution, with limited concern for economic incentives' (Lindbeck et al., 1993: p. 17). Following the crisis of the 1990s, Freeman and colleagues (1997) characterised the Swedish welfare state in apocalyptic terms, as 'nearly impossible for the country to afford' (p. 11), 'unsustainable' (p. 25) and 'dysfunctional' (p. 27). If all this was happening in the culturally homogenous, administratively more sophisticated and politically more representative countries, only worse could be expected of the developing countries.[8] The apparent demise of the welfare state seemed to render of dubious value whatever lessons it might have had for developing countries. The argument now is that, whatever merit the welfare state may have had in stimulating economic growth and in combating poverty, its time has passed – a point further reinforced by the collapse of socialism and of the ideologies of solidarity and equality that drove it. The slew of literature raising questions not only about the 'exportability' of the welfare state to developing countries but also about its 'sustainability' in the developed countries themselves reinforced this point.

As we noted above, for a brief while the basic needs and redistribution with growth strategies opened up prospects for a broader view of social policy than had hitherto been associated with development theories and practices. However, the turn to economic stabilisation and the crisis of the 1980s put paid to notions of welfare states in developing countries, as both the theories' own incipient welfare regimes and the full-blown welfare states in the advanced countries faced crises. The focus on GDP and stabilisation led to the detachment of much economics from social objectives, which made macroeconomics socially blind and inclined it to treat social policy in residual terms, a point forcefully made by Stewart and her colleagues in *Adjustment with a Human Face* (Cornia et al., 1987). The normative premises of orthodox economics, which privilege market exchange relations over other forms and rationales for social exchange, and the justification of social policies on grounds of 'market failure' paradigms based on methodological individualism and on the assumptions about markets that go along with them, were often at odds with those that had historically underpinned social policies – solidarity, nation-building and so on. In capitalist economies there are 'failures' other than those included in the 'market failure' paradigm. As Therborn (1987) suggests, in political terms the market needs the state, which operates on the basis of a logic that differs from that of the market and may pursue political objectives other than those of Adam Smith's night watchman – objectives that are not reducible to individual preferences. Furthermore, there are class conflicts which inhere in the production unit – the firm – within which processes of production and returns allocation take place in the capitalist system. These can generate their own 'failures', which have implications for social policy that go beyond the exigencies of correcting 'market failure'.

The self-imposed ideological identity around issues of protection obscured the instrumental use of social policy in developed countries. One positive aspect of the recent crisis has been that it highlighted the productive role of the welfare state. The crisis has prompted advocates of the welfare state not only to insist on its resilience, but to point out the growth aspects of the welfare regime and to assert that the much maligned service sector has actually contributed to industrial productivity (Atkinson, 1995; Goodin, 1999, Korpi, 2005). The crisis has also highlighted some commonalities that have hitherto been obscured, suggesting a new convergence between welfare regimes in developing countries and the debates on reforming welfare regimes in developed countries. A number of problems that seemed exclusive to developing countries were now seen to impinge on the developed countries as well. Thus globalisation and the quest for competitiveness have highlighted the 'imperative of developmental welfare' in developed countries (Hemerijck, 2008). There are now calls for 'social investment welfare states' (Giddens, 2000), for 'competition states' (Cerny and Evans, 1999), for movement from 'Keynesian welfare to the Schumpeterian post-national welfare' (Jessop, 1994), from welfare state to 'enabling state' (Gilbert and Gilbert, 1989), from welfare to 'workfare' (Torfing, 1999; Vis, 2007). This increased attention to production, albeit for different reasons, is reminiscent of 'developmental welfare states' in terms of production of human capital (Jessop, 1993). In addition, new indices of welfare regimes include a 'human investment index' which proxies the productivist efforts of the welfare states (Room, 2002).

In conclusion, there is an increasing recognition that 'a deep understanding of the welfare state now requires an analysis of both the traditionally protective functions of social policy and the productive functions concerned with investment in human capital' (Hudson and Kuhner, 2009: p. 35). In developing countries there is growing interest in developmental welfare states. Moreover, hitherto authoritarian developmental states have had to rethink their welfare regimes in the light of democratisation processes that are tending to push these states towards the 'European' model. These shifts on both sides of the bridge should facilitate dialogue between those preoccupied with development, with its productivist bias, and those concerned with social welfare in general.

7.6   Conclusion

In this chapter we have argued that both the new understanding of poverty and development and the concerns about welfare regimes imply a much closer normative affinity between social policies in developing and developed countries than there was in the past. This in turn demands greater recognition of the literatures dealing with economic development and welfare regimes. We have discussed some of the barriers to bridging the gap between the two literatures. The first set of barriers discussed are those associated with what we have called OECD and developing country biases. Another cause of the gap has been a linear reading of the development of the welfare state. If we understand that the institutionalisation of the welfare state was a long-term historical process in which 'learning by doing' and trial and error played a significant role, we are likely to accept that some of the experiences of welfare regimes in the more advanced countries are relevant to developing countries. Focusing attention on historical development can also serve as an important reminder of what has always been an important component of social policy in developing countries – its efficiency-enhancing side. Likewise, wage labour bias and segmentation may not be such a problem if seen from a historical point of view.

The disconnection between economic and social policy has been a feature of the literature focusing on developing countries. The literatures on human development and on endogenous growth may provide a basis for remedying this. More recently, the crisis of the welfare state has brought out some of the commonalities between the issues in developed and developing countries, and this may be helpful too.

Finally, the growing attention paid to human and social rights and the democratisation of some of the 'developmental states' has put social policy squarely on the political agenda in many countries. Moreover, many of the new democracies that may have started off on an orthodox path have gradually introduced some innovative social policy initiatives. There is a growing literature on social policies and welfare regimes in the developing countries. In addition, there is a greater awareness of the productivist aspect of welfare regimes in the advanced capitalist countries, which facilitates the conversation. Both the political conjucture and the intellectual shifts suggest new directions in research which can facilitate dialogue among researchers on social policy both in developed and in developing countries.

Notes

1. A good example is the privatisation of pensions in Chile, which Jose Pinera, the architect of the reform, saw as the beginning of a 'world pension revolution' (cited in Brooks, 2009: p. 3).
2. One should recall that the origins of welfare states were not always as morally impeccable as subsequent 'retrofitting' would suggest. In the US the origins of social security were pension schemes for ex-combatants after the American Civil War (Skocpol and Amenta, 1986). In countries such as Great Britain, the genealogy of the welfare state includes the 'warfare state', both its own and

that of adversaries (Finer, 1999). The welfare state was after all identified with 'the war aims of a nation fighting for its life' (Marshall, 1965).
3. Some writers attribute this invisibility to ethnocentricism (Walker and Wong, 2004).
4. In theory this scheme guarantees 100 days of work paid at the minimum wage to all poor rural households. It has the potential to cover around 300 million people.
5. Indeed for some, only policies on the demand side were concerned with things of intrinsic value while policies on the supply side were considered instrumentalist.
6. Such a view featured prominently in the debates on choice of techniques, in which the case for capital-intensive techniques was made on the grounds that they maximised economic surplus while keeping employment and consumption low (Galenson and Leibenstein, 1955).
7. Esping-Andersen (1997) suggested that Japan's welfare regimes may be less productivist than those of some of the Scandinavian nations.
8. There was of course literature which challenged this dark vision of the welfare state (Pierson, 2001).

References

Abramovitz, M. (1986) 'Catching Up, Forging Ahead, and Falling Behind'. *Journal of Economic History* 46 (2): 385–406.
Abramovitz, M. (1995) 'Elements of Social Capability'. In B.H. Koo and D.H. Perkins (eds) *Social Capability and Long-Term Economic Growth* (London: Macmillan).
Adesina, J.O. (2007) 'In Search of Inclusive Development: Introduction'. In J.O. Adesina (ed.) *Social Policy in Sub-Saharan African Context: In Search of Inclusive Development* (Basingstoke: Palgrave Macmillan).
Amsden, A.H. (1985) 'The State and Taiwan's Economic Development'. In P.B. Evans, T. Skocpol and D. Rueschemeyer (eds) *Bringing the State Back In* (Cambridge: Cambridge University Press).
Andersson, J. (2006) 'Growth and Security: Swedish Reformism in the Post-war Period'. In J. Callaghan and I. Favretto (eds) *Transitions in Social Democracy: Cultural and Ideological Problems of the Golden Age* (Manchester; New York: Manchester University Press; Palgrave).
Aspalter, C. (2002) *Discovering the Welfare State in East Asia* (Westport, CT: Praeger).
Atkinson, A.B. (1995) 'Is the Welfare State Necessarily an Obstacle to Economic Growth?' *European Economic Review* 39: 723–30.
Baran, P. (1957) *The Political Economy of Growth* (New York: Monthly Review Press).
Bayón, M.C., B. Roberts and G. Rojas (2000) 'New Labour Market Challenges to Social Policies in México'. In L. Haagh and C.T. Helgø (eds) *Social Policy Reform and Market Governance in Latin America* (New York: Palgrave Macmillan).
Bhagwati, J. (1966) *The Economics of Underdeveloped Countries* (London: Weidenfield and Nicolson).
Brooks, S.M. (2009) *Social Protection and the Market in Latin America: The Transformation of Social Security Institutions* (Cambridge; New York: Cambridge University Press).

Cerny, P., and M. Evans (1999) 'New Labour, Globalization, and the Competition State'. *Center for European Studies Working Paper* No. 70 (Cambridge, MA: Center for European Studies, Harvard University).

Chang, H.J. (2004) 'The Role of Social Policy in Economic Development: Some Theoretical Reflections and Lessons from Asia'. In T. Mkandawire (ed.) *Social Policy in a Development Context* (Basingstoke; New York: Palgrave Macmillan).

Chenery, H.B., C. Ahluwalia, J. Bell, J. Foluy, and R. Jolly (1974) *Redistribution with Growth* (London: Oxford University Press).

Cornia, G.A., R. Jolly and F. Stewart (1987) *Adjustment with a Human Face* (Oxford: Clarendon Press).

Devereux, S., and S. Cook (2000) 'Does Social Policy Meet Social Needs?' *IDS Bulletin* 31 (4): 63–73.

Deyo, F.C. (1992) 'The Political Economy of Social Policy Formation: East Asia's Newly Industrialized Countries'. In R. Henderson and J. Applebaum (eds) *State and Development in the Asian Pacific Rim* (Newbury Park: Sage Publications).

Dobb, M. (1969) *An Essay on Economic Growth and Planning* (New York: Monthly Review Press).

Esping-Andersen, G. (1997) 'Hybrid or Unique? The Japanese Welfare State between Europe and America'. *Journal of European Social Policy* 7 (3): 179–89.

Esping-Andersen, G. (1990) *The Three Worlds of Welfare Capitalism* (Princeton, NJ: Princeton University Press).

Evans, P. (1992) 'The State as Problem and Solution: Embedded Autonomy and Structural Change'. In S. Haggard and R. Kaufman (eds) *The Politics of Structural Adjustment: International Constraints, Distributive Conflicts and the State* (Princeton, NJ: Princeton University Press).

Figueira, C., and F. Figueira (2002) 'Models of Welfare and Models of Capitalism: The Limits of Transferability'. In E. Huber (ed.) *Models of Capitalism: Lessons for Latin America* (University Park, PA: Pennsylvania State University Press).

Finer, C.J. (1999) 'Trends in Welfare States'. In J. Clasen (ed.) *Comparative Social Policy: Concepts, Theories and Methods* (Oxford: Basil Blackwell).

Freeman, R.B., R.H. Topel, and B. Swedenborg (1997) *The Welfare State in Transition: Reforming the Swedish Model* (Chicago, IL: University of Chicago Press).

Galenson, W., and H. Leibenstein (1955) 'Investment Criteria, Productivity and Economic Development'. *Quarterly Journal of Economics* (August) LXIX: 343–70.

Gao, B. (1997) *Economic Ideology and Japanese Industrial Policy: Developmentalism from 1931 to 1965* (Cambridge: Cambridge University Press).

Gerschenkron, A. (1962) *Economic Backwardness in Historical Perspective* (Cambridge, MA: Harvard University Press).

Gibson, C., and B. Hoffman (2002) 'Dictators with Empty Pockets: A Political Concessions Model of Africa's Democratization'. Paper prepared for the *2002 Annual Meetings of the American Political Science Association,* Boston, MA, 29 August–1 September.

Giddens, A. (2000) *The Third Way and its Critics* (Cambridge: Polity Press).

Gilbert, N., and B. Gilbert (1989) *The Enabling State: Modern Welfare Capitalism in America* (New York: Oxford University Press).

Goodin, R.E. (2001) 'Work and Welfare: Towards a Post-Productivist Welfare Regime'. *British Journal of Political Science* 31 (1): 13–39.

Goodin, R.E. (1999) *The Real Worlds of Welfare Capitalism* (Cambridge; New York: Cambridge University Press).

Goodman, R., G. White and H. Kwon (eds) (1998) *The East Asian Welfare Model: Welfare Orientalism and the State* (London: Routledge).

Gough, I., G.D. Wood and A. Barrientos (2004) *Insecurity and Welfare Regimes in Asia, Africa and Latin America: Social Policy in Development Contexts* (Cambridge: Cambridge University Press).

Gough, I. (2004) 'East Asia: The Limits of Productivist Regimes'. In I. Gough and G. Wood (eds) *Insecurity and Welfare Regimes in Asia, Africa, and Latin America: Social Policy in Development Contexts* (Cambridge: Cambridge University Press).

Gregor, A.J. (1979) *Italian Fascism and Development Dictatorship* (Princeton, NJ: Princeton University Press).

Haggard, S., and R. Kaufman (2008) *Democracy, Development and Welfare States: Latin America, East Asia, and Eastern Europe* (Princeton, NJ: Princeton University Press).

Hall, A.L., and J. Midgley (2004) *Social Policy for Development* (London; Thousand Oaks, CA: Sage Publications).

Hall, P.A., and D. Soskice (eds) (2001) *Varieties of Capitalism: The Institutional Foundations of Comparative Advantage* (Oxford: Oxford University Press).

Hemerijck, A. (2008) 'The Imperative of Developmental Welfare for Europe'. *Rivista delle Poliche Sociali* 1: 57–91.

Holliday, I. (2000) 'Productivist Welfare Capitalism: Social Policy in East Asia'. *Political Studies* 48 (4): 706–23.

Holzmann, R., R.P. Hinz and H. Von Gersdorff (2005) *Old-age Income Support in the 21st Century* (Washington, DC: World Bank).

Huat, C.B. (2005) 'Welfare Developmentalism in Singapore and Malaysia'. In H. Kwon (ed.) *Transforming the Developmental Welfare State in East Asia* (Basingstoke: Palgrave Macmillan).

Huber, E. (2002) *Models of Capitalism: Lessons for Latin America* (University Park, PA: Pennsylvania State University Press).

Huber, E., and J. Stephens (2001) 'Welfare State and Production Regimes in the Era of Retrenchment'. In P. Pierson (ed.) *The New Politics of the Welfare State* (Oxford: Oxford University Press).

Hudson, J., and S. Kuhner (2009) 'Towards Productive Welfare? A Comparative Analysis of 23 OECD Countries'. *Journal of European Social Policy* 19 (1): 34–46.

Huntington, S. (1968) *Political Order in Changing Societies* (New Haven, CT: Yale University Press).

Iversen, T. (2005) *Capitalism, Democracy, and Welfare* (New York: Cambridge University Press).

Jessop, B. (1994) 'The Transition to Post-Fordism and the Schumpeterian Workfare State'. In R. Burrows and B. Loader (eds) *Towards a Post-Fordist Welfare State* (London: Routledge).

Jessop, B. (1993) 'Towards a Schumpeterian Workfare State? Preliminary Remarks on Post-Fordist Political Economy'. *Studies in Political Economy* 40: 7–40.

Kabeer, N. (2004) 'Re-visioning "the Social": Towards a Citizen-centred Social Policy for the Poor in Poor Countries'. (Brighton: Institute of Development Studies).

Kangas, O., and J. Palme (eds) (2005) *Social Policy and Economic Development in the Nordic Countries* (Basingstoke: Palgrave Macmillan).

Karshenas, M., and V.M. Moghadam (eds) (2007) *Social Policy in the Middle East* (Basingstoke: Palgrave Macmillan).

Korpi, W. (2005) 'Does the Welfare State Harm Economic Growth? Sweden as a Strategic Case'. In O. Kangas and J. Palme (eds) *Social Policy and Economic Development in the Nordic Countries* (Basingstoke: Palgrave Macmillan).

Kuhnle, S., and S.E.O. Hort (2004) 'The Developmental Welfare State in Scandinavia: Lessons to the Developing World'. *UNRISD Social Policy and Development Programme Paper* No. 17 (Geneva: United Nations Research Institute for Social Development).

Kwon, H. (ed.) (2005) *Transforming the Developmental Welfare State in East Asia* (Basingstoke: Palgrave Macmillan).

Kwon, H. (1999) *The Welfare State in Korea: The Politics of Legitimation* (New York: St. Martin's Press, in association with St. Antony's College Oxford).

Lewis, A. (1955) *The Theory of Economic Growth* (London: Allen and Unwin).

Lindbeck, A., P. Molander, T. Persson, O. Peterson, A. Sandmo, B. Swedenborg, N. Thygesen, G. Laroque and J. von Hagen (1993) 'Options for Economic and Political Reform in Sweden'. *Economic Policy* 8 (17): 220–63.

Lindert, P.H. (2004) *Growing Public: Social Spending and Economic Growth since the Eighteenth Century* (Cambridge; New York: Cambridge University Press).

Mackintosh, M., and P. Tibandebage (2004) 'Inequality and Redistribution in Health Care: Analytical Bases for Developmental Social Policy'. In T. Mkandawire (ed.) *Social Policy in a Development Context* (Basingstoke; New York: Palgrave Macmillan).

Mahalanobis, P.C. (1953) 'Some Observations on the Process of Growth of National Income'. *Sankhya: The Indian Journal of Statistics (1933–1960)* 12 (4): 307–12.

Manow, P. (2001) 'Welfare State Building and Coordinated Capitalism in Japan and Germany'. In W. Streeck and K. Yamamura (ed.) *The Origins of Nonliberal Capitalism: Germany and Japan in Comparison* (New York: Cornell University Press).

Mares, I., and M.E. Carnes (2009) 'Social Policy in Developing Countries'. *Annual Review of Political Science* 12 (1): 93–113.

Marshall, T.H. (1965) *Social Policy* (London: Hutchinson).

Martinussen, J. (1997) *State, Society and Market: A Guide to Competing Theories of Development* (London: Zed Press).

Midgley, J. (1995) *Social Development* (London: Sage Publications).

Midgley, J., and K.L. Tang (2001) 'Introduction: Social Policy, Economic Growth and Developmental Welfare'. *International Journal of Social Welfare* 10 (4): 244–52.

Mishra, R. (2004) 'Social Protection by Other Means: Can it Survive Globalisation?' In P. Kennett (ed.) *A Handbook of Comparative Social Policy* (Cheltenham; Northampton, MA: Edward Elgar).

Mkandawire, T. (ed.) (2004) *Social Policy in a Development Context* (Basingstoke; New York: Palgrave Macmillan).

Mkandawire, T. (2001) 'Social Policy in a Development Context'. UNRISD *Social Policy and Development Paper* No. 7 (Geneva: United Nations Research Institute for Social Development).

Molyneux, M. (2006) 'Mothers at the Service of the New Poverty Agenda: The PROGRESA/Oportunidades Programme in Mexico'. In S. Razavi and S. Hassim (eds) *Gender and Social Policy in a Global Context: Uncovering the Gendered Structure of 'the Social'* (Basingstoke: Palgrave Macmillan).

Morton, R. (1990) 'The State and the Effective Control of Foreign Capital: The Case of South Korea'. *World Politics* 43 (1): 111–38.

Myrdal, G. (1984) 'International Inequality and Foreign Aid in Retrospect'. In Gerald Meier and Dudley Seers (eds) *Pioneers in Development* (Washington, DC: Oxford University Press).

Palme, J. (2007) 'Sustainable Social Policies in an Era of Globalisation: Lessons from the Swedish Case'. *Social Policy Journal of New Zealand* 32: 1–16.

Peng, I. (2005) 'The New Politics of the Welfare State in a Developmental Context: Explaining the 1990s Social Care Expansion in Japan'. In H. Kwon (ed.) *Transforming the Developmental Welfare State in East Asia* (Basingstoke: Palgrave Macmillan).

Peng, I., and J. Wong (2004) 'Growing Out of the Developmental State: East Asian Welfare Reform in the 1990s'. Paper presented at the RC19 Annual Conference *Welfare State Restructuring: Processes and Social Outcomes,* Paris, 2–4 September.

Pierson, C. (2004) ' "Late Industrialisers" and the Development of the Welfare State'. In T. Mkandawire (ed.) *Social Policy in a Development Context* (Basingstoke; New York: Palgrave Macmillan).

Pierson, P. (2001) *The New Politics of the Welfare State* (Oxford; New York: Oxford University Press).

Ranis, G., F. Stewart and A. Ramirez (2000) 'Economic Growth and Human Development'. *World Development* 28 (2): 197–219.

Riesco, M. (ed.) (2007) *Latin America: A New Developmental Welfare State Model in the Making?* (Basingstoke: Palgrave Macmillan).

Rimlinger, G.V. (1971) *Welfare Policy and Industrialization in Europe, America, and Russia* (New York: Wiley).

Room, G. (2002) 'Education and Welfare: Recalibrating the European Debate'. *Policy Studies* 23 (1): 37–50.

Rostow, W.W. (1960) *The Stages of Economic Growth: A Non-Communist Manifesto* (Cambridge, MA: Harvard University Press).

Rudra, N. (2002) 'Globalisation and the Decline of the Welfare State in Less-Developed Countries'. *International Organisation* 96: 411–45.

Selwyn, B.E.N. (2009) 'An Historical Materialist Appraisal of Friedrich List and his Modern-Day Followers'. *New Political Economy* 14 (2): 157–80.

Sen, A. (1997) 'Development and Thinking at the Beginning of the 21st Century'. *STICERD Discussion Paper* No. DEDPS/2 (London: LSE).

Skocpol, T., and E. Amenta (1986) 'States and Social Policies'. *Annual Reviews in Sociology* 12 (1): 131–57.

Staniland, M. (1985) *What is Political Economy? A Study of Social Theory and Underdevelopment* (New Haven, CT: Yale University Press).

Therborn, G. (1987) 'Welfare States and Capitalist Markets'. *Acta Sociologica* 30 (3/4): 237–54.

Titmuss, R.M., B. Abel-Smith and K. Titmuss (1987) *The Philosophy of Welfare: Selected Writings of Richard M. Titmuss* (London: Allen and Unwin).

Torfing, J. (1999) 'Workfare with Welfare: Recent Reforms of the Danish Welfare State'. *Journal of European Social Policy* 9 (1): 5–28.

Vartiainen, J. (2004) 'European "Late Industrializers": The Finnish Experience'. In T. Mkandawire (ed.) *Social Policy in a Development Context* (Basingstoke; New York: Palgrave Macmillan).

Vis, B. (2007) 'States of Welfare or States of Workfare? Welfare State Restructuring in 16 Capitalist Democracies, 1985–2002'. *Policy and Politics* 35 (1): 105–22.

Wade, R. (1991) *Governing Markets: Economic Theory and the Role of Government in East Asian Industrialisation* (London: Macmillan).

Walker, A., and C. Wong (2004) 'The Ethnocentric Construction of the Welfare State'. In P. Kennett (ed.) *A Handbook of Comparative Social Policy* (Cheltenham; Northampton, MA: Edward Elgar).

Weir, M., and T. Skocpol (1983) 'State Structures and Social Keynesianism: Responses to the Great Depression in Sweden and the United States'. *International Journal of Comparative Sociology* 24 (1–2): 4–29.

Weyland, K. (1999) 'Neoliberal Populism in Latin America and Eastern Europe'. *Comparative Politics* 31 (4): 379–401.

White, G. (1998) 'Constructing a Democratic Developmental State'. In M. Robinson and G. White (eds) *The Democratic Developmental State: Political and Institutional Design* (Oxford: Oxford University Press).

Wilensky, H.L. (1975) *The Welfare State and Equality: Structural and Ideological Roots of Public Expenditures* (Berkeley, CA: University of California Press).

Yeun-wen, K. (1997) *Welfare Capitalism in Taiwan* (New York: St. Martin's Press).

Yeun-wen, K., and C.J. Finer (2007) 'Developments in East Asian Welfare Studies'. *Social Policy and Administration* 41 (2): 115–31.

Young, C. (1982) *Ideology and Development in Africa* (New Haven, CT: Yale University Press).

8
Democracy, the New Left and Income Distribution: Latin America over the Last Decade

*Giovanni Andrea Cornia and Bruno Martorano**

8.1 Introduction

Since the early 2000s, Latin America has witnessed profound economic, political and distributive changes. While the region experienced slow growth during the period 1990–97, followed by a marked crisis during the 'lost half decade' of 1998–2002, between 2003 and 2008 it recorded unprecedented growth in gross domestic product (GDP), of 5.5 per cent a year, the highest since 1967–74 (Ocampo, 2008). Such a steady expansion of output was in part a rebound from the 1998–2002 crisis, but it was supported by a sharp increase in potential output, as investment rates rose by 5 GDP percentage points compared to 2002, reaching 22 per cent of GDP in 2008. From the third quarter of 2008, Latin America was affected by the global financial crisis and particularly by its real effects (a drop in export volumes, terms of trade, remittances, tourist receipts and foreign direct investment, FDI), which reduced GDP by 1.7 per cent in 2009. Yet the region is expected to grow by 4.3 per cent in 2010, faster than any other developing region outside Asia, though still below the average for 2003–08 (CEPAL, 2009b). A second important change recorded during the last decade concerns income distribution. In contrast to the growing polarisation observed during the 1980s and 1990s, between 2003 and 2007 income inequality declined in almost every county of the region. CEPAL data for 2008 indicate that – despite a slowdown in growth – inequality continued to fall in six Latin American countries and stagnated in three. No data are yet available for 2009, though it is likely that inequality rose, despite income support measures introduced to protect the poor. Thirdly, the decline in inequality witnessed over the last decade went hand in hand with an improvement in international economic conditions, a consolidation of democracy, and a steady shift towards the election of Left-of-Centre (LOC) governments (Panizza, 2005a),[1] which – albeit with considerable variation from country to country – have gradually adopted a new policy model, more sensitive to distributive issues.

Are the recent inequality changes explained by favourable shifts in external conditions or by the adoption of new economic and social policies, especially among LOC countries? To what extent are these distributive improvements likely to be sustained in the future? These are the issues explored in the present chapter. Section 8.2 analyses changes in political orientation during what has been termed the 'Left Decade'. Section 8.3 documents the decline in income inequality, while Section 8.4 discusses the causes of this decline. Section 8.5 tests the relative importance of the various causes of this decline in inequality, while Section 8.6 discusses the sustainability of the trend. Section 8.7 draws conclusions.

8.2 Latin America's 'Left Decade'

Latin America has long been a symbol of authoritarian politics, unequal distribution of assets and income and limited redistribution by the state. However, over the last twenty years, the political landscape has gradually changed as a result of a steady drive towards democratisation and the consolidation of democracy and, from the late 1990s, a shift in political orientation towards LOC regimes. As documented by the Latinobarometro,[2] this shift can be explained to a large extent by the increasing frustration with the disappointing results of the Washington Consensus (WC) policies implemented in the 1980s and 1990s. Apart from slow growth and rising income inequality, these policies led to deindustrialisation and a shrinking of the industrial working class, a weakening of the unions, rising unemployment, and a substantial enlargement of the informal sector. The beginning of the leftward political shift can be traced to the election in 1990 of the centrist Patricio Alwyn in Chile. It continued with the election of Chavez in Venezuela in 1998, Lula in Brazil in 2002, Kirchner in Argentina in 2003, Torrijos in Panama in 2004, Tabaré Vazquez in Uruguay in 2005, Morales in Bolivia in 2005, Arias in Costa Rica in 2006, Ortega in Nicaragua and Correa in Ecuador in 2007, and Colom in Guatemala and Lugo in Paraguay in 2008, and it culminated with the election of Funes in El Salvador in March 2009. By mid-2009, of the eighteen Latin American countries analysed in this chapter, only Colombia and Mexico were run

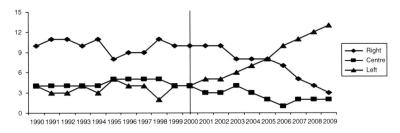

Figure 8.1   Trend in the number of Left, Right and Centre governments in 18 Latin American countries, 1990–2009
Source: Compiled by the authors from Keefer (2007) and data reported by Wikipedia for 2006–09. For more details on the assignment of governments to Left, Right and Centre, see the footnote to Figure 5 in Cornia and Martorano (2009).

by centre–right governments, while three were run by centrist regimes and thirteen by LOC governments (Figure 8.1). Such a shift clearly entailed a 'repoliticisation of inequality' after two decades of WC policies, during which political democracy and strong income polarisation had co-existed uneasily.

As noted by Panizza (2005a, 2005b) and Lustig (2009), there are significant differences between the LOC regimes. Some can be defined as social democratic, as in the case of Chile's Partido Socialista, Uruguay's Frente Amplio and Brazil's Partido dos Trabalhadores. These parties have their roots in working-class organisations, but they have evolved into broad coalitions comprising sectors of business, the middle classes, the urban and rural poor, the unemployed and informal sector workers. They have abandoned any notion of revolutionary upheaval in favour of electoral politics and respect for the institutions of liberal democracy. In contrast, a second group of LOC countries (such as Argentina and Ecuador) have developed Left–nationalist platforms, while Venezuela, Bolivia and Nicaragua have been characterised, since 2007, by a radical–populist approach which also entails a redistribution of assets, both nationally and internationally.[3] Such distinctions are not universally accepted, however (Cameron, 2009), as variations in redistributive policies could be the result of different degrees of polarisation and of the different conditions under which the LOC regimes emerged.

Matters of social justice and economic development are at the core of the new LOC parties' identity. However, in the pursuit of such objectives, these parties (including the populist ones) have avoided the ill-conceived approach to budget deficits and inflation typical of the heterodox experiments of the mid-1980s, as in the case of the Plan

Cruzado, Plan Inti and Plan Austral (Dornbusch and Edwards, 1991). In fact, the LOC economic model incorporates into its paradigm some liberal policies, such as a prudent fiscal policy and low inflation, an awareness of the inefficiencies associated with some forms of state intervention and across-the-board protectionism, the primacy of the market in determining prices, regional trade integration and openness to foreign investment.

Measures to reduce the extreme concentration of wealth which characterises much of Latin America have seldom made their way onto the agenda of LOC governments, with the exception of Bolivia (which nationalised the gas industry and is planning a land reform) and Venezuela (which unilaterally renegotiated oil royalties and nationalised key industries). The governments in these countries inherited some of the most polarised situations in the region, enjoy strong popular support and won a large majority in fair and free elections. However, they have not interpreted their electoral successes in terms of institutionalised pluralism, but rather as a sort of popular sovereignty, which pays little attention to the rights of minorities (Roberts, 2007). In contrast, the moderate stance adopted by most LOC countries is plausibly explained by the fact that – in view of the heterogeneity of several LOC coalitions in less socially polarised countries – radical reforms might have affected the business climate, sparked capital flight and undermined electoral support. As a result, in most cases the LOC model more closely resembles the 'redistribution with growth' approach (Chenery et al., 1974) than the more radical 'redistribution before growth'. In this new approach, a concern for poverty and inequality, a recognition of market failures and the implication of low taxation on the supply of public goods, the increasing importance assigned to strengthening state institutions and an awareness of the dangers of external indebtedness offer a sharp contrast to the neoliberal emphasis on shrinking the state and the self-sustained role of the markets (Panizza, 2005a). During the last decade, some non-LOC governments have also recorded macroeconomic improvements and introduced some redistributive measures. Political theory offers no obvious explanation for this trend, although it is not uncommon in Europe. Perhaps these regimes have also been affected by the new 'Great Transformation' – that is, the shift in policies towards more regulation and social protection following the demise of the Washington Consensus (Stewart, 2009). Or these changes may derive from the strengthening of institutions recorded during the last two decades and the subsequent capacity to finance pro-poor and pro-growth programmes.

8.3   The distribution of income in Latin America in historical perspective

With the exception of Uruguay and Argentina, Gini coefficients in Latin America ranged from 0.45 to 0.60 in the early to mid-1950s, in other words they were among the highest in the world (Altimir, 1996). This acute income polarisation was rooted in a very unequal distribution of land, industrial assets and educational opportunities, which benefited a tiny agrarian, mining and commercial oligarchy. The rapid GDP growth which followed the adoption of an import substitution strategy in the 1950s and 1960s had – on average – a disequalising impact, and by 1980 all medium-to-large countries had a higher income concentration than in the early to mid-1950s (Altimir, 1993).

During the 'lost decade' of the 1980s, inequality in Latin America was affected by the world recession of 1982–84, the debt crisis, a decline in commodity prices and the recessionary adjustment policies introduced to respond to them. Altogether, the 1980s were characterised by regressive outcomes, as inequality fell only in Colombia, Uruguay and Costa Rica out of eleven countries with reliable data (Altimir, 1996). Despite the return to moderate growth and extensive external liberalisation, income polarisation did not decline during the 1990s and in half of cases it worsened further, albeit at a slower pace than in the 1980s (Gasparini et al., 2009). A review of changes in inequality over the 1990s shows that inequality rose in ten countries and stagnated or declined in seven (Székely, 2003). The worsening was particularly acute during the 'lost half decade' of 1998–2002.

One of the key features of these increases in inequality was a policy-driven decline in the labour share and a parallel rise in the capital share. For instance, between 1980 and the late 1980s, the labour share declined by 5–6 percentage points in Argentina, Chile and Venezuela and by 10 points in Mexico, and this trend was not reversed during the mild recovery of 1991–98. In Chile, the fall in the labour share was due to a large extent to the relaxation of norms on workers' dismissals, to a restriction of the power of trade unions, to the suspension of wage indexation and to a reduction in the minimum wage, as well as to a reduction in wealth, capital gains and profit taxes. The fall in the labour share was also due to a slowdown in job creation (Tokman, 1986), to the spread of informal employment, to a faster decline in formal sector wages than GDP per capita, to a fall in the minimum/average wage ratio and to a widening of the skill premium in the aftermath of widespread trade liberalisation (Székely, 2003).

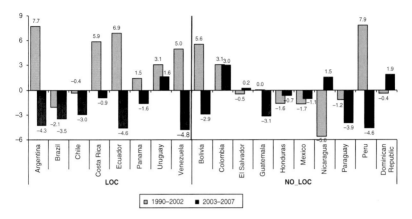

Figure 8.2 Changes in the Gini coefficients of the distribution of household income per capita, between 1990 and 2002 (light bars) and between 2003 and 2007 (dark bars) in LOC and non-LOC countries
Source: Authors' calculations based on SEDLAC data and other data where SEDLAC data were missing.

In contrast to the trends observed in the 1980s and 1990s, during the 2000s income inequality fell in most of the region, particularly after the end of the 2001–02 crisis. Indeed, over 2003–07 inequality declined in seven of the eight LOC countries and in seven of the ten Centre–Right regimes (Figure 8.2). While the average decline in the Gini coefficient was around 3 points, in countries ruled for most of the 2002–07 period by LOC governments the drop was more pronounced. Lustig (2009) arrives at similar conclusions, noting further that the decline in LOC countries was faster than in Centre–Right regimes and that the drop in inequality was more pronounced among the 'populist' than among the 'social–democratic Left' regimes.

8.4   Possible explanations for the recent decline in income inequality

8.4.1   Favourable changes in the international environment

Terms of trade gains. Since the beginning of the new century, the rapid growth of the Asian countries has had a favourable impact on the export and economic performance of Latin America. The region's export/GDP ratio rose from 13 to 24 per cent between the 1990s and 2007 due to significant improvements in both export volumes and prices (CEPAL,

2007b). As a result, in 2007 the regional terms of trade index exceeded its average for the 1990s by 33 per cent, giving rise between 2003 and 2007 to a yearly positive shock of 3.7 per cent of GDP for the region as a whole (Ocampo, 2008) and of 7–15 per cent for Bolivia, Chile, Ecuador, Peru and Venezuela. However, this regional average hides vastly different situations. For instance, between the average for the 1990s and 2007, the terms of trade index rose by 52 per cent for South America as a whole, by 21 per cent for Mexico, and by 13 per cent for Mercosur, but fell by 13 per cent in oil-dependent Central America (CEPAL, 2007b).

What was the impact of these changes on income inequality? A partial equilibrium analysis would suggest that, given the high concentration of ownership of land and mines (where the presence of foreign Trans-National Corporations (TNCs) is very important), the gains in terms of trade generated – *ceteris paribus* – a disequalising effect on the functional and size distribution of income. Indeed, production in these sectors is very land-, resource- and capital-intensive, and their employment-generation capacity is limited. Changes in terms of trade also affect inequality via changes in tax and non-tax revenue. If mining and oil rents accrue to the state (as is now the case in Bolivia), an increase in the world price of exported goods raises non-tax revenue. In addition, with constant tax effort, the rise in commodity prices generates an expansionary effect on income and consumption, which raises tax revenue. Yet the empirical evidence shows that the correlation between terms of trade and the tax/GDP ratio is very small (Figure 8.3). The correlation improves if one considers only the eight main commodity exporters and non-tax revenue (ibid.). Overall, the impact on income inequality (through the distribution of commodity rents via the budget) does not seem sufficiently general or particularly strong.

Migrant remittances. Migrant remittances grew from 1.1 to 2.3 per cent of regional GDP between 1990 and 2007 (CEPAL, 2007b). The increase benefited in particular the Central American and Caribbean countries, Mexico and Ecuador. For these countries, it might be tempting to suggest a causal link between rising remittances and falling inequality. Yet the literature on the inequality impact of remittances suggests that the short- and medium-term effect tends to be disequalising. Indeed, in most developing countries only middle-class people are able to finance the high costs of illegal migration. As a consequence, the remittances will accrue not to the poor, but to middle-income groups, while the

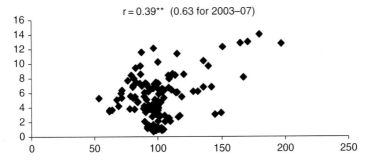

Figure 8.3 Average international terms of trade and tax revenue/GDP ratio, Latin America, 1990–2007

Note: The eight main commodity exporters are: Argentina, Bolivia, Brazil, Chile, Ecuador, Mexico, Peru and Venezuela.

Source: Authors' calculations based on the CEPALSTAT database.

migration of skilled workers tends to raise their wage rate in relation to that of unskilled workers. The final distributive effect depends on how remittance-receiving families share remittances with low-income families, and on the development of migrant networks which reduce migration costs, as in the case of Mexico. The long-term inequality impact of migration depends also on whether it triggers a brain drain, brain gain, or brain waste. Yet the evidence suggests that – as a whole – remittances do not raise the long-term growth rate of GDP (IMF, 2005). In view of all this, we would not expect that migrant remittances played a central role in reducing income inequality, either directly or indirectly.

Availability of external finance. Between 2002 and 2007 capital inflows (mostly portfolio flows to the private sector) amounted to some 2.4 per cent of the region's GDP (Ocampo, 2008). In addition, the country spreads on such funds dropped from 11.5 to 7 per cent between 2004 and 2007. This financial exuberance affected the region in several ways: to start with, the decline in international interest rates exerted a downward pressure on domestic rates; in addition, as the inflows mainly consisted of purchases of shares and securities, there was a boom in regional stock markets, the capitalisation of which quadrupled in value between mid-2004 and the end of 2007 (ibid.). Finally, the inflows facilitated the accumulation of international reserves, which helped to reduce country spreads. In contrast, the FDI stock stagnated at 22 per cent of the region's GDP, after having risen sharply between 1995 and 2002 following the acquisition of privatised assets (UNCTAD, 2008).

Yet this increased availability of finance mainly benefited large, capital- and skill-intensive companies and banks; it did not ease the problems of access to credit for labour-intensive small and medium enterprises, possibly therefore inducing adverse distributional effects. In addition, these capital inflows caused an appreciation in the exchange rate in most countries (Ocampo, 2009), which penalised the labour-intensive traded sector and the distribution of income.

General equilibrium effects of recent improvements in the external environment. In the absence of a Computable General Equilibrium model, the general equilibrium effects of the boom in terms of trade, remittances and capital inflows are difficult to map out. Improvements in the balance of payments do relax the foreign exchange constraint on growth and may stimulate production in labour-intensive industries, with the effect of reducing income inequality. An equalising effect could occur via a reduction in interest rates, which favours firms and households and penalises banks and rentiers. Yet booms in commodity prices, remittances and capital inflows also produce 'Dutch disease' effects, which slow growth in the non-commodity traded sector, with the possible effect of increasing inequality, as – often – most low-income workers are employed in the traded sector. All in all, while it is plausible that the recent bonanza had a favourable effect on growth, its impact on inequality is undetermined, as it depends to a large extent on the use made of the additional resources.

8.4.2   Business cycle effects

Growth of GDP per capita (GDPpc) doubled between the 1990s and 2003–07 in South America and rose by half a point in Central America. While all countries recorded a positive performance, growth was on average 2 percentage points higher in LOC than in non-LOC countries. Economic theory suggests that in developing countries an increase in GDPpc improves labour absorption and, under certain conditions, the wage rate, with positive distributive effects. In contrast, a GDP contraction raises inequality as wages drop, and the workers made redundant are not covered by unemployment insurance. Figure 8.4 confirms this hypothesis, by showing that, on average, a 1 per cent yearly increase in GDPpc over the business cycle (of an average duration of four to five years) reduces the Gini coefficient by 0.12 percentage points.

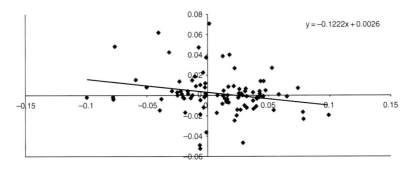

Figure 8.4 Percentage changes in Gini coefficients (y-axis) versus percentage change in GDPpc (x-axis) over the business cycle in 18 countries, 1990–2007
Source: Authors' calculation based on official GDPpc data. For the Gini see footnote 6.

Such a decline is of course far from automatic, as the growth pattern could be immiserising. Yet the empirical evidence confirms that the robust recovery recorded over 2003–08, as well as the labour policies discussed in Section 8.4.4, generated a positive effect on employment, wages and their distribution. As shown in Table 8.1, over 2002–07 the unemployment rate dropped by 5.3 points in LOC countries and 2 points in non-LOC countries, while over 5.3 million new jobs were created each year in the region, which is a much faster rate than during the previous decade. The new jobs were mainly taken by low-income workers, thus contributing to the decline in inequality.

Table 8.1 Labour market trends for LOC and non-LOC countries in Latin America, 1990–2007

		1990	2002	2007
LOC countries	Unemployment rate (%)	8.9	13.2	7.9
	Share of informal employment	40.5	38.9	38.1
	Average wage index (2000=100)	92.2	98.6	103.4
	Minimum wage index (2000=100)	86.1	100.4	138.6
Non-LOC countries	Unemployment rate (%)	8.5	10.0	8.0
	Share of informal employment	48.5	53.7	49.2
	Average wage index (2000=100)	79.5	102.2	102.0
	Minimum wage index (2000=100)	104.1	104.2	109.9

Source: Compiled by authors from the CEPALSTAT, ILO's Labour Overview (various years), and data from national statistical offices for the initial and last years.

8.4.3   Improvement in the distribution of educational achievements

A third factor that might have contributed to the recent fall in income inequality is the rise in enrolment rates recorded since the mid-1990s in both LOC and non-LOC countries and the subsequent reduction in enrolment inequality in primary and secondary education. For instance, the probability that a child from the bottom decile completed secondary education, by comparison with a child from the top decile, rose from 36.7 to 50 per cent between 1990 and 2005 (CEPAL, 2007a). The surge in enrolments also raised the average number of years of education of the work force and reduced the inequality of its distribution (Figure 8.5).

All in all, the countries of Latin America made substantial inroads in the field of human capital formation and in the reduction of many dimensions of inequality in education. In this regard, a study by Istituto de Pesquisa Economica Aplicada (cited in CEPAL, 2006) concluded that two thirds of the inequality decline observed in Brazil between 2000 and 2006 was due to a fall in wage inequality caused by a drop in educational inequality among workers and in the wage premium by education level.

8.4.4   New LOC paradigm

As noted in Section 8.2, LOC governments have developed a new economic paradigm and social contract, which binds together their traditional and emergent constituencies through a combination of macroeconomic stability, neocorporatist and participatory institutions, redistribution via the budget, labour policies and targeted social programmes. The main components of the new LOC model are reviewed hereafter.

8.4.4(a)   Macroeconomic policies

With some country variation, the measures introduced are broadly aligned with the 'pro-poor macroeconomics' paradigm (Cornia, 2006). Its key elements are:

A fiscal policy that aims to balance the budget in the context of an expansionary expenditure policy. Traditionally, Latin America has adopted pro-cyclical macroeconomic policies, which boosted growth during periods of external buoyancy but built up vulnerabilities that exploded when the favourable conditions disappeared. This stance has changed over the last decade. A decline in the budget deficit was targeted in all countries, despite an increase in public expenditure. Overall fiscal deficits were typically reduced below 1 per cent of GDP, and in several

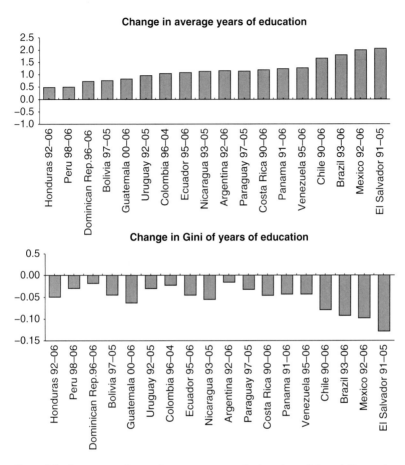

Figure 8.5 Percentage change in average years of education of the adult population and the Gini of educational achievements between the mid-1990s and the mid-2000s in 18 Latin American countries
Source: Gasparini et al. (2009: p. 45).

cases they were turned into surpluses. As a result, in 2006 and 2007 the average central government budget for the region as a whole was in equilibrium, suggesting a shift towards countercyclical fiscal management (Ocampo, 2007). A strong version of this policy, which required that the extra revenue collected during upturns be saved and used to expand public expenditure during bad years, was followed in Chile, Peru and Argentina. A weak version, consisting in balancing the budget or in achieving a small surplus and spending the extra revenue collected during the upturn, was followed in most other countries, because of the difficulties faced by democratic regimes in convincing the population of the need to maintain a policy of austerity in periods of relatively abundant revenue.

Rising tax/GDP ratios. The average regional tax and non-tax revenue of the central government, including social security contributions, rose from 15 per cent of GDP in 1990 to 17 per cent in 2000, and 20.2 per cent in 2007 (CEPAL, 2007b). Large revenue increases were recorded in Argentina and Brazil (7 percentage points of GDP), Colombia (8 percentage points), and Bolivia (10 percentage points), and only Mexico experienced a small decline. By the mid-2000s, Brazil, Argentina, Uruguay and Costa Rica had reached tax/GDP ratios similar to those of the US and Japan, while with tax/GDP ratios of 10–12 per cent most Central American countries remained mired in a 'low revenue development trap', which made them unable to fund pro-poor and pro-growth public goods. This revenue increase constitutes a major achievement, as the inability to raise taxes was a key factor in the debt accumulation of the 1970s, the debt crisis of the 1980s, and the instability of the 1990s. The increase resulted from a widespread reduction in excise duties and tariffs, a rise in indirect taxes (primarily VAT), an increase in progressive personal and corporate income tax, and stagnation at low levels of wealth taxes and social security contributions (Table 8.2). LOC countries performed somewhat better in terms of the additional revenue raised and of the progressivity of the tax instruments used (CEPAL, 2007b).

Countries benefiting from increases in export prices recorded significant revenue growth, as they taxed part of their land and mining rent by imposing special taxes on the operating revenues of mining companies. In turn, Argentina taxed the windfall profits due to rising world prices and accruing to a sector characterised by high asset and income concentration by means of a selective *ad valorem* export tax. It must be noted, however, that total revenue as a proportion of GDP started rising well before the commodity boom and resulted from efforts at broadening the direct and indirect tax base and at reducing evasion (Table 8.2).

Monetary policy and inflation targeting. With a steady decline in inflation rates (which made it easier to achieve inflation targets), monetary policy was either accommodating or neutral, tolerating (with the exception of Brazil) low or even negative real interest rates. Monetary policy also aimed to reduce the extensive dollarisation of the financial system. Argentina conducted a radical de-dollarisation during the crisis of 2002, while Peru, Bolivia and Uruguay adopted a policy of gradual de-dollarisation. There was also a general strengthening of Central Bank

Table 8.2 Central governments' tax and non-tax revenue to GDP ratios in 1990, 2002 and 2007, and changes in tax structure in LOC and non-LOC countries

Tax revenue/GDP			Non-tax revenue/GDP			Country Group	Changes over 2002–07 (percentage points of GDP)				
1990	2002	2007	1990	2002	2007		Trade taxes	Excises and other indirect taxes	VAT	Direct taxes	Social security
17.5	19.2	23.7	5.4	5.3	5.9	LOC	+0.38	−0.23	+1.35	+2.56	+0.45
9.9	14.2	16.1	2.8	2.5	3.4	Non-LOC	−0.20	−0.72	+1.19	+1.49	+0.13

Source: Authors' calculations based on the CEPALSTAT database.

independence, while capital controls were introduced to prevent the appreciation of the real exchange rate in Argentina over 2002–08, in Colombia in 2007 (Ocampo, 2009) and in Brazil in late 2009.

Exchange rate regime. With the exception of Brazil and Venezuela, most LOC and several other countries abandoned the free-float and fixed-peg regimes adopted during the previous decade, and opted for a competitive exchange rate regime or managed floats aimed at preventing a real appreciation. The clearest example of this policy is Argentina (Frenkel and Rapetti, 2008), where a competitive exchange rate shifted labour towards the labour-intensive manufacturing sector, with strong equalising effects (Damill, 2004, cited in World Bank, 2005). In 2006 and 2007, this policy approach came under pressure owing to large increases in export prices, capital inflows and remittances, and several countries experienced a mild-to-moderate real appreciation. It must be noted, however, that, without the huge accumulation of reserves and parallel sterilisation efforts, several countries would have shown stronger symptoms of 'Dutch disease' and accelerating inflation in the non-tradable sector, which – if uncontrolled – would have generated an adverse growth and distributive impact.

Trade and external indebtedness. The free trade policies adopted in the past were not overturned. Yet the Free Trade Area of the Americas seems to have stalled, while regional trade integration has developed rapidly, especially in the field of manufacturing exports. In addition, new trade agreements with industrialised and Asian countries were strengthened. LOC governments also attempted to reduce their dependence on foreign borrowing. Until 2009, short-term stabilisation agreements with the IMF were generally not renewed, while Brazil (in 2005) and Argentina (in 2006) prepaid their outstanding debt to the IMF. A few countries also restructured their foreign debt. As a result, Latin America's gross foreign debt declined from 42 to 20 per cent of the regional GDP between 2002 and 2007, while the foreign debt/GDP ratio net of currency reserves fell from 33 to 8 per cent.

8.4.4(b)   *Income, redistributive and social policies*

The LOC policy model differs markedly from the neoliberal one in terms of the degree to which public policies address the problems inherited from the 1990s – that is, unemployment, job informalisation, falling unskilled wages and social security coverage, and the weakening of institutions for wage negotiation and dispute settlement.

Income and labour market policies. Minimum wages were raised to a significant but far from excessive degree (given their low initial levels) in

LOC countries, and more moderately in non-LOC countries (Table 8.1). An assessment of the impact of minimum wages in Latin America over 1997–2001 (Kristensen and Cunningham, 2006) suggests that their recent rise probably had an equalising effect. Indeed the study shows that minimum wages raised the pay of low-income earners in both the formal and the informal sectors and were generally associated with a lower dispersion of earnings. Average wages rose slowly and, despite their recent hike, remained generally below their 2000 level. This wage restraint policy may reflect policy-makers' greater concern with creating jobs than with improving earnings. It also reflects the recognition that, unless backed by productivity gains, nominal wage raises may fuel inflation, with scant effect on real wages. The emphasis placed on job creation is confirmed by the rapid decline in unemployment in both LOC and non-LOC countries and by the faster rise in wage employment than in self-employment. Moreover, the wage premium declined due to a growing supply of educated workers (Section 8.4.3) and to a shift in production towards the unskilled labour-intensive tradable sector. Finally, several countries introduced large-scale public works programmes and attempted to extend the coverage of formal employment and to revive trade unions. In Uruguay, for instance, the Frente Amplio administration reinstated tripartite collective bargaining bodies comprising representatives of the business sector, unions and government.

Rising public social expenditure and redistribution. Public social expenditure had already begun to rise in the early-to-mid 1990s and continued growing in the early 2000s (Table 8.3). Most of the increase was in social security, social assistance and education (ibid.). The rise was nearly universal, and in 2005–06 only in Ecuador was the social expenditure/GDP ratio lower than in 1990–91. While there is still a huge intra-regional variation in social expenditure,[4] it appears that the 2003–06 rise was greater by about 1 GDP point among the LOC than among the non-LOC countries. One factor in the rise in public expenditure was the increase in tax/GDP ratios. But changes in the structure of public expenditure also played a role. For instance, the debt cancellation enjoyed by Heavily Indebted Poor Countries (HIPC) permitted a reallocation to social activities of funds previously used to service the foreign debt.

The rise in social expenditure generated positive redistributive effects. Analyses of the incidence of social expenditure by income quintile for eighteen countries over 1997–2003 (CEPAL, 2007b; Gasparini et al., 2009) show that all the components of social expenditure are less concentrated than private incomes are; expenditures on primary education

Table 8.3   Average regional social public expenditure/GDP in LOC versus non-LOC countries

Year	Social public expenditure as a percentage of Gross Domestic Product (GDP)				
	Total	Education	Health	Social security	Housing
1990	9.0	2.8	2.1	3.3	0.7
1996	10.9	3.4	2.4	4.0	1.0
2003	12.8	4.3	2.8	4.6	1.1
Around 2006	13.3	4.3	2.9	4.6	1.4
LOC Δ (2003–06)	1.33	0.20	0.38	0.46	0.29
Non-LOC Δ (2003–06)	0.48	−0.12	0.06	0.11	0.43

Notes: The data refer to the 18 countries analysed in this study, including Bolivia (using national data) omitted in similar studies by CEPAL (2005 and 2007b).
Source: Authors' calculations based on the CEPALSTAT database.

and social assistance are strongly progressive; those on secondary education and healthcare are mildly progressive or proportional; and those on tertiary education are as concentrated as the income distribution. In turn, social security outlays (pensions, unemployment benefit) are somewhat less concentrated than private incomes, as they focus on formal sector workers. The limited progressivity of expenditure on social insurance raises the question of how best the government can expand its coverage: by actively extending the formal sector or by setting up solidarity-based, non-contributory, universal or targeted funds providing basic benefits to informal sector workers and pensioners. Both approaches have been followed in recent years, though the latter has been more common. For instance Argentina, Brazil, Bolivia, Chile, Costa Rica, and Uruguay introduced universal or means-tested non-contributory social pensions costing between 0.2 and 1.3 per cent of GDP a year, providing a monthly benefit of US$20 to 140, and covering between 5 and 69 per cent of the relevant population.[5]

Social assistance. Over the last fifteen years, the region has also experienced a major strengthening of targeted social assistance programmes (Barrientos and Santibanez, 2009). This new emphasis has entailed the development of large-scale programmes focusing on unconditional income transfers such as non-contributory pensions; conditional transfers such as most of those listed in Table 8.4; and integrated anti-poverty programmes (such as Chile Solidario). These new transfers are well funded by the state (they absorb 0.5–1 per cent of GDP), and cover a large share of the population at risk (Table 8.4). Several studies document

Table 8.4   Summary of some of the main social programmes recently introduced in the region

Programme (reference year)	Cost GDP %	Beneficiaries (N)	Monthly subsidy ($)
Plan Jefas y Jefes (Argentina, 2002)	0.80	1.85 million workers	US$45 (2002) US$150 (2007)
Plan Nacional Emergencia (Bolivia, 2002)	0.86	1.6% of active pop.	US$63 for manual workers
PANES (Uruguay, 2005)	0.50	7.2% of active pop.	US$55
Bolsa Familia (Brazil, 2005)	0.36	11.1 million families	R$62 for poor families R$15 for children R$30 for young people
Chile Solidario (Chile, 2005)	0.08	256,000 families	US$8–21 depending on poverty intensity
Oportunidades (México, 2006)	0.40	5 million families (18% of pop.)	US$12–74 depending on educational level US$17 family health
Bono desarrollo umano (Ecuador, 2005)	0.60	5 million people (40% of pop.)	US$15
Familias en accion (Colombia, 2007)	0.20	1.7 million families	US$8–33 (educational subsidy/child) US$ 30 (health subsidy/family)

Source: Compiled by authors based on Fiszbein and Schady (2009) and Bouillon and Tejerina (2007).

the favourable impact of such transfers. However, the existing evidence suggests that these programmes had greater success in ensuring invest-ment in human capital (e.g. enabling children to attend schools and clinics) than in lifting the poor out of poverty (ibid.).

8.5   Relative weight of the above factors in the recent decline in inequality

Disentangling the relative importance of the sources of the 3–4 Gini point decline recorded between 2002/3 and 2007 in the region entailed the compilation of a data set on income inequality and a large number of explanatory variables[6] with annual observations for the eighteen countries covered and for the years 1990–2007. The regression analysis carried out using the fixed-effects method provided satisfactory results (Cornia, 2010: Table 9), as almost all variables have the sign expected *ex ante* on the basis of the theories discussed in Section 8.4 and are statistically significant. When introduced alone, the dummy variables 'populist government' and 'social democratic government' are both significant; but the former has a somewhat bigger redistributive effect (1.9 Gini points) than the latter (1.4 Gini points). As expected, GDP growth reduces inequality and is generally significant, but has a limited impact on inequality, as a 6 per cent growth in GDPpc reduces the Gini coefficient only by 0.2–0.4 points. In contrast, educational inequality is strongly related to income inequality, as the observed average regional drop of 2–3 points in the Gini coefficient of the years of education of the workforce over 2002–07 accounts for an average decline of 1.5–2 points in the Gini of disposable income. As for the impact of the international environment, the 33 per cent average improvement in terms of trade reduced income inequality by about 0.4–0.6 Gini points. Migrant remittances and capital inflows are non-significant in all specifications, while FDI/GDP appears to be significantly disequalising but to have played a negligible role during the last decade. In turn, a 20 per cent devaluation of the real exchange rate reduced income inequality by about 1.2 points.

As for the impact of redistributive policies, the regression analysis corroborates the predictions of Section 8.4. For instance, doubling the minimum wage index (while assuming a 3 percentage point expansion of formal employment) induces a drop in income inequality of 1.2 Gini points. Likewise, the 1.3 point rise in the ratio of public social expenditure to GDP observed in LOC countries over 2003–06 (Table 8.3) induced a statistically significant drop in the Gini coefficient of income inequality of 0.4 points. Finally, the ratio of direct to indirect taxes has a modest but significant impact on income inequality. These results refer to the regional average, and must therefore be interpreted with caution in making reference to a specific country. They must also be tested for the possibility of reverse causation and endogeneity. Reverse causation is not easily tested on the above data set, which includes at most eighteen observations for each country and variable, and it is thus more appropriate to deal with this problem from a theoretical standpoint (see Cornia, 2010, for a discussion of this problem). In turn, a solution to the possible problems of endogeneity requires the development of a simultaneous equation system, which is difficult in a panel with only eighteen observations. This means that the above results should be interpreted as correlations rather than causal explanations, though the theoretical discussion in Section 8.4 lends support to a cautious causal interpretation of the results obtained.

All in all, among the variables considered, those with the biggest impact on income inequality are (in descending order): improvements in educational enrolment and inequality due to sustained investments in education over 1990–2007 which affected the skills premium; the choice of an appropriate real exchange rate; the labour market and social expenditure policies discussed in Section 8.4; and the 'social democratic' and 'populist' dummies which measure the effect on inequality of policies and conditions other than those explicitly considered in the regression analysis. The terms of trade gains and growth recovery also contributed to the decline in inequality over 2002–07, but in a less important way, while migrant remittances and portfolio flows were not significant and the FDI/GDP stock (which stagnated over 2002–07) did not affect inequality during this period. Although we must exercise prudence due to the data limitations and specification problems mentioned above, these results appear to contradict the conclusions of several commentators (e.g. Perez Caldentey and Vernengo, 2008), who argue that the recent decline in inequality is driven by favourable international conditions and not by policy changes introduced by governments in the economic and social sphere.

8.6 The distributive impact of the financial crisis

The rapid growth which began in 2003 was abruptly interrupted in the third quarter of 2008 and 2009 by the global financial crisis. Unlike in the 1980s and 1990s, the region did not suffer a financial crisis because of the greater solidity of its domestic financial sector following a reduction in foreign debt, accumulation of reserves and improved macroeconomic management. Yet the region suffered a series of real economy shocks, including, first of all, a considerable decline in the terms of trade and export volumes. By mid-2009 the terms of trade had worsened by between 20 and 28 per cent in the Andean countries, by 6.2 per cent in the Mercosur, by 4.5 per cent in Mexico, and had turned positive in the oil-importing Central American countries. The combined effect of falling commodity prices and export volumes led to a 23.4 per cent drop in the value of exports, which was the main factor affecting Latin America's performance in late 2008 and 2009 (Ocampo, 2009). Second, in 2009 the region suffered a 10 per cent decline in remittances, while tourist receipts dropped by less and affected only a few countries. Thirdly, FDI declined by 37 per cent in 2009 from its historical peak in 2008 due to the fall in the prices of primary commodities. Fourthly, there was a substantial drop in portfolio inflows and an increase in capital outflows. As a result, the net capital inflow turned negative after mid-2008, causing a decline in the international reserves of the region from a peak of US$510 billion in mid-2008 to US$490 billion in mid-2009. Meanwhile, average interest rate spreads rose by 500 basis points between the lowest point reached in 2007 and mid-2009, though this increase was considerably lower than that observed during the Russian and Argentinean crises of 1998–99 and 2001–02 (of 1,100 and 1,400 basis points respectively), and had already started declining by mid-2009.

These exogenous shocks weakened the balance of payments and revenue collection. As a result, the regional primary deficit worsened from +1.4 to −1 per cent of GDP between 2008 and 2009, while the total budget deficit increased from −1.2 to −2.6 per cent over the same period. Much of this increase was due to a drop in tax and non-tax revenue. Yet, as Jimenez and Gomez-Sabaini (2009) noted, the decline in revenue collection varied considerably depending on the economic and tax structure of the different countries. Commodity-exporting countries saw their revenue/GDP ratio fall by 3.8 per cent, while in the others the drop was only half a point. Finally, the growing deficit in the current account balance triggered a wave of devaluations of the nominal exchange rate, which for the largest economies rose by between 15 and 35 per cent (CEPAL, 2009b). These devaluations were, however, a blessing in disguise, in view of the appreciation of most currencies in 2006–07, thus providing export incentives and a stimulus to diversify the economic structure. As a result of all this, the regional growth rate of GDP dropped from 4.2 per cent in 2008 to −1.7 per cent in 2009, to recover to an estimated 4.3 per cent in 2010 (ibid.). The recovery is projected to be 1.2 percentage points faster in LOC countries, due to greater fiscal stimuli and active credit policies, larger domestic markets, greater export diversification and closer trade ties with China (ibid.).

What about the distributive impact of the global economic crisis? The Gini coefficient of the distribution of income for 2008 shows that income inequality continued to decrease in six countries, while remaining constant in three. In contrast, inequality is likely to have risen in 2009, though the increase might be smaller than initially feared. Indeed, the regional output contraction of 1.7 per cent was accompanied by a modest 0.8 per cent increase in the regional unemployment rate, the remaining redundant labour moving to the informal sector. Meanwhile, the fall in world commodity prices reduced inflation substantially between 2008 and 2009, with the effect that average real wages grew by 4.6 per cent in 2009, in contrast to the stagnation of 2008. Finally, the targeted social spending programmes introduced in South America and Mexico effectively moderated the negative consequences of the crisis (CEPAL, 2009a).

All in all, it appears that the growth and distributive impact of what is considered the worst crisis since the Great Depression was less severe than initially anticipated, and that the recent growth and inequality gains recorded in the region are therefore unlikely to be derailed in either LOC or non-LOC countries. Indeed, the current crisis has hit a region which is in a much better condition than that prevailing during the crises of 1982–84 and 1998–2002. To start with, the region avoided a domestic financial crisis like that experienced during the 1980s and 1990s. This means that fewer funds were needed to recapitalise ailing banks, and that fiscal policy could concentrate on pro-poor and pro-growth interventions. Secondly, the impact of the crisis was moderated by the improvements in the macroeconomic stance (see Section 8.4) recorded over 2003–07, which made it possible to follow countercyclical fiscal policies over the short term. There is evidence that the adoption of these policies, especially among LOC countries, sustained growth during the most acute phase of the crisis and accelerated the recovery in the second part of 2009 (CEPAL, 2009b), as the increase in public consumption partially offset the contraction of other components of aggregate demand. Meanwhile, with few exceptions, central banks carried out more flexible monetary and credit policies, ensuring sufficient liquidity to financial markets, while public banks in part offset the credit squeeze of private banks. Thirdly, the trade diversification of the first part of the 2000s reduced the impact of the trade shocks in part of the region. For instance, the Southern Cone nations were less affected because of their increasing trade ties with East Asia, while Mexico was more affected because of its integration with the US economy. Fourthly, most countries have introduced important public works and cash transfer programmes in recent years (Table 8.4), and, as a result, in 2009 85 million Latin Americans received a subsidy under some kind of transfer scheme (UNDP, 2009). This prior institutional development facilitated the expansion of safety nets during the crisis and helped to preserve some of the recent inequality declines.

8.7   Conclusions: Is the current crisis reversing recent inequality gains?

At the end of 2009, it is unclear whether the LOC regimes in the region are here to stay, or whether the current difficulties and, in some cases, the regimes' own political mistakes have eroded the consensus which brought them to power. The coup in Honduras in June 2009, the election of a Centre–Right president in Panama in July 2009 and the results of the elections in Chile in early 2010 may signal that the trend has reached its zenith. At the same time, the recent re-election of LOC candidates in Brazil, Bolivia and Uruguay suggests that progressive governments may be able to endure the problems caused by the crisis and by the resistance of powerful interest groups.

One key issue regarding the sustainability of the recent reforms and inequality gains in LOC countries concerns the stability of the new pact on redistribution via the budget and the related need to sustain government revenue in the future. Historically, government revenues, public spending and deficits have been much more volatile in Latin America than in developed countries. Because of this legacy, several authors question whether the recent fiscal changes have been structural in nature, or whether they are purely due to cyclical factors (Izquierdo and Talvi, 2008). Braun (2007) further argues that, while the recent increases in expenditure are permanent, the revenue improvements appear to be mostly transitory. And, as shown by the case of Ecuador and Venezuela, where a large share of government revenue depends on volatile commodity prices, the structural fiscal balance improved much less than in other parts of the region.

Yet in most countries the new fiscal pact seems to be stably anchored in a permanent change in fiscal policies. In this regard, Vladkova-Hollar and Zettelmeyer (2008) report that, though structural fiscal balances improved less between 2002 and 2007 than overall fiscal balances, they still improved significantly, especially in many LOC countries. Likewise, the Organisation for Economic Co-operation and Development (OECD) (2009) shows that deficit and revenue volatility fell by one third in 1990–94 and by a quarter in 2000–06. One of the developments ignored by pessimistic commentators is what Lora (2008) calls the 'silent institutional revolution' which has taken place in the region between the 1980s and the 2000s, a change which he sees as a major determinant of the macroeconomic stability now enjoyed by the region. This revolution has focused on political, legal, property rights, fiscal and social protection institutions. The reform of electoral systems increased political competition, while the judiciary became more independent of the executive and legislative powers. As for fiscal reforms, restrictions on deficits were imposed in twelve out of the eighteen countries under study, and some of them (starting with Chile) introduced fiscal responsibility rules which set limits on the level of expenditure, deficit and public debt, adopted procedures to strengthen the spending authority of the ministry of finance, and improved tax administration and the transparency of and access to tax information. Evidence of the structural nature of the increase in tax/GDP ratios in LOC and, to a lesser extent, in moderate non-LOC governments is also provided by their timing and extent, as taxation rose during periods of low commodity prices and in countries (such as Brazil) that hardly depend for their revenue on commodity prices.

In addition to the new fiscal pact, there have been important changes in public spending on education, cash transfers, and other forms of social assistance. Micro- and macro-evidence supports the view that higher public and private spending reduced inequality in education and improved the distribution of human capital among the workforce. Redistribution was also pursued via macroeconomic policies favouring the labour-intensive traded sector and changes in labour market policies and institutions. In this case, too, the changes introduced were far from radical, and yet they helped to raise labour participation, increase the proportion of workers covered by formal contracts and reduce unemployment.

Beyond the problems posed by the current financial crisis, the Latin American governments face formidable hurdles to deepening the reforms that are under way. First, the trend towards rising taxation and social expenditure needs to continue in much of the region, with the objective of building a lean welfare state that avoids the high costs and dis-incentives of the European model while providing increasingly universal coverage. Secondly, the revenue needed to sustain public expenditure in the future will have to come from a diversification of the economy into new labour- and skill-intensive sectors, and a diversification of exports by industry and areas of destination. Thirdly, an intensification of the new policy model by LOC governments will have to overcome considerable political opposition, as shown by the cases of Bolivia and Argentina, where policy mistakes and the opposition of interest groups nearly stalled moderate attempts at redistribution. Perhaps the main danger of the current crisis is that it may create a gap between the responses expected from LOC governments and what they can actually do. A deterioration in living conditions might lead to a collective perception that the crisis is due to inadequate policy responses. Failure to stay the policy course adopted in recent years – albeit with the necessary corrections – may cause a credibility gap, undermine support for LOC governments and push the region towards its traditional path of unequal development or towards more radical solutions, possibly overturning the inequality gains of the recent past.

Notes

*Section 8.4 of this paper draws in part on Cornia (2010).

1. The countries covered in this chapter are Argentina, Bolivia, Brazil, Chile, Colombia, Costa Rica, the Dominican Republic, El Salvador, Ecuador, Guatemala, Honduras, Mexico, Nicaragua, Panama, Paraguay, Peru, Uruguay, and Venezuela. The LOC countries are those that were ruled for at least four of the six years between 2002–07 by Left-of-Centre regimes, i.e. Argentina, Brazil, Chile, Costa Rica, Ecuador, Panama, Uruguay and Venezuela.
2. Corporación Latinobarómetro is a non-profit NGO based in Santiago, Chile. Since 1995 it has carried out polls on a variety of political topics by surveying 19,000 households from 18 countries in the region (http://www.latinobarometro.org).
3. There is no agreement among political scientists over the term 'populist', which many see as a catchall category comprising diverse political regimes sharing only a common aversion to technocratic neoliberalism and US hegemony, weak institutional parties, and dominance by new movements (Roberts, 2007). For instance, populist regimes range from top-down '*chavismo*' in Venezuela where the community-based *chavista* organisations are closely controlled from the centre, to Bolivia's Movement Towards Socialism which is an autonomous, largely indigenous movement which arose from the mass protests of 2000–04 against the privatisation of municipal water supplies, foreign control over gas exports, and US-sponsored drug eradication programmes, and demanding the return of land to indigenous communities (ibid.).
4. In 2006, Cuba, Uruguay, Brazil, Argentina, Costa Rica, and Panama had social expenditure/GDP ratios of 15–20 per cent (as in the OECD), while in the Caribbean, Central American and Andean countries they were below 10 per cent.
5. Data taken from HelpAge International, www.helpage.org.
6. For more detailed information on the variables included in the database see Cornia (2010: footnote 15). The majority of the 324 observations of the Gini coefficient of income inequality are taken from the SEDLAC database (which computes the Gini coefficients on the basis of survey micro data according to a standardised procedure), and to a lesser extent from WIDER's WIID2c database and WDI 2007. A total of 98 data-points were interpolated by filling gaps of one or two years in time series with stable trends. In most cases, the Gini coefficients refer to disposable household income per capita.

References

Altimir, O. (1996) 'Economic Development and Social Equity'. *Journal of Interamerican Studies and World Affairs* 38 (2/3): 47–71.

Altimir, O. (1993) 'Income Distribution and Poverty Through Crises and Adjustment'. Paper presented at the ECLAC/UNICEF Workshop on *Public Policy Reforms and Social Expenditure*, Santiago, Chile, 14–15 June.

Barrientos, A., and C. Santibanez (2009) 'New Forms of Social Assistance and the Evolution of Social Protection in Latin America'. *Journal of Latin American Studies* 41 (1): 1–26.

Bouillon, C.P., and L. Tejerina (2007) *Do We Know What Works?: A Systematic Review of Impact Evaluations of Social Programs in Latin America and the Caribbean* (Washington, DC: Inter-American Development Bank).

Braun, M. (2007) 'Fiscal Policy Reform in Latin America'. Paper prepared for the *Consulta de San Jose*, San José, Costa Rica, 22–25 October.

Cameron, M.A. (2009) 'Latin America's Left Turns: Beyond Good and Bad'. *Third World Quarterly* 30 (2): 331–48.

CEPAL (Comisión Económica para América Latina y el Caribe) (2009a) *Panorama Social de América Latina, 2009*. LC/G.2423-P/P (Santiago de Chile: CEPAL).

CEPAL (Comisión Económica para América Latina y el Caribe) (2009b) *Balance Preliminar de las Economías de América Latina y el Caribe, 2009*. LC/G-2424-P (Santiago de Chile: CEPAL).

CEPAL (Comisión Económica para América Latina y el Caribe) (2007a) *Panorama Social de América Latina, 2007*. LC/G.2351-P (Santiago de Chile: CEPAL).

CEPAL (Comisión Económica para América Latina y el Caribe) (2007b) *Balance Preliminar de las Economías de América Latina y el Caribe, 2007*. LC/G.2355-P (Santiago de Chile: CEPAL).

CEPAL (Comisión Económica para América Latina y el Caribe) (2006) *Panorama Social de América Latina, 2006*. LC/G.2326-P (Santiago de Chile: CEPAL).

CEPAL (Comisión Económica para América Latina y el Caribe) (2005) *Panorama Social de América Latina, 2005*. LC/G.2288-P/E (Santiago de Chile: CEPAL).

Chenery, H., M. Ahluwalia, C. Bell, J. Duloy and R. Jolly (1974) *Redistribution with Growth* (London: Oxford University Press).

Cornia, G.A. (2010) 'Income Distribution under Latin America's New Left Regimes'. *Journal of Human Development* 11 (1): 85–114.

Cornia, G.A. (2006) *Pro-Poor Macroeconomics: Potential and Limitations* (Basingstoke: Palgrave Macmillan).

Cornia, G.A., and B. Martorano (2009) 'What Explains the Decline of Income Inequality During the Last Decade?' Paper presented at the conference *Overcoming Persistent Inequality and Poverty* in honour of Frances Stewart, Oxford, UK, 17–18 September.

Dornbusch, R., and S. Edwards (1991) *The Macroeconomics of Populism in Latin America* (Chicago and London: University of Chicago Press).

Fiszbein, A., and N. Schady (2009) *Conditional Cash Transfers: Reducing Present and Future Poverty* (Washington, DC: World Bank).

Frenkel, R., and M. Rapetti (2008) 'Five Years of Competitive and Stable Real Exchange Rate in Argentina, 2002–2007'. *International Review of Applied Economics* 22 (2): 215–26.

Gasparini, L., G. Cruces, L. Tornarolli and M. Marchionni (2009) 'A Turning Point? Recent Developments on Inequality in Latin America and the Caribbean'. *Documento de Trabajo Nro. 81* (La Plata: CEDLAS, Universidad Nacional de La Plata).

Izquierdo, A., and E. Talvi (2008) *All That Glitters May Not Be Gold: Assessing Latin America's Recent Macroeconomic Performance* (Washington, DC: Research Department, Inter-American Development Bank).

IMF (International Monetary Fund) (2005) *World Economic Outlook, April 2005: Globalization and External Imbalances* (Washington, DC: International Monetary Fund).

Jimenez, J.P., and J.C. Gomez-Sabaini (2009) *The Role of Tax Policy in the Context of the Global Crisis: Consequences and Prospects'*. LC/L.3037 Montevideo, 19–20 May 2009.

Keefer, P. (2007) *DPI2006 Database of Political Institutions: Changes and Variable Definitions* (Washington, DC: Development Research Group, World Bank).

Kristensen, N., and W. Cunningham (2006) 'Do Minimum Wages in Latin America and the Caribbean Matter? Evidence from 19 Countries'. *World Bank Policy Research Working Paper No. 3870* (Washington, DC: World Bank).

Lora, E. (2008) 'La Revolución Silenciosa de las Instituciones y la Estabilidad Macroeconómica'. *Documento de Trabajo 649* (Washington, DC: Inter-American Development Bank).

Lustig, N. (2009) 'La Pobreza y la Desigualdad en América Latina, y los Gobiernos de Izquierda' *Cuadernos del Consejo Mexicano de Asuntos Internacionales* 7 (Mexico DF: Consejo Mexicano de Asuntos Internacionales).

Ocampo, J.A. (2009) 'Impacto de la Crisis Financiera Mundial sobre América Latina'. *Revista de la CEPAL 97*: 9–32.

Ocampo, J.A. (2008) 'The Latin American Economic Boom'. *Revista de Ciencia Política* 28 (1): 7–33.

Ocampo, J.A. (2007) 'The Macroeconomics of the Latin American Economic Boom'. *CEPAL Review 93*: 7–28.

OECD (Organisation for Economic Development and Co-operation) (2009) *Latin American Economic Outlook 2009* (Paris: OECD).

Panizza, F.E. (2005a) 'Unarmed Utopia Revisited: The Resurgence of Left-of-Centre Politics in Latin America'. *Political Studies* 53 (4): 716–34.

Panizza, F.E. (2005b) 'The Social Democratisation of the Latin American Left'. *Revista Europea de Estudios Latinoamericanos y del Caribe 79*: 95–103.

Perez Caldentey, E., and M. Vernengo (2008) 'Back to the Future: Latin America's Current Development Strategy'. Online: www.networkideas.org/featart/aug2008/fa02_Back2Future.htm, accessed 12 June 2009.

Roberts, K.M. (2007) 'Repoliticizing Latin America: The Revival of Populist and Leftist Alternatives'. *Woodrow Wilson Center Update on the Americas*, November 2007, Program on Democratic Governance and the 'New Left' (Washington, DC: Woodrow Wilson International Center for Scholars).

Stewart, F. (2009) 'Power and Progress: The Swing of the Pendulum'. Address to the 2009 meeting of the *Human Development and Capability Association*, Lima, Peru, 10–11 September.

Székely, M. (2003) 'The 1990s in Latin America: Another Decade of Persistent Inequality but with Somewhat Lower Poverty'. *Journal of Applied Economics* 6 (2): 317–39.

Tokman, V. (1986) 'Ajuste y Empleo: Los Desafíos del Presente'. *Mimeo* (Santiago, Chile: PREALC, Regional Employment Programme for Latin America and the Caribbean).

UNCTAD (United Nations Conference on Trade and Development) (2008) *Handbook of Statistics*. Online: http://stats.unctad.org/handbook, accessed 12 July 2009.

UNDP (United Nations Development Programme) (2009) 'The Global Financial Crisis: Social Implications for Latin America and the Caribbean' *Crisis Update No. 2* (Regional Bureau for Latin America and the Caribbean).

Vladkova-Hollar, I., and J. Zettelmeyer (2008) 'Fiscal Positions in Latin America: Have They Really Improved?' *IMF Working Paper* WP/08/137 (Washington, DC: International Monetary Fund).

World Bank (2005) *Argentina: Seeking Sustained Growth and Social Equity: Observations on Growth, Inequality and Poverty* (Washington, DC: World Bank).

Part IV
Conflict, Ethnicity and Inequality

9
Understanding Horizontal Inequalities: The Role of Civil Society

Graham K. Brown

9.1 Introduction

Horizontal inequalities between ethnic and religious groups are increasingly recognised to be an important causal factor in violent ethnic conflict in the developing world (Stewart, 2008). An important general conclusion that arises from the case study and econometric work associated with the concept is that the impact of socioeconomic horizontal inequalities on conflict likelihood is crucially mediated by political factors. To date, however, attention to this political dimension has largely focused on the role of the state and of ethnic leaders. Civil society as a distinct realm of political activity is a relatively unexplored dimension of horizontal inequalities, and one which deserves closer attention.

This chapter provides a preliminary conceptual analysis of the role of civil society in mediating, resolving or exacerbating horizontal inequalities. Identifying two distinct approaches to understanding civil society itself – a liberal democratic approach that focuses on institutions, institutional arrangement and a privileged relationship with democracy; and a Gramscian approach that focuses on the discursive and hegemonic potential of civil society – I show how these approaches would lead to very different theoretical interpretations of the relationship between civil society and horizontal inequalities in multiethnic societies. I then deploy two different types of empirical data as appropriate for each theoretical perspective – quantitative cross-sectional survey data; and qualitative interpretive analysis respectively – to show in exploratory investigation that both approaches may offer important insights.

The institutional dimension of civil society is strongly linked to ethnic cleavages. While civil society is often reified as a 'bringing together' phenomenon which is thought to promote democracy, tolerance and 'communicative action', in Habermas' terminology, it can also be a site of exclusion, intolerance, and even oppression (Whitehead, 1997; Alexander, 1998). Civil society is also theorised to be institutionally reflective of the underlying political economy of the country – an idea that has led to its enshrinement at the centre of the 'modernisation' thesis linking economic development with democratisation (White, 1994; Brysk, 2000; Zuern, 2000). Yet where political economies are severely divided along ethnic or religious lines, so by implication may civil society be divided (Tan and Singh, 1994; Kaneko, 2002; Verma, 2002).

Secondly, civil society plays a crucial role in the public *interpretation* of inequality. Inequalities, particularly horizontal inequalities, will not lead to social mobilisation and conflict unless they are perceived to be severe and unjust. While previous research on horizontal inequalities has focused on the role of political elites in providing public interpretation of such inequalities, this paper argues that civil society also plays this role, in a way that can both mitigate and exacerbate ethnic tensions; indeed civil society is rarely a homogenous entity, and different sectors of it may pursue these different interpretive stances at the same time.

9.2   Theoretical perspectives on civil society and ethnic conflict

In order to explicate the central argument of this chapter, we need first to clear some analytical ground and distinguish between different theoretical perspectives on civil society. This will be important because, as we shall see, while recent scholarship has usefully advanced our understanding of the relationship between civil society and social conflict in ethnically divided societies, this work has largely been located within an (implicitly) liberal conceptualisation of civil society, which focuses on institutions and networks and privileges a particular relationship between civil society and democratisation. While not disputing the importance of such networks, a central argument of this paper will be that civil society also plays a parallel role in societies beset by severe horizontal inequalities, in which the *meanings* and *understandings* attached to such inequalities are contested – as, hence, are the options for remedial action. To explore this dimension of civil society, I will argue, requires us to adopt a dualistic perspective on civil society, understanding it both as an institutional realm of association and, in a more Gramscian vein, as an arena of discursive contestation. Methodologically, this broadly locates the account to be developed here across both the 'explanation' and 'understanding' axes of the 'double hermeneutic' of social sciences (Giddens, 1979): we will explore the 'objective' relationships between the social phenomena of horizontal inequalities and civil society in order to provide 'explanation'; and we will explore the second hermeneutic of social interpretation by society itself, in order to provide 'understanding'.

Civil society is perhaps one of the most pedigreed concepts in modern political theory, with antecedents stretching back as far as Plato and, in the modern period, Thomas Hobbes, although its use and meaning have undergone many revisions during the centuries between them.[1] Plato's conceptualisation of civil society as 'a politically organised commonwealth', which guarded against the 'dangers of private interest' and state power, finds many echoes in modern writings on the subject (Ehrenberg, 1999: pp. 3–4). His emphasis on the power of 'reason' in the realm of civil society to arrive at a unitary 'Good', however, would strike many modern theorists, particularly those of a Gramscian bent, as in itself overly oppressive and of as much danger as the state itself.

Contemporary conceptualisations of civil society find their common roots in Alexis de Tocqueville's work on democracy. Comparing America with his native France, Tocqueville concluded that, in the United States, a 'weak' state complemented by robust civic associations was far more conducive to democracy than the 'strong' state and weak social groupings in France (Tocqueville, 1954, 1955). Civil society – the intermediary level of association between the state and the individual – was the key to resisting state oppression.

If Tocqueville remains the anchor for modern conceptualisations of civil society, Foley and Edwards have noted that this phrase now encompasses 'a complex set of arguments, not all of which are congruent' (Foley and Edwards, 1996: p. 37). Broadly speaking, however, two distinct approaches to civil society can be identified in the contemporary period. The first, and probably dominant, approach is the liberal perspective, which is primarily concerned with civil society as a constituent of democratisation and of the democratic process. Is democracy viable without a robust civil society? Does such a mature civil society engender democratisation? These are the types of question that concern liberal theorists. On the other hand, the Marxist approach is more concerned with civil society as the legitimising extension of a hegemonic state. Clearly, a full picture of civil society would address both these concerns. Chandhoke neatly sums up the shortcomings of exclusive focus on one or the other approach thus:

> Liberals concentrate on the oppressions of the state, but they do not inquire into the oppressions of civil society. And the Marxist

concentration upon the oppressions of this sphere has led them to neglect any analysis of the institutions and values of civil society.

(Chandhoke, 1995: p. 162)

In the liberal tradition, civil society is employed in a largely Tocquevillean sense to signify 'an intermediate associational realm between state and family populated by organisations which are separate from the state, enjoy autonomy in relation to the state and are formed voluntarily by members of society to protect or extend their interests or values' (White, 1994: p. 379). The liberal interpretation of civil society ascribes to it a strongly democratic dimension, in some cases viewing it almost functionally, as part of a 'transition' process that leads from authoritarianism to democracy. Socially, this process is linked to the emergence and growth of a strong middle class, itself predicated upon strong economic growth. In a widely cited essay, Larry Diamond thus identifies ten 'democratic functions' of civil society, ranging from its limiting effect on state power to its role in the selection and training of future political leaders (Diamond, 1996).

Particularly within the context of development studies, liberal accounts of civil society are increasingly linked to the concept of social capital. Often couched in economistic terms as a public good, social capital accounts for the less tangible qualities of civil society. In the words of Robert Putnam, one of the foremost proponents of the theory, social capital 'refers to features of social organization such as networks, norms, and social trust that facilitate coordination and cooperation for mutual benefit' (Putnam, 1995: p. 67). The general thesis put forward by proponents of social capital is that democratic civil society functions best – or only – where social capital is strong. In his acclaimed empirical study of local government in Italy, Putnam thus argued that local government was far more successful in the north of the country because of dense networks of civil engagement, which were lacking in the south (Putnam, 1993). By contrast, however, he saw a steady erosion of social capital in the United States, epitomised by his now famous phrase that America goes 'bowling alone' (Putnam, 2000).

Where Putnam's conceptualisation of social capital has also been criticised is in his assumption that social capital is, in all its forms and at all times, of net social benefit.[2] Critics have pointed to the 'negative externalities' of social capital, noting that 'group solidarity ... is often purchased at the price of hostility towards out-group members' (Fukuyama, 2001: p. 8). In liberal conceptualisations of civil society, this problematic dimension of social capital is reflected in wider concerns. Alexander, for instance, has noted a 'bifurcating discourse' in civil society, in which the 'citizen' is postulated against the 'enemy' (Alexander, 1998). Civil society, for Alexander, is both liberal and repressive: liberal towards its citizens, but repressive towards its enemies. Alexander's primary concern is international relations; others, such as Whitehead, have identified a similar contradiction on a national level. All conceptualisations of civil society, Whitehead argues, 'admit a third category of "uncivil citizens", or persons enjoying political rights, but not submitting themselves to the constraints imposed by "civil society"' (Whitehead, 1997: p. 95). As Whitehead notes, this leaves an arena of 'uncivil interstices', into which he puts such groups as religious fundamentalists and mafia organisations – generators, one might suggest, of 'antisocial capital'.

Liberal theories of civil society, then, face two major challenges in their accounts of democracy and democratisation. First, their broad failure to consider 'uncivil' tendencies in voluntary spheres of social activity (the realm of 'civil' society) has resulted in often over-optimistic evaluations of civil society's democratising 'function'. Secondly, they have been unable to counter convincingly charges that the direction of causality in their argument is the wrong way round. Implicit in both these problems is an unresolved 'End of History' teleology (Fukuyama, 1989). Whilst few analysts would still openly support Fukuyama's thesis that liberal democracy has 'won' the future, liberal accounts nonetheless continue to assume that it has at least a privileged relationship with civil society.

For liberal theorists, then, civil society and its infrastructural constituent social capital enjoy a privileged and mutually reinforcing relationship with democracy. Civil society is seen as a rein on the excesses of state power; a vibrant civil society leads to an accountable state. For many Marxist analysts, particularly those influenced by Gramsci, almost the direct opposite is true. In this paradigm, civil society is understood as the arena in which the state perpetuates its power through hegemonic rather than coercive means.

Modern Marxist theorisations of civil society have been dominated by the legacies of Antonio Gramsci. Within Gramsci's own writings, however, there is some confusion as to the exact role of civil society. In one note Gramsci writes, 'State = political society + civil society, in other words hegemony protected by the armour of coercion' (Gramsci, 1971: p. 263). Elsewhere, in a formulation more akin to those of liberal theorists, he suggests that civil society stands 'between the economic structure and the State' (Gramsci, 1971: p. 208). Inconsistencies aside, however, it is clear that Gramsci viewed civil society as the primary vehicle for the state's hegemonic project. Civil society fulfils this role for Gramsci in two ways. First, it is the arena of the 'intellectuals', who themselves have a vital role in giving a sense of consensual legitimacy to the state. Secondly, civil society exerts the state's hegemonic influence through 'so-called private organisations, like the Church, the trade unions, the schools' (Gramsci, 1971: p. 56).

Gramsci saw civil society as more than just an extension of the state, however, but rather as the realm in which the state's hegemonic project was extended *and* contested. He identified two potential counter-hegemonic approaches: the 'war of position', in which class alliances are forged and broken, and the revolutionary 'war of movement'. While the state is a more dominant actor in Gramscian readings of civil society, then, Gramscians do accept that civil society has at least the potential to provide opposition to the state – a role which the liberal tradition conversely privileges. In one Gramscian formulation, for instance, Chandhoke identifies a process of

> the neutralization of the emancipatory potential of civil society and of its appropriation by the dominant classes and the state...The appropriation of this space by dominant practices does not, however, invalidate it.
>
> (Chandhoke, 1995: p. 203)

For Chandhoke, as for the influential modern Gramscian theorists Laclau and Mouffe (1985), civil society is primarily an arena of discursive contestation. In particular, Chandhoke identifies the concept of rights as historically critical to the civil society discourse. States, he argues, have legitimised themselves through civil society by the extension of (discursive) rights to their citizens. Civil society, in turn, has grasped these rights and 'progressively widened' them. Thus Chandhoke accepts that civil society may engender democracy, but argues that the often non-inclusive nature of civil society – an objection mirroring those of Alexander and Whitehead – gives rise to a 'crippled form of democracy' (Chandhoke, 1995: p. 204).

How then, do we try to bring horizontal inequalities into the picture? I want to suggest here that we can see two broad routes for exploring the relationship between civil society, horizontal inequalities and conflict. These different routes are located within the different theoretical realms outlined above, and also lend themselves largely to different methodological and epistemological approaches. Briefly summarised, these approaches are as follows:

- *A social capital approach.* Working with a broadly liberal conceptualisation of civil society, one could seek to explore the relationship between horizontal inequalities and the formation and deployment of between- and within-group social capital. Lending itself to positivist quantitative cross-sectional analysis, this would provide an account located within an 'explanatory' causal framework, seeking to explain how civil society mediates – either positively or negatively – the impact of horizontal inequalities on conflict; and
- *A social meaning approach.* The alternative approach would be to work within a more Gramscian conceptualisation of civil society and to explore the ways in which the social meanings attached to inequalities – and hence their impact on conflict dynamics – are contested in civil society as a political arena. Necessitating an embrace of Giddens's 'double hermeneutic', this would require a more interpretivist, qualitative approach, located on the 'understanding' axis of social enquiry.

Each approach has its merits and limitations, and in the following two sections I explore each one in turn, providing some preliminary evidence on possible relationships before concluding with suggestions for future research.

9.3 The social capital approach: Horizontal inequalities and trust in multicultural societies

Probably the best-known contemporary study of civil society and violent ethnic conflict is Ashutosh Varshney's study of Hindu–Muslim communal violence in India (Varshney, 2002). Varshney's thesis is simple but compelling – in order to account for the variation in levels of ethnocommunal rioting in India, there is little point in looking for 'root causes' of conflict, as these are presumably the same across large areas of the country, whereas the incidence of Hindu–Muslim violence is highly concentrated geographically. Instead, we need to examine the conditions that allow religious tensions to escalate into violent conflict. Through a series of paired comparisons, Varshney argues that in those cities in which 'associational networks' between Hindu and Muslim civil groups are dense and cooperative, the 'sparks' of conflict did not escalate into violence; where civil society is communally divided, however, conflict more easily escalated into violence. Although he does not explicitly frame it in these terms, Varshney's thesis hence bears similarities to the social capital version of civil society, particularly in those formulations that make a distinction between 'bridging' and 'bonding' forms of social capital (Fukuyama, 2001). Moreover, like the social capital argument, Varshney's has been criticised for getting the causal direction wrong (Portes, 1998; Rothstein, 2003) – peaceful cities, it could be argued, are more likely to see the emergence of cross-communal networks rather than vice versa. Varshney does address this possibility through a more historical analysis of one of his paired comparisons, but the general critique remains important.

While Varshney's approach does not explicitly consider horizontal inequalities, there is a clear compatibility between his thesis and a social capital view of horizontal inequalities. The hypothesis here is that severe horizontal inequalities impede the development of bonding social capital between groups because these give rise to civic organizations geared towards making different, and potentially conflicting, claims upon the state. In her collaborative work on group behaviour with Rosemary Thorp and Judith Heyer, Frances Stewart made the important point that, rather than depending on social capital for their efficacy, associational groups[3] can in fact play an important role in generating social capital (Heyer et al., 2002). Moreover, this can transcend ethnic boundaries and contribute towards 'bridging' as well as 'bonding' capital. Co-authoring with Thorp and Amrik Heyer, Stewart cites the example of irrigation projects in Sri Lanka that brought together Sinhalese and Tamil farmers (Thorp et al., 2005, citing Uphoff and Wijayaratna, 2000). This 'positive externality' of group behaviour has clear parallels with Varshney's account of the role of civil society in preventing violent conflict.

But such potential benefits of group behaviour for bridging social capital clearly depends upon some commonality of need or aspiration other than the 'identity group' – in the cited case, this was the fact that there were farmers of both Sinhalese and Tamil extraction in want of better irrigation facilities. It is in this respect that horizontal inequalities enter the picture as a potentially important barrier to bridging social capital. Where inequalities between groups are high, the possibility of 'bridging' social capital emerging as a result of inter-group collaboration for development aims is likely to be considerably reduced. In an extreme scenario, where there is a strong 'ethnic division of labour' – akin to Hechter's notion of 'internal colonialism' (Hechter, 1975) – the barriers to the formation of trans-ethnic associational groups are likely to be high.

Given the problems of causal mechanism associated both with Varshney's account and with the broader social capital literature, it is important to be careful here about the causal links we hypothesise. In a 'perfectly ranked' (Horowitz, 1985) society where ethnicity and economic functions are entirely segregated, one could argue that horizontal inequalities would not, in themselves, constitute a causal factor for social conflict and violence, but are rather a symptom of a broader underlying problem of social stratification and segregation.

In this section I provide a preliminary quantitative exploration of the relationship between horizontal inequalities and the level of social capital within a society. With limited data, I do not take the approach further, to explore evidence of a causal link with violent conflict. I use the World Values Surveys (WVS), a standardised survey instrument that has been carried out in fifty-five developed and developing countries, in four waves, since the early 1980s. While these data are problematic in many ways (discussed below), they make the only major cross-country and longitudinal survey that asks questions relevant to this topic. The surveys ask a range of questions about values and behaviour, and they are widely used as a source for cross-national empirical studies of social capital (e.g. Norris, 2002; Inglehart and Welzel, 2005). Following Norris, I take as a basic indicator of social capital responses to the question asked in most of the WVS surveys about whether respondents felt that, generally speaking, that other people in society could be trusted. I begin by examining the determinants of individual-level responses to this question, which I term 'social trust'; I then explore the determinants of national-level social capital, defined as overall levels of trust within a society.

To explore social trust, I run a series of logit regressions to predict the likelihood that individuals express generalised social trust. Our main variables of interest are:

- The levels of ethnic and religious diversity within society. Mainstream views on the relationship between ethnicity and social capital typically assume that ethno-religious diversity *per se* is a barrier to social trust, without paying attention to the inequality dimension. I use two different measures of diversity: the proportion of the total national population in the respondent's own group; and the level of group 'fractionalisation', calculated using the standard Ethnolinguistic Fractionalization (ELF) concentration index.[4] In addition, I compute these measures separately for ethnicity and religion, producing a total of four measures of diversity.

- The level of horizontal inequality within society. Again, I use two different measures of horizontal inequality. The first is a ratio of the average income of the respondent's group to the average income across the whole country. The second is the population-weighted coefficient of variation in the average incomes of all groups (GCov: see Mancini et al., 2008, for a discussion of this and other possible aggregate measures of horizontal inequalities [HIs]). As above, I compute these measures separately for ethnicity and religion.

At this point, it is important to note that the income data gathered by the WVS surveys are rather granular, with ten income bands rather than specific amounts collected. Moreover, these income bands are unlikely to match up well in different countries, so we must take the measures of HI produced here as broadly indicative, but not necessarily terribly accurate.

In addition to these core variables, I control for the following variables:

- Age of the respondent.
- Gender of the respondent, operationalised as a dummy variable scoring 1 for males and 0 for females.
- Personal income level, operationalised as the ratio between the respondent's income band and the average income band within the survey.
- Education index, operationalised as the age at which the respondent finished schooling.

I also include a series of dummy variables for each survey to hold for country specific effects, although these are not reported in the tables. Finally, I exclude members of groups that make up less than 10 per cent of the population, as the surveys are not large enough to produce representative group-level results for small groups.

Table 9.1 shows the first set of regression results, which focus on measures of demographic diversity but not on horizontal inequality. Model I presents a 'base' model in which the probability of expressing general trust in other people is regressed against the individual characteristics of age, gender, employment status, education level and income level. Higher levels of personal income are most strongly associated with higher levels of trust, and this result holds across the rest of the models. Age and the education index are also positively correlated with

Table 9.1   Demographic diversity and social trust

Variable	I	II	III	IV	V
Age	0.004***	0.004***	0.004***	0.002*	0.002***
	(0.001)	(0.001)	(0.001)	(0.001)	(0.001)
Gender	−0.011	−0.011	−0.011	0.005	0.003
[Dummy: Male respondent]	(0.028)	(0.028)	(0.028)	(0.023)	(0.023)
Personal Income Index	0.135***	0.141***	0.134***	0.179***	0.179***
	(0.023)	(0.023)	(0.023)	(0.02)	(0.02)
Employment Status	0.022	0.023	0.021	0.018	0.024
[Dummy: In employment]	(0.028)	(0.028)	(0.028)	(0.024)	(0.024)
Education Index	0.005**	0.005*	0.005**	0.009***	0.01***
	(0.002)	(0.002)	(0.002)	(0.002)	(0.002)
Size of Ethnic Group		0.283***			
		(0.092)			
Ethnic Fractionalisation			0.558*		
			(0.251)		
Size of Religious Group				0.018	
				(0.066)	
Religious Fractionalisation					−0.841***
					(0.208)
Constant	−1.268***	−1.386***	−1.599***	−1.42***	−0.918***
	(0.158)	(0.162)	(0.217)	(0.103)	(0.157)
N	34155	34155	34155	47374	47374
N. Country dummies	25	25	25	35	35
Pseudo-R²	0.089	0.089	0.089	0.076	0.076

Note: Standard errors in parenthesis; asterisks signify level of significance * < 5 per cent ** < 2.5 per cent *** < 1 per cent. Results for country dummies not reported.

social trust, and these results likewise hold largely constantly across the different models, although in some cases at weaker levels of significance. Models II and III introduce respectively two measures of ethnic diversity: the proportion of the respondent's ethnic group in the population as a whole, and the overall measure of ethnic fractionalisation. Models IV and V introduce the equivalent measures, which are based on religion instead of ethnicity. For ethnicity, the size of the respondent's ethnic group is strongly and positively correlated with social trust: members of groups that constitute a larger proportion of the population tend to have higher levels of general social trust. The level of ethnic fractionalisation of the population as a whole is also, surprisingly, positively correlated with social trust, although the coefficient is only marginally significant.

In contrast, the results do not show any significant relationship between the size of a respondent's religious group and the likelihood that he or she will express general levels of social trust (Model IV), but they do show a strong negative relationship between the overall level of religious fractionalisation in a society and the level of social trust.

The second set of results, reported in Table 9.2, replace the measures of social diversity with measures of ethnic and religious horizontal inequalities. Model VI includes a measure of the relative standing of the individual's ethnic group, in addition to his/her own economic standing; Model VII includes the overall measure of ethnic inequality determined by the GCov index; Model VIII includes both. Models IX to XI include the respective measures based on religious rather than ethnic

Table 9.2   Horizontal inequalities and social trust

Variable	VI	VII	VIII	IX	X	XI
Age	0.005***	0.004***	0.005***	0.002**	0.002***	0.002***
	(0.001)	(0.001)	(0.001)	(0.001)	(0.001)	(0.001)
Gender	−0.015	−0.011	−0.015	0.005	0.003	0.003
	(0.028)	(0.028)	(0.028)	(0.023)	(0.023)	(0.023)
Personal income index	0.172***	0.133***	0.170***	0.176***	0.178***	0.172***
	(0.025)	(0.023)	(0.025)	(0.020)	(0.020)	(0.020)
Employment status	0.023	0.025	0.026	0.019	0.023	0.023
	(0.028)	(0.028)	(0.028)	(0.024)	(0.024)	(0.024)
Education index	0.005**	0.006***	0.006***	0.009***	0.012***	0.012***
	(0.002)	(0.002)	(0.002)	(0.002)	(0.002)	(0.002)
Ethnic group income index	−0.294***		−0.303***			
	(0.071)		(0.071)			
Ethnic HI		−1.598***	−1.622***			
		(0.349)	(0.350)			
Religious group income index				0.380		0.589***
				(0.199)		(0.201)
Religious HI					−6.567***	−6.690***
					(0.509)	(0.511)
Constant	−1.277***	−0.958***	−0.963***	−1.408***	−1.173***	−1.163***
	(0.158)	(0.172)	(0.172)	(0.099)	(0.101)	(0.101)
N	34155	34155	34155	47374	47374	47374
N. Country dummies	25	25	25	35	35	35
Pseudo-R^2	0.089	0.089	0.090	0.076	0.079	0.079

groups. Of the control variables, age, personal income and education remain significant across all these models, as in the first set of models. When we consider ethnicity as the dividing factor, the relative wealth of a respondent's ethnic group is significantly and *negatively* correlated with social trust: while one's own wealth may translate into higher levels of trust, members of richer ethnic groups tend to express lower levels of trust. This may reflect insecurities felt by relatively wealthy economic minorities, such as the Chinese in much of Southeast Asia and the Lebanese in West Africa. Overall, levels of ethnic horizontal inequality are also strongly negatively correlated with levels of social trust (Model VII), and both these results remain significant when they are included together (Model VIII): irrespective of the overall economic standing of the respondent's own ethnic group, levels of social trust are lower where economic disparities between ethnic groups are higher. When we turn to look at religion as the dividing factor, the relative standing of a respondent's religious group, when entered by itself, is not significantly correlated with levels of social trust (Model IX), but the overall level of religious inequality in society is strongly and negatively correlated with levels of social trust, with a coefficient four times larger than the equivalent measure for ethnic horizontal inequalities (Model X). When both terms are included in one regression, however, the overall level of religious horizontal inequalities remains significantly negative, while the relative standing of the respondent's own religious group gains a significant coefficient. In contrast to the findings on ethnic groups, however, these results return a *positive* coefficient on the relative standing of the respondent's own group: while richer ethnic groups tend to express less social trust, richer religious groups tend to express more. In interpreting these results, however, it is important to bear in mind that the observed range of ethnic inequalities far exceeds the range of religious inequalities, with a maximum observed value of 0.59 for ethnic inequalities (South Africa in 1996) vis-à-vis 0.23 for religious inequalities (Singapore in 2002). Figure 9.1 maps out the predicted probability of the average respondent expressing social trust at different levels of ethnic and religious horizontal inequality only across the observed range of inequalities. It is clear from this that, even at relatively modest levels of horizontal inequality, religious disparity appears to be far more damaging to levels of social trust than ethnic disparities, although both have a clear negative impact.

Thus far, we have considered the extent to which ethnic and religious diversity and horizontal inequalities affect 'social trust' at the

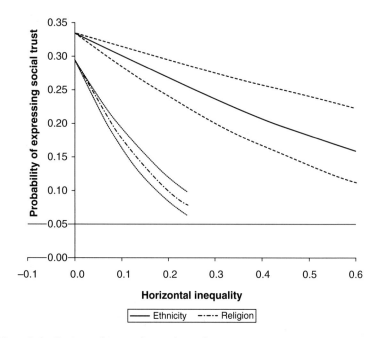

Figure 9.1   Horizontal inequality and social trust
Calculated from Models VII and X; country dummies all set to 0; all other control variables
held at mean value; dashed lines represent 95 per cent confidence interval.

individual level. We have found that both factors affect social trust
in the expected directions, but with slightly different inflections for
ethnicity and religion. For ethnicity, the size of a respondent's group
appears to be positively correlated with social trust, while the relative
wealth of the group is negative correlated. For religion, the size of group
is less relevant than the overall level of religious fractionalisation, and
there is some evidence that the relative wealth of the respondent's religious group may be positively correlated with social trust. Across both
definitions of group, however, the overall level of horizontal inequality in society is clearly and strongly negatively correlated with social
trust.

To get a picture of social capital rather than of what we have termed
here 'social trust', we can aggregate up to higher levels and explore the
impact of ethno-religious diversity and disparity at the national level.
I do this with a simple set of OLS regressions that regress each of the
national-level measures of diversity and disparity against the overall

level of trust within society, which we have taken as our indicator of social capital. I control only for the level of GDP per capita in the country. The results are presented in Table 9.3 and broadly confirm the individual-level results, although much more weakly. While all four ethno-religious diversity measures are negatively correlated with social capital, the levels of significance are generally quite low. The exception here is the measure of religious horizontal inequalities, which is highly significant in its negative correlation with social capital, although the level of religious fractionalisation is only weakly so: religiously diverse societies do not appear to have significantly lower levels of social capital than religiously homogenous societies in general; but, where these religious differences coincide with income differentials, there is a substantial reduction in social capital.

The results of these preliminary quantitative investigations, then, clearly suggest that there is an important relationship between civil society and horizontal inequalities in ethnically and religiously diverse societies, a relationship that revolves around a crucial issue of trust and social capital. In ethnically and, particularly, religiously unequal societies, people tend to have less trust in each other, and the level of trust exhibited by an individual is significantly affected by the relative standing of his or her ethnic and religious group, over and above his or her

Table 9.3   Ethno-religious diversity, horizontal inequality and social capital

	XII	XIII	XIV	XV
GDP per capita	0.0034**	0.0035**	0.0049***	0.0046***
[USD 000s PPP, 2000]	(0.0015)	(0.0015)	(0.0015)	(0.0015)
Ethnic Fractionalisation	−0.0976 (0.0553)			
Ethnic HI		−0.2763* (0.1505)		
Religious Fractionalisation			−0.1385* (0.0665)	
Religious HI				−0.8218*** (0.3253)
Constant	0.2647*** (0.0299)	0.2566*** (0.0267)	0.2777*** (0.0349)	0.2715*** (0.0294)
N	74	74	72	72
R^2	0.1208	0.1238	0.1559	0.1789

own individual position within society. This quantitative social capital-based approach to understanding the relationship between horizontal inequalities and civil society allows us to identify important general patterns; however, deployed in an exploratory way such as this one, it cannot offer firm conclusions about the nature of this relationship and about the ways in which it might contribute to ethnic mobilisation, and ultimately to group violence. To develop the tools to understand, rather than explain, the relationship between civil society, horizontal inequalities, and ethnic conflict, we turn to the role that civil society plays in giving 'social meaning' to inequality.

9.4   The social meaning approach: Civil society and the public interpretation of inequality

An alternative approach to exploring the relationship between horizontal inequalities and civil society would trace the link between civil society and horizontal inequalities in a more discursive vein, drawing more on the Gramscian tradition outlined above than on liberal accounts of civil society. Methodologically, the concern here is more with the second dimension of Giddens's double hermeneutic – the extent to which the societies we are studying themselves interpret inequality, and how this impacts upon the dynamics of mobilisation.

The basic observation that would ground this type of approach is that, by itself, 'inequality' – whether horizontal or vertical – *does* nothing; socioeconomic variables have no agency of their own. What is important is how inequality is *perceived* by actors with agency. Some studies of horizontal inequality have – either explicitly or implicitly – assumed that perceived inequalities broadly reflect 'objective' inequalities, and this is probably a reasonable assumption to make, especially when one is trying to unpick general trends using quantitative analysis. But when we are concerned with the social processes that translate 'objective' inequalities into mobilisation, conflict, and violence, the way in which meanings are attached to inequalities becomes of paramount importance, and it is here that civil society may play an important role.

It is important at this stage to dissect this notion of perceived inequalities. In particular, we can identify three dimensions of inequality perception relevant to political action:

- *Accuracy*. How far do perceptions of inequality reflect 'actual', objective inequalities? In many parts of Africa and elsewhere, for instance, it is typically assumed that much inequality is 'hidden' because those who have accumulated illicit wealth store it overseas. In contrast, in many parts of urban Southeast Asia, the popular perception of ethnic Chinese wealth may be exaggerated by the extent to which Chinese culture has a tendency towards overt displays of opulence during festival seasons. The 'accuracy' of popular perceptions of underlying inequalities is undoubtedly an important issue for scholars of horizontal inequalities to investigate, and may be particularly problematic for quantitative analyses, but will play a less important role in the account explored here.

- *Meaning.* Whatever the perceived level of inequalities – and whether or not these perceptions are 'accurate' – inequality can often be ascribed or interpreted in many different ways. To give a simplistic example, which might seem familiar to scholars of West Africa, imagine a country divided into two regions. The northern region is largely rural, arid, agricultural and (hence) poor. The southern region, on the other hand, is temperate, relatively urbanised and industrial. Moreover, each region is largely – though not exclusively – populated by different ethnic groups. There are obviously likely to be severe inequalities in this country, but the *meaning* attached to these inequalities may differ widely. They could be interpreted as primarily *regional* inequalities (between the North and South regions); as primarily *ethnic* inequalities (between the 'northern groups' and the 'southern groups'); or even as vertical/class inequalities. The apportionment of meaning to inequality is of crucial importance to social conflict for two reasons. First, it seems plausible – and this will be explored further below – to assert that the interpretation of inequalities and the attribution of a particular (horizontal) dimension to existing inequalities involve some degree of attribution of 'blame'. This 'blame' may be historical – a colonial system that preferred certain groups to others – or it may be contemporary – a government that practises deliberate social exclusion – but will surely have implications for the mobilisation of grievances. Secondly, and linked to this, the attribution of meaning to inequalities also inscribes different routes to 'correction'. In our (not too) fictional example, if prevailing inequalities are interpreted as primarily regional and primarily due to climatic differences that have favoured the cash-cropping South, corrective measures are most likely to be sought in relatively technocratic measures designed to promote investment and industrialisation in the impoverished North. In contrast, if the same inequalities are interpreted as ethnic and their cause is attributed to ethnic exclusion from government, then remedial measures might be sought in affirmative action and ethnic rebalancing in politics. Moreover, these two paths would clearly have major differences in terms of the kinds of mobilisational politics that might emerge to make these claims.

• *Tolerability.* The final dimension of perception that it is important to highlight is the degree to which inequality is seen as socially tolerable or, to put it another way, how much inequality can exist without provoking conflict.[5] Inequalities may persist with a given attributed meaning for a long period without provoking conflict if these inequalities are seen to be at a socially tolerable level. Similarly, as Stewart and colleagues (2008) note, if governments implement policies *aimed* at reducing horizontal inequalities, the tolerability of current inequalities may increase if there is an expectation of their reduction in the future. Conversely, the tolerability of horizontal inequalities may change rapidly in the other direction, particularly through the work of 'ethnic entrepreneurs' who seek to highlight and politicise politically dormant inequalities.

Having identified these different but interrelated dimensions of the social perceptions of inequality, what role might civil society play? Clearly, perceptions of inequality – accuracy, meanings and tolerability – are not likely to be homogenous within a society. Certain sections of the population may perceive the prevailing inequalities in ways that are very different from other sections, and these may or may not coincide with cultural or regional groupings. We have already alluded to some of the ways in which different actors may impact upon the perception of inequalities – ethnic entrepreneurs might seek to emphasise a particular dimension of inequality; states might enact policies aimed at reducing inequalities. Within the more Gramscian theory outlined above, civil society can be understood as the discursive realm beyond the state, in which precisely such meanings of inequality are contested.

In the remainder of this section I explore these issues further, using a case study of horizontal inequalities in share ownership and control of the economy more broadly, in Malaysia. Since 1969, Malaysia has implemented a series of affirmative action policies for the Malays and other indigenous groups (together termed the *bumiputera*, or 'sons of the soil') under the broad rubric of the New Economic Policy (NEP). While the NEP has addressed a wide range of economic and social horizontal inequalities, from educational and income disparities to employment in professional industries (Stewart, 2000; Brown, 2005; Stewart et al., 2008), one of the original targets – 30 per cent of total share ownership in the country for Malays and other *bumiputera* – has remained a totemic and highly politicised goal of the restructuring programmes. As we will see, different sectors of civil society have, in various ways, contested all three dimensions of this goal – the accuracy, the meaning, and the tolerability of inequitable share ownership.

At the time of independence, *bumiputera* investors accounted for barely 1.5 per cent of share capital ownership in the country, with Chinese Malaysian investors dominating domestic share ownership (Jomo, 2004: p. 11). As part of its package of targeted affirmative action measures, the NEP sought to achieve 30 per cent share ownership on the part of Malays and other *bumiputera* by the year 1990. This was to be achieved through two main mechanisms: companies wishing to list on the stock exchange or to issue additional share offerings were obliged to set aside a 30 per cent quota for *bumiputera* investors; and the government set up a number of '*bumiputera* trust agencies', notably Pemodalan Nasional Berhad (PNB, National Capital Ltd.), which bought and held stock in 'trust' for the *bumiputera* as a whole. By 1990, official figures suggested that progress had fallen far short of this target, with only around 20 per cent of share capital in *bumiputera* hands, around a quarter of this being held by the *bumiputera* trust agencies. Since then the figure has largely stagnated, and indeed it slipped somewhat following the Asian Financial Crisis in 1997. While the Ninth Malaysia Plan, which ran from 2006 to 2010, revised the target down to a goal of 20–25 per cent share ownership by 2010, the latest available figures from the Mid-Term Review of the Ninth Malaysia Plan (Malaysia, 2008) indicate that *bumiputera* ownership is still falling just short of this target.

Contestation over the meaning and accuracy of equity ownership disparities predates the NEP, however. A key civil society figure in the pre-NEP era who contested the ethnic dimension of economic control was the dissident left-wing intellectual and lawyer James Puthucheary. An Indian-born student activist and unionist in British-controlled Singapore and Malaya, Puthucheary was imprisoned by the British briefly in 1951, and then again, for a more extended period, in 1956. In this latter period of detention, Puthucheary wrote a book entitled *Ownership and Control in the Malayan Economy* (Puthucheary, 1960), which argued that interethnic disparities in control of the economy were something of a smoke-screen for the dominance of foreign capital, which was both iniquitous in itself and a barrier to genuine economic growth, due to its overwhelmingly extractive orientation. Puthucheary took issue with the dominant view that Malay farmers were ostracised from the market, leaving Chinese to dominate the local economy; he argued instead that the Malay peasants, and the Chinese and Indian labourers, who together formed the bulk of the working population, were integrated into the market economy, but on severely inequitable terms, which put them all on the margins of subsistence. Puthucheary did not deny that the class of middlemen and brokers who interceded between these subsistence workers and the colonial and foreign elites *were* predominantly Chinese, but he argued that this merely served to 'deflect attention away from more powerful and central actors [i.e. the colonial economic powers]' (Hirschman, 1998: p. 73). This level of colonial control, Puthucheary further argued, served to inhibit the development of 'secondary' industries in Malaya that might form the basis of more equitable growth strategies, because colonial control was geared towards extractive industries and profits were repatriated rather than reinvested in Malaya.

Puthucheary, then, can be seen as the first protagonist in a long, civil society-based struggle to contest both the *accuracy* and the *meaning* of horizontal inequalities in economic control in Malaysia. Moreover, in an analysis that has parallels with more recent arguments about share ownership, Puthucheary saw these two dimensions as being inherently linked: for him, the *accuracy* of population perceptions that the economy was controlled by Chinese was deeply flawed, and the *meaning* he read behind these inequalities had far more to do with diverting attention from the extractive nature of the colonial economy than with ethnic rivalries within Malaya.

Despite being released from prison in 1959 by Singapore's new prime minister, Lee Kuan Yew, Puthucheary remained sidelined from politics for many years; his opposition to the merger of Singapore and Malaya (along with the East Malaysian states of Borneo) to form Malaysia in 1963 saw him briefly imprisoned again, and then banned from entering Singapore until 1990. At the same time, the union-based left-oriented civil society activism of the 1950s was subjected to harassment and oppression by the departing British colonial powers and the new Malay[si]an government (Harper, 2000; Leong, 2000), leaving Puthucheary's critique to fade from mainstream view, although his book remained a first-year text for economics students in Malaysian universities for many years.

Instead, the 1960s witnessed the emergence in Malaysia of a civil society landscape characterised by ethnic segmentation (Brown, 2004;

Weiss, 2005). A key development here was the two 'Bumiputera Economic Congresses' held in 1965 and 1968. Hosted by the government Ministry of National and Rural Development – headed by Abdul Razak Hussain, who would later, as prime minister, implement the NEP – the congresses brought together a wide range of *bumiputera* civil and economic elites and gave voice to a growing sense among many Malays that the ethnic bargain of independence and the broadly *laissez-faire* policies of the first prime minister, Tunku Abdul Rahman, were allowing Malay economic participation to slip ever further behind. Within the framework proposed here, these congresses can be understood as primarily contesting the *tolerability* of existing horizontal inequalities, including in economic control, and led to concrete outcomes through the subsequent creation of an array of bodies, including Bank Bumiputera and the Majlis Amanah Rakyat (People's Trust Council), which would play important institutional roles in the implementation of the NEP.

These *bumiputera* congresses were, moreover, part of a broader civil and political movement among the Malays, often dubbed the Malay *ultras*, who numbered among their elite the rising political activist Mahathir Mohamed: his 1970 book *The Malay Dilemma* (Mahathir, 1970) was considered so provocative when it was published that it was banned until the author himself became prime minister in 1981. In many ways, *The Malay Dilemma* was similar in its ambit and ambitions to Puthucheary's *Ownership and Control*, although it was less heavily researched and more sociological in its orientation. Moreover, Mahathir's conclusions were often diametrically opposed to Puthucheary's. Whereas Puthucheary saw domestic horizontal inequalities in economic control as a distraction from colonial domination, Mahathir argued that these inequalities had emerged out of a deliberate policy of collusion between the colonial powers and the 'immigrant races', particularly the Chinese. But – and this was the controversial heart of his argument – Mahathir also placed part of the blame at the feet of the Malays themselves, arguing that their cultural inclination towards tolerance and non-confrontation (together with other purported cultural weaknesses, such as an alleged tendency towards in-breeding) had led them to allow themselves to be marginalised in this way. Whereas Puthucheary had linked the *accuracy* of dominant perspectives over horizontal inequalities with their historical and sociological *meaning*, Mahathir sought to link the *meaning* of horizontal inequalities with their *tolerability* in an explicit way. For Mahathir, the solution must be direct government intervention in the form of affirmative action. These ideas were also echoed in the less controversial call, launched by Senu

Abdul Rahman, another leading figure in the Malay *ultras*, for a *Revolusi Mental* ('mental revolution') among the Malays.

With the implementation of the NEP after the ethnic riots of May 1969, the Malay *ultras* entered the political mainstream, and *bumiputera* share ownership became a totemic goal of the affirmative action policy. Over the ensuing two decades, however, a resurgent critical voice emerged from a network of new civil society organisations and from actors who were committed to moving beyond ethnic politics in Malaysia. Key here was the NGO Aliran Kesedaran Negara (Aliran, Movement for National Consciousness), formed in the late 1970s by the prominent political scientist and Muslim intellectual Chandra Muzaffar. Through its regular publication, *Aliran Monthly*, Chandra and his collaborators attempted to revive the critique of Puthucheary, modified for the post-independence era. Their central claim was that the focus on ethnic disparities in capital ownership was still a distraction from more fundamental issues; but, instead of colonial domination, the hidden dimension of inequality they now saw was the accumulation of economic control in the hands of a small, politically linked elite of all ethnic groups. They argued that the 'trust agencies', purportedly accumulating capital for the *bumiputera*, 'benefitted [Malay elites] much more than the vast majority of Bumiputras for whom they are intended' (Chandra Muzaffar, 1989: p. 7) and that analysis of the distribution of share ownership in individual unit trust investment vehicles showed that share ownership was vastly skewed towards a small number of individuals. Like Puthucheary, Chandra and Aliran did not directly dispute the *accuracy* of prevailing horizontal inequalities in share ownership: they contested their *meaning*. Similar arguments were also put foward by the Harvard-trained Malaysian economist and civil society activist Jomo Kwame Sundaram in his doctoral thesis, published in 1986 as *A Question of Class: Capital, the State, and Uneven Development in Malaya* (Jomo, 1986). Both in his academic and in his civil society activities, however, Jomo went further than Chandra and Aliran, in contesting not only the meaning of horizontal inequalities in Malaysia, but also – with specific reference to the share ownership target – their *accuracy*. In a 1990 academic article, Jomo argued that the existing government figures that showed *bumiputera* share ownership had improved, but were still falling far short of the 30 per cent target underestimated actual *bumiputera* ownership (Jomo, 1990). This was because politically linked *bumiputera* investors were buying up capital through nominee companies and other locally controlled (unlisted) ones, which accounted for over 20 per cent of share ownership but were deemed non-*bumiputera* in the government's calculations.

Throughout the 1990s, these debates continued to reverberate around civil society, but were largely muted by the phenomenal economic growth of the decade and by the partial liberalisation of the NEP by the Mahathir administration. Jomo himself noted in 1995 that rapid economic growth had produced 'much more to share and less to complain about'.[6] Following the Asian Financial Crisis and the concomitant drop in *bumiputera* share ownership, however, the issue re-emerged in the early years of the new century. Malay politicians such as Khairy Jamaluddin, son-in-law of Mahathir's successor Abdullah Ahmad Badawi, began speaking of the need for a 'final push' to achieve the 30 per cent target. While the Ninth Malaysia Plan, as we have seen, revised down the target, it nonetheless refocused debate on the issue, and new civil society organisations pushed this debate in two very different directions.

In 2006, the Centre for Public Policy Studies (CPPS), a research bureau of the Asian Strategy and Leadership Institute (ASLI) think tank, published a report on the state of equity ownership in Malaysia. The report's authors argued that the methods used by the government to calculate share ownership were flawed because they were based on the par value of shares at the time of public offering, not at their current market value. This, they argued, distorted the calculations considerably, because much Malay wealth was invested in large old companies like Malayan Banking Berhad, which had market values tens or even hundreds of times greater than their par value. The CPPS hence reported re-estimated *bumiputera* corporate wealth based on the market value of publicly listed companies, and concluded that the correct figure was around 45 per cent, rather than the 20 per cent found in official government estimates. The report provoked huge public debate and ASLI, which was headed by Mahathir's son Mirzan Mahathir, disowned the report, prompting its chief author, Lim Teck Ghee, to resign.

While the CPPS report was the first major civil society initiative explicitly to dispute the *accuracy* of horizontal inequalities in corporate ownership, at around the same time another sector of civil society was mounting a renewed challenge to the *tolerability* of existing horizontal inequalities. Rather than originating in Malay discontent, however, this new initiative emerged out of an increasingly vocal ethnic Indian movement, arguing that the kinds of affirmative action measures afforded the Malays should be extended to ethnic Indians, including share ownership. In 2001, the Eighth Malaysia Plan had announced a target of 3 per cent equity ownership for Indians; but, amid an escalation in ethnic tensions surrounding the destruction of Hindu temples standing in the way of development projects, a new civil society organisation called the Hindu Rights Action Front (HINDRAF) was formed, which issued a petition of demands to address Indian marginalisation through explicit affirmative action policies. HINDRAF was able to mobilise massive Indian support in a series of demonstrations across the country, provoking a harsh government crackdown, including the detention of its leaders, without trial, under Malaysia's notorious Internal Security Act. From our perspective here, however, it is important to note that HINDRAF's agenda, in contrast to those of Aliran and of the other civil society movements discussed above, was in many ways a conservative one. Hence, for instance, a failed class action suit, brought by HINDRAF to the British courts seeking £4 trillion compensation for the descendants of indentured labourers, merely reinforced the 'official' Malay nationalist position that horizontal inequalities had their roots in an exploitative colonial policy, but sought to position Indians alongside Malays as the victims of this policy. HINDRAF did not seek to contest the *meaning* or *accuracy* of horizontal inequalities, merely to extend the remedial policies to Indians – that is, to contest the *tolerability* of Indian, as well as Malay, marginalisation. In doing so, however, it appears to have been remarkably successful; in the 2008 general elections, shortly after the HINDRAF saga, the government lost considerable Indian support – a swing of up to 80 per cent by some estimations (Brown, 2008) – and the leader of the main Indian party in the government coalition, Samy Vellu, lost his seat, while two of the HINDRAF leaders under detention without trial were elected to parliament.

In this section we have traced the ways in which civil society actors and organisations have contested the public understanding of horizontal inequalities in Malaysia, with a particular focus on the totemic issue of share capital and control of the economy more broadly. It is clearly beyond the scope of a preliminary case study such as this one to draw broader conclusions about the relationship between this discursive dimension of civil society and horizontal inequalities. One broad observation that can be made, however, is that, while contestations of the *meaning* of horizontal inequalities in Malaysia have in many ways been the most progressive, seeking to move political debate beyond narrow ethnic lines, civil society initiatives and movements that have contested the *tolerability* and *accuracy* of horizontal inequalities have had a far greater impact upon political debate within the country. Whether this pattern holds beyond Malaysia must be the subject of further investigations, but it is certainly a hypothesis that bears research, particularly in relation to the ways in which horizontal inequalities may contribute to the work of 'ethnic entrepreneurs' who deliberately seek to manipulate such inequalities for violent mobilisation.

9.5 Conclusions

This chapter has argued that the role of civil society in the dynamics of horizontal inequalities has been insufficiently studied, and has suggested two different approaches that such investigations might take: a 'social capital' approach, which would focus on the role of horizontal inequalities in impeding the emergence of trans-ethnic 'bridging' social capital, and a 'social meaning' approach, which would focus on the ways in which civil society plays an important role in contesting the social construction of horizontal inequalities. The chapter has gone on to provide two preliminary sketches of how these approaches might proceed in practice. The limitations of these initial studies are clear – neither has spoken directly to the issue of the link between horizontal inequalities and violent conflict. But they have provided indicative evidence that civil society *does* play an important role in both perspectives. Making the link with mobilisation to violent conflict must be the subject of further investigation.

Notes

1. This chapter cannot hope to provide a detailed historical analysis of the development of the concept. A number of existing works provide such analyses; especially useful are Cohen and Arato (1992); Ehrenberg (1999); and, for a more critical perspective, Kumar (1993).
2. In fact, Putnam's later writings accept this darker side to social capital.
3. I use the term 'associational groups' here to distinguish 'groups' in this sense from 'group' in the sense of ethnic groups.
4. This measure, effectively a Herfindahl concentration index, calculates the probability that two randomly chosen individuals from a population will belong to different groups.
5. This notion of the 'tolerability' of inequality draws on Arnim Langer's ideas about the 'bounds of acceptability' of horizontal inequality.
6. Quoted in *New Straits Times*, 21 March 1995.

References

Alexander, J.C. (1998) Citizen and Enemy as Symbolic Classification: On the Polarizing Discourse of Civil Society. In J.C. Alexander (ed.) *Real Civil Societies: Dilemmas of Institutionalization* (London: Sage).

Brown, G.K. (2004) Civil Society and Social Movements in an Ethnically-divided Country: The Case of Malaysia, 1981–2001. *PhD Thesis*, School of Politics, University of Nottingham.

Brown, G.K. (2005) 'Balancing the Risks of Corrective Surgery: The Political Economy of Horizontal Inequalities and the End of the New Economic Policy in Malaysia'. *CRISE Working Paper No. 20* (Oxford: Centre for Research on Inequality, Human Security and Ethnicity, University of Oxford).

Brown, G.K. (2008) 'Federal and State Elections in Malaysia, March 2008'. *Electoral Studies* 27 (4): 740–44.

Brysk, A. (2000) 'Democratizing Civil Society in Latin America'. *Journal of Democracy* 11 (3): 151–65.

Chandhoke, N. (1995) *State and Civil Society: Explorations in Political Theory* (New Delhi: Sage).

Chandra, M. (1989) 'Quotas and Percentages – the Solution?' *Aliran Monthly* 9 (4): 7–11.

Cohen, J.L., and A. Arato (1992) *Civil Society and Political Theory* (London: MIT Press).

Diamond, L. (1996) 'Towards Democratic Consolidation'. In L. Diamond and M.F. Plattner (eds) *The Global Resurgence of Democracy* (Baltimore, MD: Johns Hopkins University Press).

Ehrenberg, J. (1999) *Civil Society: The Critical History of an Idea* (New York: New York University Press).

Foley, M.W., and B. Edwards (1996) 'The Paradox of Civil Society'. *Journal of Democracy* 7 (6): 38–52.

Fukuyama, F. (1989) 'The End of History?' *The National Interest* 16: 3–18.

Fukuyama, F. (2001) 'Social Capital, Civil Society and Development'. *Third World Quarterly* 22 (1): 7–20.

Giddens, A. (1979) *Central Problems in Social Theory* (Berkeley, CA: University of California Press).

Gramsci, A. (1971) *Selections from the Prison Notebooks*. Translated by Q. Hoare and G. Nowell (London: Lawrence and Wishart).

Harper, T.N. (2000) *The End of Empire and the Making of Malaya* (Cambridge: Cambridge University Press).

Hechter, M. (1975) *Internal Colonialism: The Celtic Fringe in British National Development, 1536–1966* (Berkeley, CA: University of California Press).

Heyer, J., F. Stewart and R. Thorp (eds) (2002) *Group Behaviour and Development* (Oxford: Oxford University Press).

Hirschman, C. (1998) *'Ownership and Control of the Malaysian Economy* Revisited: A Review of Research in the 25 Years Since the Publication of J.J. Puthucheary's Classic'. In D.J. Puthucheary and K.S. Jomo (eds) *No Cowardly Past: James J. Puthucheary Writings, Poems, and Commentaries* (Kuala Lumpur: INSAN).

Horowitz, D.L. (1985) *Ethnic Groups in Conflict* (Berkeley, CA: University of California Press).

Inglehart, R., and C. Welzel (2005) *Modernization, Cultural Change, and Democracy: The Human Development Sequence* (Cambridge: Cambridge University Press).

Jomo, K.S. (2004) 'The New Economic Policy and Interethnic Relations in Malaysia'. *UNRISD Identities, Conflict and Cohesion Programme Paper* No. 7 (Geneva: United Nations Research Institute for Social Development).

Jomo, K.S. (1990) 'Whither Malaysia's New Economic Policy?' *Pacific Affairs* 63 (4): 469–99.

Jomo, K.S. (1986) *A Question of Class: Capital, the State and Uneven Development in Malaya* (Singapore: Oxford University Press).

Kaneko, Y. (2002) 'Malaysia: Dual Structure in the State-NGO Relationship'. In S. Shigetomi (ed.) *The State and NGOs: Perspectives from Asia* (Singapore: Institute of Southeast Asian Studies).

Kumar, K. (1993) 'Civil Society: An Inquiry into the Usefulness of an Historical Term'. *British Journal of Sociology* 44 (3): 375–95.

Laclau, E., and C. Mouffe (1985) *Hegemony and Socialist Strategy* (London: Verso).

Leong, Y.F. (2000) 'The Emergence and Demise of the Chinese Labour Movement in Colonial Malaya, 1920–1960'. In K.H. Lee and C.-B. Tan (eds) *The Chinese in Malaysia* (Shah Alam: Oxford University Press).

Mahathir, M. (1970) *The Malay Dilemma* (Singapore: Time Books).

Malaysia (2008) *Mid-Term Review of the Ninth Malaysia Plan* (Putrajaya: Economic Planning Unit).

Mancini, L., F. Stewart, and G.K. Brown (2008) 'Approaches to the Measurement of Horizontal Inequality'. In F. Stewat (ed.) *Horizontal Inequalities and Conflict: Understanding Group Violence in Multiethnic Societies* (Basingstoke: Palgrave Macmillan).

Norris, P. (2002) *Democratic Pheonix: Reinventing Political Activism* (Cambridge: Cambridge University Press).

Portes, A. (1998) 'Social Capital: Its Origins and Applications in Modern Sociology'. *Annual Review of Sociology* 24: 1–24.

Puthucheary, J.J. (1960) *Ownership and Control in the Malayan Economy: A Study of the Structure and Ownership of Control and its Effects on the Development of Secondary Industries and Economic Growth in Malaya and Singapore* (Singapore: Eastern Universities Press).

Putnam, R.D. (2000) *Bowling Alone: The Collapse and Revival of American Community* (New York: Simon and Schuster).

Putnam, R.D. (1995) 'Bowling Alone: America's Declining Social Capital'. *Journal of Democracy* 6 (1): 65–78.

Putnam, R.D. (1993) *Making Democracy Work: Civic Traditions in Modern Italy* (Princeton, NJ: Princeton University Press).

Rothstein, B. (2003) 'Social Capital, Economic Growth and the Quality of Government: The Causal Mechanism'. *New Political Economy* 8 (1): 49–71.

Stewart, F. (ed.) (2008) *Horizontal Inequalities and Conflict: Understanding Group Violence in Multiethnic Societies* (Basingstoke: Palgrave Macmillan).

Stewart, F. (2000) 'Crisis Prevention: Tackling Horizontal Inequalities'. *Oxford Development Studies* 28 (3): 245–62.

Stewart, F., G.K. Brown and A. Langer (2008) 'Policies Towards Horizontal Inequalities'. In F. Stewart (ed.) *Horizontal Inequalities and Conflict: Understanding Group Violence in Multiethnic Countries* (Basingstoke: Palgrave Macmillan).

Tan, B.K., and B. Singh (1994) *Uneasy Relations: The State and NGOs in Malaysia* (Kuala Lumpur: Gender and Development Programme, Asian and Pacific Development Centre).

Thorp, R., F. Stewart, and A. Heyer (2005) 'When and How Far is Group Formation a Route out of Chronic Poverty?' *World Development* 33 (6): 907–20.

Tocqueville, A. de (1954) *Democracy in America*, Vol. 1 (New York: Vintage).

Tocqueville, A. de (1955) *The Old Regime and the French Revolution* (New York: Doubleday Anchor).

Uphoff, N.T., and C.M. Wijayaratna (2000) 'Demonstrated Benefits from Social Capital: The Productivity of Farmer Organizations in Gal Oya, Sri Lanka'. *World Development* 28 (11): 1875–90.

Varshney, A. (2002) *Ethnic Conflict and Civic Life: Hindus and Muslims in India* (New Haven, CT: Yale University Press).

Verma, V. (2002) *Malaysia: State and Civil Society in Transition* (Boulder, CO: Lynne Rienner).

Weiss, M. (2005) *Protest and Possibilities: Civil Society and Coalitions for Political Change in Malaysia* (Stanford, CA: Stanford University Press).

White, G. (1994) 'Civil Society, Democratization and Development: Clearing the Analytical Ground'. *Democratization* 1: 375–90.

Whitehead, L. (1997) 'Bowling in the Bronx: The Uncivil Interstices Between Civil and Political Society'. In R. Fine and S. Rai (eds) *Civil Society: Democratic Perspectives* (London: Frank Cass).

Zuern, E. (2000) 'The Changing Roles of Civil Society in African Democratisation Processes'. In H. Soloman and I. Liebenberg (eds) *Consolidation of Democracy in Africa: A view from the South* (Aldershot: Ashgate).

10
Horizontal Inequalities and Militancy: The Case of Nigeria's Niger Delta

Arnim Langer and Ukoha Ukiwo

10.1 Introduction

The upsurge of violent conflicts in the early 1990s unexpectedly animated academic and policy interest in social cohesion and in political stability. Given the political, humanitarian and economic costs of violent conflict, most studies on intra-state conflicts have focused on the causes of such violence (see Van de Goor et al., 1996). A huge range of perspectives has emerged in the field of conflict analysis, but the new political economy approach that focuses on the economic dimension of civil war has become particularly prominent (see Berdal and Malone, 2000; Collier and Hoeffler, 2000). The absence of superpower support for rebel groups has of necessity strengthened the tendency for rebellion to be self-financing (see Sherman and Ballentine, 2003). Scholars and policy-makers have explored the role of feasibility and opportunity costs at the onset of conflicts. The 'greed' of rebel leaders and of their recruits is considered to be the central explanatory variable, because a variety of factors – such as the availability of 'lootable' natural resources, low commodity prices and the presence of an army of unemployed youths – are shown to have a positive correlation with the onset of civil wars (see Le Billon, 2000; Humphreys and Weinstein, 2008; Nillesen and Verwimp, 2009). This argument triggered the so-called greed and grievance debates between scholars who focus on the economic interests of rebel leaders and combatants, and scholars who focus on the political, social, economic and cultural grievances of identity-based groups.

One of the emergent perspectives that provide fresh insights into the role of grievance in violent group mobilisation is the horizontal inequality perspective pioneered by Frances Stewart. 'Horizontal inequality' refers to inequalities between culturally defined (and politically salient) groups (see Stewart, 2000). Unlike the greed-based perspective, which focuses mainly on economic factors and on individuals, the horizontal inequalities perspective is multidimensional and its level of analysis is the group. Stewart's work has inspired several studies which explore the linkages between the presence and persistence of horizontal inequalities and the likelihood of conflict and its dynamics (see Brown and Langer, 2010).

This chapter is the product of one such study. It explores the role of horizontal inequalities in militancy in the Niger Delta, which has mostly been attributed to the greed of elites and youths in the region and to the emergence of a war economy based on 'blood oil' (see Reno, 2000; Ikelegbe, 2005; Collier, 2007; Oyefusi, 2007; Watts 2008; Asuni, 2009). The study is based on surveys which elicited the views of combatants and civilians on the causes of militancy in the region. By militancy we refer to the activities of non-state armed actors who use guerrilla tactics to destabilise the state and disrupt strategic production activities in order to advance specific political demands on behalf of, or in the name of, a specific group. We show that militancy in the region appears to be driven by perceptions of horizontal inequalities between the people of the oil-producing Niger Delta and other major ethnic groups in Nigeria.

The Niger Delta has about 30 million residents and comprises nine out of the thirty-six states in the Nigerian Federation. The marshy areas of the Niger Delta are extremely important for Nigeria because oil and gas, which currently account for approximately 40 per cent of Gross Domestic Product (GDP) and 80 per cent of public revenue, are derived from the region. The region is also home to Nigeria's southern minority ethnic groups, notably Ijaw, Edo, Ibibio, Urhobo, Itsekiri, Isoko, Ikwerre and Ogoni. Since the early 1990s, most of the ethnic groups have protested over the share of oil revenues that is allotted to the region and demanded more representation in the federal government. The groups have historically attributed poor representation and poor dividends from oil to their minority status in the Nigerian polity, which is dominated by the three major ethnic groups (see Osaghae, 1995).

The first armed groups in the region were formed to defend ethnic and communal groupings in violent conflicts between neighbouring communities and confrontations with Nigerian security agents (see, for example, Osaghae, 1998; Ibeanu, 1999; and Ibeanu and Luckham, 2006). These ethnic militias have transformed into non-ethnic and pan-regional armed groups such as the Movement for the Emancipation of the Niger Delta (MEND), which conducted sporadic attacks on strategic oil infrastructure and military targets between 2005 and 2009. In 2009 the federal government, which had incurred huge losses in revenues as a result of the activities of the militant groups, granted amnesty to leaders and members of the groups (see Ukiwo, 2007; Ukiwo, 2010).

The chapter proceeds as follows. The next section discusses the survey methodology as well as some socioeconomic and demographic background information on the respondents to both surveys. In Section 10.3 we present the results of both surveys on key questions intended to identify the underlying causes of the widespread violence and militancy in the Niger Delta. In the final section we draw some conclusions and discuss the implications of the findings of the survey.

10.2   Survey methodology and background of respondents

The assumptions of a particular 'theory' of conflict usually influence the methodology chosen to investigate that theory and the associated risks and biases. Thus, for instance, most studies that assume a greed 'model' of group mobilisation tend to focus on the socioeconomic characteristics (such as employment status and educational attainment) of militia members or would-be members. The tendency for uneducated, unemployed and unmarried youths to enlist in militia groups is then usually seen as evidence of the predominant role of the 'greed' factor in the mobilisation process. Studies by scholars who take a grievance-based approach display a similar methodological bias in that they often focus exclusively on group grievances and inequalities, thereby ignoring entirely, or at least neglecting, individuals' personal incentive structures and motivations for joining militia groups.

In the growing literature on the competing greed and grievance explanations of armed conflicts there are few social surveys that target both individual combatants and members of their communities. An exception is Ikelegbe's study of Egbesu Boys in the Niger Delta, which focused on ten militia members and opinion leaders in the community (see Ikelegbe, 2006). The tendency is for analysts to target individual recruits (see Humphreys and Weinstein, 2008) or communities (see Osaghae et al., 2007; Oyefusi, 2007; Nillesen and Verwimp, 2009). By collecting and analysing survey data among both demobilised militants and ordinary citizens, we demonstrate that the horizontal inequalities perspective is able to offer a rich insight into the causes of conflicts by reflecting both individual and group positions. By targeting both militants and community members, we aim to understand better the social context of militancy, which may be obscured in a restrictive focus on individual militants. Moreover, surveying the rank-and-file and ordinary citizens helps us to avoid the elitist focus of previous research on conflict, which tends to reinforce the 'elite manipulation' thesis. This methodology is particularly significant, because an important concern for scholars using the horizontal inequalities perspective is to transcend state-centric analysis by bringing civil society back into the analysis of violent group mobilisation (see Brown and Langer, 2010).

We conducted two surveys in Rivers State in August 2009: one among a group of demobilised militants (referred to subsequently as the Former Militants Survey); and one among ordinary citizens in four communities in and around Port Harcourt, the state's capital (the Community Survey). Rivers State was chosen because it is one of the states with the highest oil production, has been a rallying point for minority agitations and has witnessed some of the worst incidents of armed violence. In addition, most of the international oil corporations and service companies have their headquarters or major operational bases in Port Harcourt. Importantly, Rivers State was also one of the first Niger Delta states to commence a disarmament and rehabilitation programme for 'repentant' militants. Under the programme, militants who handed in their weapons were admitted to a rehabilitation camp run by the Rivers State Social Rehabilitation Committee.

A total of 100 demobilised militants were interviewed in the Former Militants Survey. Security was the principal reason for targeting demobilised militants rather than active ones. There were serious risks involved in visiting the militia camps following the escalation of hostilities between Nigeria's armed forces and militia groups from March 2009. The questionnaires were not administered inside the rehabilitation camps due to our inability to secure official permission for this, but at two alternative venues. About half of the questionnaires were administered at the Government House Chapel in Port Harcourt following weekly prayer meetings organised by a faith-based organisation who worked with demobilised militants. The remaining interviews were conducted at weekly welfare meetings, which were attended by a large group of demobilised militants.

It is important to note here that only a very few former militants declined to be interviewed; the vast majority were quite keen to be included in the study, as long as confidentiality was guaranteed. In order to ensure that our largely pragmatic decision to interview former militants after two different types of gatherings did not introduce a selection bias into our results, we systematically compared the answers of respondents interviewed at both venues. We found no systematic differences of opinion between the two groups, and therefore we assumed that our interview selection strategy did not result in any (observable) selection bias.

The Community Survey was conducted in the following four communities: Borokiri in Port Harcourt Local Government Area (LGA), Okrika in Okrika LGA, Degema and Harris Town in Degema LGA and Baen in Khana LGA. All four communities were selected for the study because they have served as key recruiting grounds and/or operational bases for the main militia groups in Rivers State. The four locations were also selected to reflect the ethno-regional structure of the state.

Borokiri is a lower-class waterside neighbourhood in Port Harcourt and a major recruiting ground for several street gangs and militia groups, such as the Outlaws, the Icelanders and the Greenlanders. It has also been a major battleground between rival militia groups. Okrika has experienced several armed conflicts involving militia groups. The island is also the base of the Niger Delta Volunteer Service (NDVS), Icelanders and the Bush Boys militias. Harris Town and Degema in Degema LGA are recruiting grounds for the Niger Delta Strike Force (NDSF), led by Prince Farah Dagogo. Baen in Khana LGA has also been an important recruitment ground for the Gberesaakoo Boys and Seresibra militia groups (see Joab-Peterside, 2007; Naagbanton, 2007).

In each of the selected communities, fifty questionnaires were administered to individuals who were at least 18 years old. Both purposive and random sampling methods were adopted in the Community Survey. The purposive sampling was used to guarantee equal representation to both genders in the survey. A random sampling method was adopted for the selection of households as well as of respondents within households.

Although the Community and Former Militants surveys dealt with many of the same issues, the questionnaires were not exactly the same. For instance, while the Former Militants questionnaire had a number of questions on the recruitment process, on life inside the militia and on demobilisation and reintegration issues, these questions were obviously absent from the Community questionnaire. In addition, some issues, such as the perceived causes of militancy, were approached somewhat differently in the two surveys. Thus, while in the Community questionnaire respondents were asked directly about the main causes of the widespread violence and militancy in the Niger Delta, in the Former Militants questionnaire this issue was approached by asking respondents their main reasons for joining a militia group.

10.3 Discussion of survey results

10.3.1 Background characteristics

This section provides some general background information on respondents to both surveys. The Community Survey covered 200 respondents with an equal number of males and females as a result of our 50–50 gender quota. A large majority of respondents were between 18 and 40 years old (68 per cent) and 60 per cent of them had one or more children. The respondents' educational attainment was relatively high. While 38 per cent of respondents had completed secondary schooling, 37 per cent had also attended post-secondary education. These figures seem surprisingly high in a country where the average school life expectancy was eight years in 2004 (see UNDP, 2006). However, the national average is not representative of the high educational attainments in some regions, especially in the South. Most respondents in the Community Survey were employed. Eleven per cent of respondents said they were unemployed and 16 per cent said they were students.

The most common occupations were: civil servant (14 per cent), businessperson – either in a company or self-employed (14 per cent) – teacher (7 per cent), farmer/fisherman (6 per cent) and trader/hawker/vendor (5 per cent). Only 1.5 per cent of the respondents worked in the oil industry. Apart from farming and fishing, the proportion of respondents from each occupational group was consistent with demographic trends. Farmers were poorly represented in the survey because interviews were conducted in the daytime, when most farmers were on their farms. It is worthy of note that the occupational grouping with the lowest number of respondents (1.5 per cent) was that of oil workers. This is not surprising, because the failure of the oil industry to provide employment to youths has been a factor in most anti-state and anti-oil company mobilisations in the region.

To determine socioeconomic status, respondents were further asked to indicate how often in the past year they or anyone in their family had gone without certain necessities, such as enough food to eat, medical treatment, money for rent or money for school fees (Table 10.1). We can roughly distinguish three socioeconomic groups: a relatively well-to-do group of 20–25 per cent of respondents (those who declared that they had 'never' gone without these things in the past year); a poor group of 45–50 per cent of respondents (those who declared they had gone without these things 'once or twice' or 'sometimes' in the past year); and a very poor group of 20–25 per cent of respondents (those who declared that they had gone without these things 'many times' or 'always' in

Table 10.1   Frequency with which respondents of the Community Survey had to go without the following in the past year (per cent)

	Never	Just once or twice	Sometimes	Many times	Always
Enough food to eat	24.6	15.8	37.4	17.2	3.0
Medical treatment	24.6	16.3	30.5	20.7	3.9
Money to pay rent	52.2	7.4	19.2	11.8	3.9
School expenses*	21.3	20.6	35.3	19.1	3.7

*Only respondents with children were asked this question.

the past year). These results are largely consistent with existing figures showing that the Niger Delta region has the highest level of self-assessed poverty in the country (see World Bank 2008).

In the Former Militants Survey a large majority of respondents were male (81 per cent) and relatively young (78 per cent of respondents were between 20 and 30). Most of them had never been married (76 per cent) and had no children of their own (66 per cent). The educational attainment level of respondents in the Former Militants Survey was somewhat lower than in the Community Survey. In particular, while 57 per cent of former militants had completed secondary school, the corresponding figure in the Community Survey represented 75 per cent. The survey also showed that most respondents grew up in poverty. This is illustrated by Figure 10.1, which shows the frequency with which respondents had to go without the items outlined above – enough food to eat, medical treatment, money to pay rent and money to pay for education – during childhood. We should stress, however, that these responses should not be taken entirely at face value: memories of childhood may not be very accurate, and it is also possible that the former militants painted a gloomy picture to justify their decision to join militant groups. It is nonetheless important that the former militants thought they faced severe hardships as children, as perception is highly significant in group mobilisation.

10.3.2   Perceived causes of militancy in the Niger Delta

Let us now turn to those questions that dealt with the perceived causes of militancy in the Niger Delta. In the Community Survey, respondents

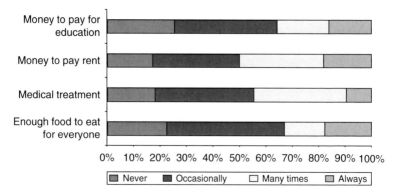

Figure 10.1 Frequency with which respondents to the Former Militant Survey had to go without particular items during childhood

were asked to indicate to what extent they thought that different potential factors had contributed to the emergence of militias in the region. Figure 10.2 shows their responses. It is noteworthy that most respondents (more than 80 per cent) felt horizontal inequalities in the form of socioeconomic 'marginalisation' and 'unfair distribution of oil resources' were the major causes of militancy in the region. More than 70 per cent of respondents also identified environmental pollution, corruption and the high rate of youth unemployment as factors. Moreover, a considerable proportion of respondents said the 'greed' and the 'selfish interests' of elites and militants were causes of militancy in the Niger Delta. The results clearly indicate the complexity of militancy in the Niger Delta, in common with armed conflicts elsewhere, and the limitations of the greed and grievance perspectives.

Not only did most respondents in the Community Survey think that horizontal inequalities were the underlying causes of militancy in the region, but a substantial number of them also had similar grievances themselves. This is illustrated in Figure 10.3, which presents respondents' answers to the three questions aimed at eliciting views on some dimensions of horizontal inequalities. The results of the first question indicate that a majority of respondents felt that the Niger Delta region was insufficiently represented at the federal level in comparison to other regions. The results of the second question indicate that most respondents also felt that their region was seriously disadvantaged in socioeconomic terms in comparison to other regions. This finding is clearly consistent with respondents' self-assessment of their socioeconomic situation, discussed above. The results of the third

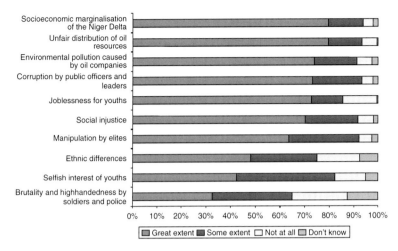

Figure 10.2 Perceived causes of violence and militancy in the Niger Delta according to respondents in the Community Survey

question suggest that a large majority of respondents thought that their region's socioeconomic and political marginalisation was the result of discrimination.

In order to determine how former militants perceived the causes of militancy, they were presented with a list of fifteen reasons why people might be likely to enlist in militant groups and asked to specify how important each of the reasons was in their decision to join. The results are shown in Figure 10.4. As in the Community Survey, most of the respondents mentioned horizontal inequality-related issues – such as 'unfair distribution of oil resources', 'socioeconomic marginalisation of your community' and 'political exclusion of your community' – as key motivating factors in the decision to enlist in militias. Respondents' discontent with their personal socioeconomic situation (in particular with being unemployed) was also a very important reason for deciding to join a militia group. With respect to the latter, it is noteworthy that more than 80 per cent of the respondents in the Former Militants Survey were unemployed at the time they joined a militia group. Unsurprisingly, therefore, when asked to rate their living conditions in the year before joining a militia group, more than 70 per cent of respondents said they were 'bad' (35 per cent) or 'very bad' (36 per cent). Only 9 per cent of former militants rated their living conditions as 'good' in the year before they joined a militia.

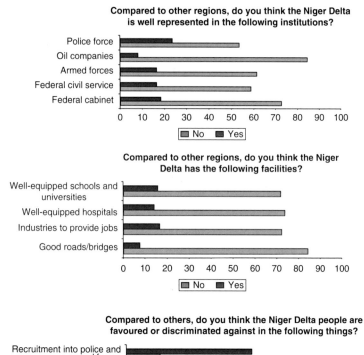

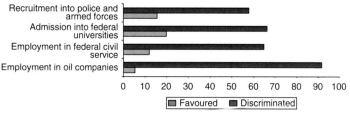

Figure 10.3   Perceptions of horizontal inequalities by respondents in the Community Survey

While 'individualistic' motives, such as discontent with one's personal socioeconomic situation, played an important role in respondents' decision to join a militia group, only a relatively small proportion of respondents (about 20 per cent) admitted that obtaining material and non-material benefits for themselves was a very important reason for joining a militia group. Again, although group motives were more prominent, a considerable percentage of the respondents (between 40 and 70 per cent) admitted to being motivated by a range of so-called 'individualistic' reasons. It seems, however, that some of these

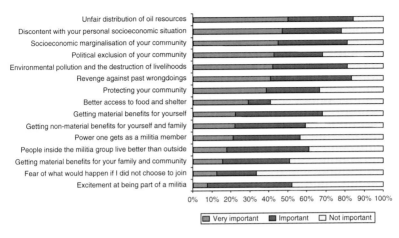

Figure 10.4   Reasons for joining a militia group (Former Militants Survey)

expectations were not met, as most of the former militants interviewed said their living conditions inside a militia group were generally not much better than the conditions they faced before joining. We shall return shortly to some of the apparent contradictions between group and individual motives.

10.3.3   Citizens' perceptions of militia groups and their activities

In order to determine how ordinary citizens perceived militia members, respondents were asked to choose between the following two statements: (a) 'Militants are heroes fighting for the interest of the Niger Delta'; and (b) 'Militants are criminals using the resource control issue as a cover to get unearned money.' As Figure 10.5 shows, about 41 per cent of respondents considered militants to be 'Niger Delta heroes', while 50 per cent perceived them as 'greedy' criminals. Thus, although more than 80 per cent of respondents perceived horizontal inequality-related issues and grievances to be very important causes of the problem of militancy and violence in the region, only about 41 per cent thought the militants were actually fighting for the interests of the Niger Delta. It is important to understand the context of this apparent inconsistency. We suggest that the 50/41 per cent split among respondents shows that, while the community identifies with the goals of the militant groups, it disapproves of their activities. In fact, given the bad press the militants were getting

242

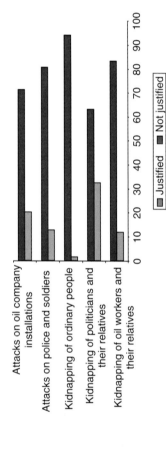

Figure 10.5 Perceptions of militia activities by respondents in the Community Survey

at the time of the survey, it is significant that up to 41 per cent of community members interviewed still considered them to be heroes.

This point is reinforced by survey results which show that, although 41 per cent of respondents in the Community Survey considered militants to be 'Niger Delta heroes', a large majority of respondents (78 per cent) generally disapproved of them. In particular, when asked how they perceived the militia groups, a large majority of respondents in the Community Survey said they had either a 'negative' (40 per cent) or a 'very negative' (38 per cent) view of them. Moreover, 40 per cent of respondents in the Community Survey also admitted to fearing militia groups, 24 per cent said that they were angered by them and 13 per cent said that they distrusted them. Again, only a small proportion of respondents expressed more positive attitudes towards them.

Most of the respondents in the Community Survey also disapproved of the strategies and methods the militants employed. While about 38 per cent said that militants were justified in using violence, more than 58 per cent considered the use of violence 'not justified at all'. Figure 10.5 shows which violent activities the respondents in the Community Survey disapproved of the most. While these results reaffirm a general disapproval of the use of violence by the militia groups, there were some notable differences between the perceived acceptability of different violent activities conducted by or associated with militias in the Niger Delta. Thus, while only a very small number of respondents in the Community Survey thought that militants were justified in kidnapping ordinary people, more than 30 per cent of respondents thought that militias were justified in kidnapping politicians and their relatives in order to achieve their goals. This result sheds further light on the community's exasperation with political leaders, which is reflected in the fact that up to 95 per cent of respondents said that 'corruption by politicians and leaders' was to 'a great extent' – or at least to 'some extent' – a cause of militancy (see Figure 10.2).

A considerably lower proportion of respondents (about 12 per cent) considered the kidnapping of oil workers and their relatives to be a justifiable action. Attacks on oil installations had a higher level of acceptability among citizens (20 per cent). This response suggests that, among those respondents who sanctioned the use of violence, there was a clear perception of who was responsible for the horizontal inequalities and thus of who would be the likely targets of violence.

In line with the overall negative perceptions of militia groups and their activities, only 8 per cent of respondents in the Community Survey had considered joining a militia themselves (among respondents younger than 30 years, this proportion was 10 per cent).

It is worthwhile noting that, while 60 per cent of former militants thought that communities generally perceived the militia groups in 'negative' (45.8 per cent) or 'very negative' (14.6 per cent) terms, 40 per cent still thought that communities had a 'positive' (32.3 per cent) or even 'very positive' (7.3 per cent) view of the militia groups. Given that almost 80 per cent of respondents in the Community Survey expressed negative attitudes towards the militia groups, it is evident that a substantial proportion of former militants underestimated the extent of public distrust and negative feeling directed at them. Within their own family circle, however, a substantially higher proportion of former militants were aware of the negative attitudes towards militias. Consequently, only 15 per cent of former militants said that their membership of a militia group was a source of pride to their families. This finding is significant, as it suggests that the former militants were inspired more by community expectation than by family and therefore by personal interests.

In line with the negative views towards militia groups found among community members, community members appear to have given very little support to the militants. In particular, 87 per cent of respondents in the Community Survey said that their community had given 'very little' (20.0 per cent) or 'none or almost no support whatsoever' (67.2 per cent) to the militias. While this response may reflect the fact that community members wanted to be 'politically correct', in line with the government's stance on militants, it is noteworthy that the former militants largely confirmed that they had received very little community support.

This finding contrasts with that of Ikelegbe (2005), who found that militants enjoyed extensive support from their communities. A number of reasons can be suggested for these different results. First, Ikelegbe's study was based on a survey of a particular ethnic militia, the Egbesu Boys. Their strong community support stemmed from the fact that Egbesu was embedded in Ijaw traditions of vigilantism and defence. Secondly, while the governing elite in Bayelsa State (where Ikelegbe's survey was conducted) saw the militants as 'heroes' at the time, the present governing elite in Rivers State considers militants to be 'villains and criminals'.

10.3.4 Reasons for demobilising and long-term solutions to the Niger Delta conflicts

In order to get a better understanding of the causes and possible solutions to the problem of violence and militancy in the Niger Delta, the former militants were asked why they had decided to leave their militia groups. The three most important reasons were: the federal government's efforts to resolve the crisis; hope for a better future outside a militia group; and the offer of amnesty. Furthermore, while a minority of former militants (18 per cent) said that under certain circumstances they might rejoin their militia group, about half of them (50 per cent) said that they would not consider rejoining. The circumstances that could influence demobilised militants' decision to rejoin their militia groups included a worsening of the injustices against the Niger Delta (27 per cent), failure of the amnesty deal (15 per cent), a military invasion of the region by Nigeria's armed forces (11 per cent) and a worsening of the individual's personal socioeconomic conditions (11 per cent). With regard to the latter issue, it is noteworthy that most respondents (about 66 per cent) considered life after leaving their militia group to be 'the same' (28 per cent) or 'better' (38 per cent) than on the inside. Only 11 per cent of former militants thought that their life was better when they were active militants.

Both questionnaires also elicited respondents' views on how they thought the Niger Delta crises could be resolved. It is interesting to note that almost 80 per cent of respondents to both surveys thought that the provision of jobs for youths was the most important measure that could be undertaken to resolve the militancy problem in the Niger Delta. An improvement in social amenities was another measure that many respondents in both surveys thought could contribute to a resolution of the problems. Giving the Niger Delta a higher share of oil revenues and improving the region's democratic governance performance were only considered to be important measures by respondents in the Community Survey (20–30 per cent), and not generally by former militants.

It is also significant that more respondents in the Community Survey than in the Former Militants Survey considered youth employment to be a solution. In addition, the fact that very few respondents in the Community Survey suggested a security solution, notably arrest and prosecution of militants, seems to contradict the widespread perception among them that the militants are 'criminals'.

It is apposite at this juncture to comment on some of the apparently inconsistent and contradictory findings of the survey. Although a large majority of respondents to the Community Survey thought that horizontal inequalities were very important causes for the widespread militancy in the Niger Delta, 42 per cent also perceived the 'self-interest of youths' to play a major role in this respect. Some interpretations can be adduced for this contradiction.

First, we might attribute it to the now standard classification of armed groups in the region into 'genuine militants' and 'criminals'. Since the question was asked in broad terms and did not specify particular groups, it is plausible that the contradictory response reflected the effort of respondents to incorporate both categories into their answers. Government officials and leaders of civil society have been divided on how to describe militants. Debates over this classification started when Governor Rotimi Amaechi of Rivers State described militants as 'armed robbers' and 'criminals'. Chief E. K. Clark, a prominent Ijaw leader and former federal minister of education, warned against such a classification by noting that 'not all militants are criminals'. Since then, attempts have been made to distinguish between 'genuine militants' and 'criminals'.[1] The labelling is often made loosely, without much rigour, the same people using different labels at different times. For instance, Governor Amaechi has always offered a more social and political interpretation of militancy when his audiences were the oil companies, the international community and federal authorities.[2] The obvious reason for his use of this discourse is the desire to impress on such audiences their culpability and thus their responsibility in the phenomenon of militancy in the region. However, government officials have increasingly taken a stronger stance against militants because the latter have targeted politicians and public figures and their activities have resulted in a loss of revenues to some states and local government councils.[3]

Secondly, it is plausible that the response reflects the respondents' views that there have been multiple motives at different phases of the conflict. Thirdly, the response could also signal a rejection of the *approaches* adopted by militant groups: the survey showed that, while respondents generally believe that the region has been marginalised, they do not identify with the approach adopted by militants to overturn that marginalisation. Frequent reports of involvement by militants in commercial hostage-taking and illegal theft of oil have estranged the public from the militias. This is because some of the activities of the militants have had negative short-term consequences for the livelihood of communities. The blow-out of pipelines leads to environmental pollution and endangers the subsistence of farmers and fishermen. Incessant disruption of oil production has forced some companies to shut down or downsize, aggravating the unemployment situation in many communities. This also explains why a majority of respondents in the Community Survey identified with group grievances as underlying causes of militancy, but had a negative attitude toward militants and admitted giving them little or no support.

Fourthly, it is also plausible that respondents were influenced by the official labelling of militants as 'criminals' in the state, but were at the same time conscious of the causal linkages between the behaviour of militants and perceptions of marginalisation and social injustices. This possibility is supported by the solutions to militancy preferred by community members. It is instructive that most respondents recommended socio-political and economic solutions rather than legal and security solutions to militancy.

Finally, it is possible that the contradictory response is a reflection of what some scholars consider the difficulty of disentangling grievance or greed-based motivations (see Murshed, 2002; Murshed and Tadjoeddin, 2007) and ascertaining good proxies. A case in point here is unemployment, which is often presented as an individualistic motivation for enlistment into armed groups. In the Niger Delta, however, youth unemployment is considered a symptom of marginalisation and is strongly resented, because of the perception that available jobs have been taken up by non-indigenes. The high level of unemployment among youths in the richly endowed Niger Delta is considered unacceptable and is a source of both individual grievance and community grievance (see Ukiwo, 2005). This probably explains why a majority of the respondents in the community survey who described militants as greedy 'criminals' recommended youth employment and other socio-political initiatives instead of security and legal solutions to militancy.

10.4 Concluding remarks

Violent conflict is a complex phenomenon, which cannot be fully understood through the application of perspectives that offer monocausal explanations. The contribution of the horizontal inequalities perspective to the understanding of the nexus between conflict and development is that its multidimensional focus facilitates an appreciation of the interconnected factors associated with violent group mobilisation. Our study showed the salience of horizontal inequalities in militancy in the Niger Delta. Among other factors, such as corrupt political leadership, environmental degradation, elite manipulation and the selfish interests of youths, horizontal inequalities stood out as the factor that most respondents considered to be implicated in the militancy in the region. The surveys did not test the relationship between the variables, but it was possible to tease out some relations where the pattern of responses seemed to be inconsistent. For instance, the apparent disconnection between prognosis and prescription disappears when we understand that youth unemployment is considered an indicator of horizontal inequalities, as unemployment is seen principally as a group problem. The advantage of the horizontal inequalities perspective over others is that, by situating individual motivations within the larger social context, it allows for prescriptions that target both individual and group grievance. Thus, unlike the 'greed' model, which would result only in a recommendation that employment be provided for youths (see Oyefusi, 2007), the horizontal inequalities perspective would support youth employment alongside fundamental changes aimed at promoting more social inclusion.

The horizontal inequalities perspective is also more useful because it provides insights into how perceptions of such inequalities contribute to identity mobilisation and formation. Although our study did not investigate this aspect, it is interesting to see how respondents who come from different ethnic groups have identified with the Niger Delta identity (see also Ukiwo, 2007). Finally, horizontal inequalities provide the raw material for 'elite manipulation'. Elites can only connect with the people if they are able to make them visualise a 'we' and a 'they'. Thus, identity construction and mobilisation are more effective if the people see there are inequities in political representation, recognition of cultural status and access to social entitlements. Evidently, therefore, policies aimed at tackling horizontal inequalities will most likely have an indirect impact on other factors linked to violent group mobilisation (see Stewart et al., 2008). Policies designed to correct horizontal inequalities, such as promoting inclusive political institutions and ending discrimination of access to employment and social services, tend to reorder the incentive structures both for elite mobilisation and for mass participation in violent conflict.

Acknowledgement

We acknowledge the research assistance of Paul Dasiemokuma, Solomon Fubara, Roland Nwikinawa, Aribiton Awoju, Joseph Ledum Kukang, Grace Barikpor Nwinor, Blessing B. Job and Samuel Karikpo.

Notes

1. See 'Clark Cautions Amaechi: Not All Militants Are Criminals'. *Vanguard*, 8 August 2008.
2. See Aisha Umar, 'Militants Are Fighting a Just Cause, Amaechi'. *Daily Trust*, 23 May 2009.
3. Since derivation revenues are allocated according to monthly production levels in each state, states which experience disruptions in oil production have had to forego a substantial proportion of such revenues.

References

Asuni, J.B. (2009) 'Blood Oil in the Niger Delta', *USIP Special Report* (Washington DC: United States Institute for Peace).
Ballentine, K., and J. Sherman (eds) (2003) *The Political Economy of Armed Conflict: Beyond Greed and Grievance* (Boulder, CO: Lynne Rienner).
Ballentine, K., and H. Nitzschke (2005) 'Introduction'. In K. Ballentine and H. Nitzschke (eds) *Profiting from Peace: Managing the Resource Dimensions of Civil War* (Boulder, CO: Lynne Rienner).
Berdal, M., and D. M. Malone (eds) (2000) *Greed and Grievance: Economic Agendas in Civil Wars* (Boulder, CO: Lynne Rienner).
Brown, G., and A. Langer (2010) 'Horizontal Inequalities and Conflict: A Critical Review and Research Agenda'. *Conflict, Security and Development* 10 (1): 27–55.
Collier, P. (2007) *The Bottom Billion: Why the Poorest Countries are Failing and What Can Be Done about it* (Oxford: Oxford University Press).
Collier, P., and A. Hoeffler (2000) 'Greed and grievance in civil war', Policy Research Working Paper Series 2355 (Washington: The World Bank).
Humphreys, M., and J. Weinstein (2008) 'Who Fights? The Determinants of Participation in Civil War'. *American Journal of Political Science* 52 (2): 436–55.
Ibeanu, O. (1999) 'Ogoni: Oil, Resource Flow and Conflict'. In T. Granfelt (ed.) *Managing Globalized Environment* (London: Intermediate Technology Publications).
Ibeanu, O., and R. Luckham (2006) *Niger Delta: Political Violence, Governance and Corporate Responsibility in a Petro-State* (Abuja: CDD).
Ikelegbe, A. (2005) 'The Economy of Conflict in the Oil Rich Niger Delta Region of Nigeria'. *Nordic Journal of African Studies* 14 (2): 208–34.
Ikelegbe, A. (2006) 'Beyond the Threshold of Civil Struggle: Youth Militancy and the Militarization of Resource Conflicts in the Niger Delta Region of Nigeria'. *African Studies Monographs* 27 (3): 87–122.
Joab-Peterside, S. (2007) 'On the Militarization of Nigeria's Niger Delta: The Genesis of Ethnic Militias in Rivers State'. *Economies of Violence Working Paper* No. 21 (Berkeley, CA: University of California).
Le Billon, P. (2000) 'The Political Ecology of Transition in Cambodia, 1989–1999: War, Peace, and Forest Exploitation'. *Development and Change* 31: 785–805.
Murshed, M.S. (2002) 'Conflict, Civil War and Underdevelopment: An Introduction'. *Journal of Peace Research* 39 (4): 387–93.
Murshed, M.S., and M.Z. Tadjoeddin (2007) 'Reappraising the Greed and Grievance Explanations for Internal Civil Conflict'. *MICROCON Research Working Paper* No. 2 (Brighton: MICROCON).

Naagbanton, P. (2007) 'The Proliferation of Small Arms, Armed Groups and Violent Conflicts in the Niger Delta Region of Nigeria'. Paper presented at the *International Workshop on Conflict in the Niger Delta*, PRIO, Oslo.

Nillesen, E., and P. Verwimp (2009) 'Rebel Recruitment in a Coffee Exporting Economy'. *MICROCON Research Working Paper* No. 11 (Brighton: MICROCON).

Osaghae, E. (1995) 'The Ogoni Uprising: Oil Politics, Minority Agitations and the Future of the Nigerian State'. *African Affairs* 94: 325–44.

Osaghae, E. (1998) 'Managing multiple minority problems in a divided society: The Nigerian experience', *Journal of Modern African Studies* 36 (1): 1–24.

Osaghae, E., A. Ikelegbe, O. Olarinmoye and S. Okhonmina (2007) 'Youth Militias, Self-determination and Resource Control Struggles in the Niger Delta Region of Nigeria'. *Research Report* (Leiden: African Studies Cente).

Oyefusi, A. (2007) 'Oil and the Propensity to Armed Struggle in the Niger Delta Region of Nigeria'. *Post-Conflict Transitions Working Paper* No. 8 (Washington, DC: World Bank).

Reno, W. (2000) 'Shadow States and the Political Economy of Civil Wars'. In M. Berdal and D. Malone (eds), *Greed and Grievance: Economic Agendas in Civil Wars* (Boulder, CO: Lynne Rienner), pp. 43–68.

Stewart, F. (2000) 'The Root Causes of Humanitarian Emergencies'. In W. E. Nafziger, F. Stewart and R. Väyrynen (eds) *War, Hunger and Displacement: The Origins of Humanitarian Emergencies, Vol. 1: Analysis* (Oxford: Oxford University Press).

Stewart, F., G. Brown and A. Langer (2008) 'Policies Towards Horizontal Inequalities'. In F. Stewart (ed.) *Horizontal Inequalities and Conflict: Understanding Group Violence in Multiethnic Societies* (Basingstoke: Palgrave Macmillan).

Ukiwo, U. (2005) 'The Study of Ethnicity in Nigeria'. *Oxford Development Studies* 33 (1): 7–23.

Ukiwo, U. (2007) 'Le Delta du Niger Face a la Democratie Virtuelle du Nigeria'. *Politique Africaine* 106: 128–47.

Ukiwo, U. (2007) 'From "Pirates" to "Militants": A Historical Perspective on Anti-state and Anti-oil Company Mobilization Among the Ijaw of Warri, Western Niger Delta'. *African Affairs* 106: 587–610.

Ukiwo, U. (2010) 'The Nigerian State and the Resolution of the Niger Delta Crisis: Amnesty and Beyond'. In Cyril Obi and Siri Aas Rustad (eds) *Oil and Insurgency in the Niger Delta: Managing the Complex Politics of Petroviolence* (London: Zed Books).

UNDP (United Nations Development Programme) (2006) *Niger Delta Human Development Report* (Abuja: UNDP).

Van de Goor, L., K. Rupesinghe and P. Sciarone (eds) (1996) *Between Development and Destruction: An Enquiry into the Causes of Conflict in Post-colonial States* (Basingstoke: Palgrave Macmillan).

Watts, M. (2008) 'Anatomy of an Oil Insurgency: Violence and Militants in the Niger Delta, Nigeria'. In K. Omeje (ed.) *Extractive Economies and Conflict in the Global South: Multiregional Perspectives on Rentier Politics* (Aldershot: Ashgate), pp. 51–74.

World Bank (2008) 'Niger Delta Social and Conflict Analysis' (Washington DC: World Bank).

11
Seeking Representativeness: Affirmative Action in Nigeria and South Africa Compared

Abdul Raufu Mustapha

11.1 Introduction

Africa is one of the most ethnically fragmented regions of the world. In some countries, ethnic and racial diversity interact with socioeconomic and political dynamics to create distinct group inequalities – horizontal inequalities. High levels of political, economic and cultural horizontal inequality can predispose such societies to conflict (Stewart, 2008). Managing diversity is therefore an important aspect of statecraft in Africa (see Mustapha, 1999, 2002), even if the results have not always been successful. One key aspect of managing diversity is the attempt to make state institutions more representative. States in Africa have moved at different speeds in their pursuit of representativeness. Some, like Ghana, have informal – but virtually institutionalised – mechanisms for accommodating different segments of the population in the political, economic and cultural life of the country; in others, like Côte d'Ivoire, the inclusive mechanism has been highly personalised and dependent on the goodwill of the president (Langer, 2007). This paper examines two types of formal inclusiveness: the Federal Character Principle in Nigeria and Broad-Based Black Economic Empowerment in South Africa.

Political and cultural inclusion is a mark of recognition of rightful membership in a community, while economic inclusion implies recognition of the right to services and productive assets. Full inclusion implies the recognition of legitimate interests, which need articulation and promotion. But inclusion can also be tokenistic; that is, in form only, without granting the possibility of articulating legitimate interests. Africa is replete with examples of both forms of inclusion, substantive and tokenistic. Representation is a more nuanced form of inclusion, and there are obvious overlaps between the two concepts (Krislor, 1974: p. 63). We often think of representation when we are considering institutions that are responsible for policy judgements, such as legislatures and juries, but not when we are thinking of institutions responsible for policy implementation, such as administrators (ibid.: p. 21). When we think of the latter category of functionaries, we invariably think in terms of merit or specialist skills and capacities. In a similar vein, we think of the modern economy as an entity regulated by the forces of supply and demand and through the efficient allocation of resources.

In both Nigeria and South Africa, important questions of inclusion and representativeness have been raised with respect to both the bureaucracy and the economy. Given the importance of the bureaucracy in many African countries, it is true that 'parts of government other than elected representatives serve representative functions' (Pennock, 1968: p. 4). Similarly, in South Africa, because property rights under apartheid were so reliant on political force for their establishment and maintenance, 'nothing obeyed market principles less than the market' (ANC, nd: p. 5). In both Nigeria and South Africa, therefore, legitimate issues of inclusion and representativeness have been raised with respect to both state institutions and the economy. This chapter looks at the ways in which both countries have addressed this challenge.

Section 11.2 looks at the Nigerian experience with the Federal Character Principle (FCP), while Section 11.3 examines the South African experience with Broad-Based Black Economic Empowerment (B-B BEE). Section 11.4 looks at the effectiveness of both policies, while Section 11.5 concludes the analysis by comparing salient aspects of the two approaches.

11.2 The Federal Character Principle in Nigeria

11.2.1 Ethno-regional inequalities, governance and conflict

Nigeria's population of 140 million[1] is made up of between 250 and 400 ethnic groups. These groups are broadly divided into 'majority' and 'minority' ethnicities. The majority groups are the composite Hausa-Fulani of the northwest, the Yoruba of the southwest, and the Igbo of the southeast. These three constituted 57.8 per cent of the population in 1963.[2] The Hausa (without the Fulani) constituted 20.9 per cent, the Yoruba 20.3 per cent, and the Igbo 16.6 per cent (Jibril, 1991). Eleven of the largest ethnic minorities together were constituting 27.9 per cent of the population (Afolayan, 1983). The hegemonic strength of

the political and bureaucratic systems by making them more inclusive. These reforms ultimately led to the Federal Character Principle.

11.2.2   The Federal Character Principle (FCP) and the Federal Character Commission (FCC)

A major task of governance is to gain social acceptance for policies with the minimum of resistance from those governed. No matter how well conceived, public policy needs societal support, and 'one of the oldest methods of securing such support is to draw a wide segment of society into the government to convey and to merchandise a policy' (Krislor, 1974: pp. 4–5). This need for the 'administrative penetration' of society through representativeness is even more acute in post-colonial countries, where bureaucrats exercise enormous discretionary powers. Though regional quotas were introduced for military recruitment in the 1950s, the quest for reforms after 1966 has meant the entrenchment of affirmative action within Nigeria's political and constitutional systems. Affirmative action, that is, 'planning and acting to end the absence of certain kinds of people – those who belong to groups that have been subordinated or left out – from certain jobs and schools' (Bergman, 1996: p. 7), is the key premise of the FCP. Such affirmative action is often defended on three grounds: (1) to offset past discrimination; (2) to counteract present unfairness; and (3) to achieve future equality. The first is often referred to as 'compensation', the second as 'a level playing field' and the third as 'diversity' (Cahn, 2002: p. xiii). In Nigeria, all three motives for affirmative action were implied in the drive for reforms.

Two distinct waves of reform culminated in the creation of the Federal Character Commission (FCC). The first wave started in 1967 and included the dismantling of the regional institutional framework and its replacement by smaller states. The objectives were: (a) to deny regional elites an institutional framework; (b) to create administrative cleavages within ethnic majorities; (c) to give administrative autonomy to ethnic minorities; and (d) to tilt the balance of power away from the regions and towards the centre. Informal quotas were also introduced as the basis for representation within the federal cabinet and in the admission process in federal educational institutions.

The second wave was triggered by constitutional debates about the nature of the post-military political settlement. These started in 1979, with the introduction of a majoritarian presidency that must: (a) get a *national* majority of votes cast; and (b) cross a *threshold* of not less than 25 per cent of votes, cast in at least two thirds of the states. Pan-ethnic rules for the formation of political parties and the constitutional entrenchment of consociational power-sharing rules (the Federal Character Principle) were also introduced. These were all institutional designs that aimed to force politicians out of their ethno-regional cocoons. It is this reform process that led ultimately to the creation of the Federal Character Commission, which was to give administrative teeth to the FCP.

Emphasis on balanced representation and power-sharing was given formal constitutional backing in 1979. The drafters of the constitution believed that the fear of domination and exclusion were salient aspects of Nigerian politics. They therefore felt it was essential to have specific provisions to ensure that there was no predominance of persons from a few states or from a few ethnic or other sectional groups in the composition of the government and in its agencies (CDC, 1977: p. xi). Accordingly, Section 14, Subsection 3 of the 1979 Constitution stated that state institutions must reflect the ethno-regional composition of their constituencies – Federal Character. This section was non-justiciable. However, other justiciable sections which reiterated the Federal Character Principles were: (a) Section 135, which stipulated that the president must appoint at least one minister from among the indigenes of each state; (b) Section 157, which compelled the president to take due regard of the Federal Character in appointing persons to numerous offices of state; (c) Section 197 (2), which stipulated that the officer corps and the other ranks of the armed forces must reflect the Federal Character; and (d) Section 199, which called for the establishment of a body to ensure that the composition of the armed forces complied with the Federal Character Principle. These Federal Character provisions have been incorporated into all subsequent Nigerian constitutions in one form or another.

In Section 150 of the 1989 Constitution, many new institutions, such as the governing bodies of state-owned companies and the governing councils of the universities, were brought under the purview of the Federal Character Principle. The National Constitutional Conference, convened by then-head of state Sani Abacha in June 1994, went furthest in promoting consociational power-sharing[6] and also came to the conclusion that a Federal Character Commission was to be established, to 'monitor and enforce Federal Character application and proportional representation'.

By the time the FCC was established by Decree No. 34 of 1996, its powers were enormous, including the powers (Section 4, Subsection 1c) to prosecute heads of ministries and parastatals. The scope of its operations had also been extended beyond governmental bureaucracies, to address inequalities in social services and infrastructural development, along with inequalities in the private sector (Section 4, Subsections 1di and 1dii). This socioeconomic dimension is referred to as the 'second mandate'. The FCC also had powers: (a) to work out a quota formula for the redistribution of jobs; and (b) to establish, by administrative fiat, the principle of proportionality within the Federal Civil Service (FCS) (FCC, 1996). Though it argued that the commission 'must not be used as a lever to elevate the incompetent' or be associated 'with the lowering of standards' (ibid.: pp. 30–31), it nevertheless established that, within the FCS, indigenes of any state should not constitute less than 2.5 per cent or more than 3 per cent of the total positions available (ibid.: p. 33).

Where there were only two posts, one must go to the North and the second to the South; where there were six posts, one must go to each of the six geo-political zones of the country. In short, the FCC leaned heavily towards the quota model of affirmative action (Cahn, 2002: p. xiii).[7] Where a state was unable to find a candidate to fill its slot, that fact was officially noted and a candidate from another state in the same zone was sought. Indigenes of a zone should constitute a minimum of 15 per cent and a maximum of 18 per cent of the senior-level positions in each establishment.

A major function of the FCC is the collection of fairly reliable data on the composition of the core federal bureaucracy. The Statistical Division of the FCC monitors the composition of different institutions, categorizing the thirty-six states of the federation into: NR (not represented) – 0 per cent; GUR (grossly underrepresented) – under 1.5 per cent; UR (underrepresented) – between 1.5 per cent and 2.4 per cent; AR (adequately represented) – between 2.5 per cent and 3 per cent; OR (overrepresented) – between 3.1 per cent and 3.9 per cent; and GOR (grossly overrepresented) – above 4 per cent. Ironically, between 2000 and 2004, nine largely southern states remained in the 'grossly overrepresented' states category, while the number of adequately represented states went down from five in 2000 to three in 2004, suggesting that the FCC was not achieving its objective.

11.3 Broad-Based Black Economic Empowerment in South Africa

11.3.1 From apartheid to black empowerment

Apartheid was the constitutional enshrinement of segregation and inequality between the four racial groups it recognised: Blacks (Africans),

Whites, Indians, and Coloureds. It has been asserted that the 'dominant themes of South Africa's economic history are inequality and exclusion'; South Africa's Gini was the highest recorded in the world (Leibbrandt et al., 1999: p. 3). The labour market, asset ownership and access to state welfare services are identified as key drivers of inequality (Hoogeveen and Ozler, 2005). In 1992/3, the infant mortality rate of the Black population was six times greater than that of the White population (McIntyre and Gilson, 2000).

In the terminal apartheid period, between 1975 and 1991, the Gini remained static, but masked an increasing polarisation within all the races, as the rich got richer while the poor got poorer. Within the Black population, this polarisation saw the income share of the poorest 40 per cent of earners fall by 48 per cent, while the share of the richest 10 per cent rose by 43 per cent. By the 1990s, within-group inequalities accounted for three fifths of overall inequality, suggesting the importance of both within-group and between-group dynamics. In this context of within- and between-race inequalities, Leibbrandt and colleagues wrote of 'the racial fault line in South African inequality' (Leibbrandt et al., 1999: p. 4). Comparing the relationships between race and inequality in Malaysia and South Africa, they point out that, while the between-group share in overall inequality was about 13 per cent in Malaysia, in South Africa the same figure is 36 per cent. 'In South Africa..., income inequality between the four racial groups, and particularly between African and White, is a crucial predictor of total income inequality in the society'; the 'key inequality wedge' is said to be between White and Africa households (ibid.: pp. 3–9).

When apartheid ended formally, it was inevitable that this pattern of systematic racial horizontal inequality would have to be addressed. The constitution made explicit provisions for affirmative action; Chapter 3, Section 8 established the right to equality and equal protection by the law. It made unlawful any 'unfair discrimination'. Section 3a made provision for measures 'to achieve the adequate protection and advancement of persons or groups or categories of persons disadvantaged by unfair discrimination, in order to enable their full and equal enjoyment of all rights and freedoms'. Similarly, Schedule 4 of the Constitutional Principles declared that the constitution should provide for 'a democratic system of government committed to achieving equality between men and women and people of all races...' Schedule 4 also demanded the promotion of a public service 'broadly representative of the South African community' and stated that the Constitutional Court must be representative of the country 'in respect of race and gender'. Deracialisation and 'engendering' were constitutional imperatives at the end of apartheid. In 2007, Blacks made up about 79.7 per cent of the population, Whites 9.1 per cent, Coloureds 8.8 per cent, and Indians/Asians 2.4 per cent, which included a small long-established Chinese population of approximately 100,000 people (SSA, 2007). Of those aged 15 years or more, there were more women than men in the population.

White business had its own vision of post-apartheid transformation. In the early 1990s, companies were quickly recruiting Blacks with the right connections to sit on boards. But such Blacks were generally regarded as 'fakes'.[8] To avoid the resulting stigma and embarrassment, many Blacks approached by White businesses started demanding 'real shares', not just seats in the boardroom. This led to the fabrication of intricate financial instruments, which conjured up 'paper shares' 'where people owned shares they did not [apparently] own....' (ibid.). In 1993, for example, Sanlam, a symbol of the Afrikaner financial renaissance, sold 10 per cent of its stake in Metropolitan Life to a Black consortium (DTI, 2007a: p. 10). Many companies listed on the Johannesburg Stock Exchange followed suit. However, these business-driven initiatives foundered because 'nowhere is inequity greater in South Africa than in relation to equity... Black people are producers and consumers but not owners' (ANC, nd: p. 5). Financing Black acquisition of shares became highly dependent on complex corporate processes under the control of White business, bankers and lawyers. The resulting financial consortia or special-purpose vehicles behaved more like investment funds than like actual owners and controllers of businesses. Amid the global financial volatility of 1997 and the Asian stock market crash of 1998, many new Black owners were left with huge debts instead of stocks (DTI, 2007a: pp. 10–11). Still, these problematic deals 'provided empowerment with a high profile and brought forth a new generation of business leaders' (DTI, 2007a: p. 11).

Starting in 1994 with its Reconstruction and Development Programme (RDP), the ANC-controlled state sought to make South African society and economy more inclusive. The B-B BEE is the culmination of this intervention. From the mid-1980s, as it prepared for change in South Africa, the ANC grappled with the question of what to do with apartheid-era inequalities. The Constitutional Committee under Oliver Tambo had two options pressed upon it. One sought the scrapping of apartheid laws, the enactment of a democratic constitution and of a Bill of Rights, and respect for private property. This would have amounted to a continuation of the economic *status quo*. The second option called for confiscation of the 'spoils of apartheid' and their redistribution to the dispossessed. Rejecting both options, the committee and the ANC settled for affirmative action (ANC, nd). By 1994, when it came to power, the ANC was confirmed in this decision by constraints imposed by international economic trends as well as by the inherited fiscal difficulties of the state (Carter and May, 2001).

The RDP sought to redirect resources to the poor through job creation, land redistribution and major infrastructural developments (Hoogeveen and Ozler, 2005). Between 1993 and 1998, while 24 per cent of the budget went towards debt servicing, an increasing proportion of the balance was diverted into social spending: 60 per cent in 1997–98, compared to 54 per cent in 1994. Education, health, social security and housing were the main beneficiaries (Carter and May, 2001). The RDP's wider goal was to deracialise the economy 'through focused policies of black economic empowerment' (DTI, 2007a: p.10). In 1996, the Growth, Employment, and Redistribution (GEAR) programme replaced the RDP. GEAR was an export-led macroeconomic strategy which included trade liberalisation, tight monetary policies and fiscal restraint. But, despite the RDP and the GEAR, the promise of black empowerment remained unfulfilled, as unemployment increased and little land redistribution took place (Hoogeveen and Ozler, 2005).

A series of legislative acts also sought to promote Black economic interests. The National Small Business Act of 1996 provided financial and technical advice largely to Black entrepreneurs. The 1997 Green Paper on Procurement reforms led to the Preferential Procurement Policy Regulation of 2001, which leveraged government business in support of Black empowerment. The year 1998 saw the enactment of the Employment Equity Act (EEA), the Skills Development Act, the Competition Act and the National Empowerment Fund Act. The EEA argued that employment equity could not be achieved simply by repealing apartheid laws. It therefore required all firms employing more than fifty persons to take affirmative action to ensure a representative body of employees at all levels of organisation and in all occupations. No quotas were set, however. The procurement process itself was restructured to 'unbundle' tenders into smaller units, making it possible for smaller Black businesses to participate. The Competition Act exempted companies from anti-competition laws where such anti-competitive practices were aimed at strengthening Black businesses. The National Empowerment Fund (NEF) Act created the NEF Corporation, which held equity on behalf of disadvantaged groups. It also promoted savings and investments within these groups and supported business ventures run by them (DTI, 2007a).

These initiatives led to some gains, particularly in the public sector, but the efforts were unfocussed and Black disadvantage persisted. Between 1995 and 2000, broad unemployment increased from 29 per cent to 38 per cent, with unskilled Black labour bearing much of the brunt. As a consequence, while some Black households had made economic gains, many had lost ground; Coloureds, Indians, and Whites showed 'modest improvements' in their overall poverty levels by 2000. By 2000, therefore, 'poverty is virtually zero among Whites, and Africans are the poorest ethnic group followed by Coloureds and Asians... – closely mimicking the order established by the Apartheid regime' (Hoogeveen and Ozler, 2005).

11.3.2   Broad-Based Black Economic Empowerment

Addressing the National Conference of the Black Management Forum (BMF) in 1999, President Thabo Mbeki pointed out: 'Five years after the arrival of the democratic order, we have not made much progress and may well be marching backward with regards to the de-racialization of the productive property. Clearly something is not right' (ANC, 2001). From July 2000, various leading organs of the ANC revisited the theme of 'economic transformation'. It was in this context that the BEE Commission (BEECom) under the auspices of the Black Business Council released the 'National Integrated BEE Strategy' in 2000, helping to define the process, its objectives and a strategy for their achievement (DTI, 2007b). In March 2001, the ANC's Economic Transformation Committee (ETC) met to discuss the BEECom report with other stakeholders, such as the Congress of South African Trade Unions (COSATU). The ANC National Conference in Stellenbosch in 2002 adopted resolutions that supported BEE and affirmative action. Some argued that a young democracy built on White property and Black political power was unsustainable and that 'there is no other practical and effective instrument for South Africa to deracialise the economy within a reasonable time' (Macozoma, 2005). Amid this increasing political pressure, the mining industry released the Mining Industry Charter for Black Economic Empowerment in October 2002 (Goniwe, 2004). It was this combination of initiatives from Black business interests, the ANC and some established White business interests that propelled the BEE process, leading in March 2003 to the release of the strategy for B-B BEE by the DTI and to the enactment of the Broad-Based Black Economic Empowerment Act in 2003.

The B-B BEE is defined as an economic transformation strategy driven by the moral requirement to deracialise and 'engender' the South African economy, and by an economic imperative to broaden the base of economic activity and to promote growth. The new strategy sought to provide a more focussed approach, based on innovative funding mechanisms. The policy's objectives included: (a) a substantial increase in the number of Black people who owned and controlled existing and new businesses; (b) a substantial increase in the number of Black people owning and controlling existing and new enterprises in designated priority sectors of the economy; (c) a significant increase in Black enterprises, Black-empowered enterprises, and Black-engendered enterprises; (d) a significant increase in the number of Black people in executive and senior management positions in enterprises; (e) an increase in the control and management of enterprises by community and broad-based groups such as trade unions, employee trusts and community groups; (f) increased ownership of land and other assets, and improved access to infrastructure and skills in thirteen designated underdeveloped areas; (g) accelerated and shared economic growth; and (h) increased income levels for Black people and the reduction of between- and within-race income inequalities (DTI, 2007a).

These were the objectives of the B-B BEE Act 2003. It defined the beneficiary 'Black people' as those disadvantaged by apartheid – Africans, Coloureds and Indians; in 2008 the Chinese Association of South Africa obtained a court injunction stipulating that the 'South African Chinese people fall within the ambit of the definition of "black people" '.[9] Firstly, the act created an enabling framework which empowered the minister responsible for the DTI to issue guidelines to industry, and established an Advisory Council to advise the president. Secondly, various regulatory instruments were to be used to guide the economy towards the objectives of B-B BEE. A Generic Scorecard was introduced to measure progress achieved by particular enterprises and whole industrial sectors. Specifically, this scorecard measured three core elements of B-B BEE: (a) direct empowerment of Black people through ownership and control of enterprises and assets; (b) human resources development and employment equity; (c) indirect empowerment through preferential procurement and enterprise development. Through the promotion of employment equity and preferential procurement, the B-B BEE process tied in previous efforts to deracialise the economy. Thirdly, the restructuring of state-owned enterprises (SOE) was to be used to transfer assets to Black people. Fourthly, clear procurement targets were to be set to increase the level of preference for Black enterprises. Fifthly, the forging of partnerships with the private sector, trade unions, and community groups in 'structured collaboration' was to be used to drive the B-B BEE process. Given past experience, financing was a major aspect of the new strategy.

Two key monitoring processes are involved in the B-B BEE: the Generic Scorecard and the work of the Commission for Employment Equity (CEE). Through the Code of Good Practice, the minister guides the B-B BEE process by setting targets and determining when those targets have to be met. The code includes the scorecard, which contains eight specific measurement principles for monitoring and evaluating compliance with the three core elements of B-B BEE outlined above – direct empowerment, human resources development and indirect empowerment. All organs of state and all publicly quoted entities are subject to the code by law. Sectors of the economy are encouraged to develop Sector or Transformation Charters collaboratively, in corporatist consultations between the employers, workers unions and community interests. The charters contain targets on the eight specific measurements of the scorecard. These sectoral charters must be certified by the minister and officially gazetted. Enterprises with no sectoral charters are expected to adopt the guidelines contained in the Code of Good Practice. Measurable indicators and principles, a weighting system, and conversion factors for determining the performance level of enterprises have been established, along with a scoring and ranking framework. Enterprises are ranked in three categories: (1) 65 per cent and above overall performance, good performers; (2) 40 per cent to 64.9 per cent, satisfactory; and (3) below 40 per cent, limited performers. The actual evaluation of an enterprise is carried out by private verification agencies. These agencies, accredited by the South African National Accreditation System (SANAS), issue certificates of performance to enterprises which pass these on to the DTI.

Monitoring and verification of compliance with the EEA, on the other hand, is done through the Inspectorate Division of the Department of Labour and the Labour Court. Designated employers subject to the EEA include employers with more than fifty employees; employers with fewer than fifty employees but with an annual turnover above the threshold for small businesses; and all state and municipal authorities. In effect, the EEA is applicable to both public and private sector organisations. The EEA seeks to promote equal opportunity and affirmative action through preferential treatment and numerical goals, but excluding quotas – the 'trumping' model of affirmative action. There is also a corporatist element to the EEA. Employers are obliged by law to collect and analyse all relevant information on their workforce, including racial profiles by professional category. This analysis is then the subject of consultation with workers and trade unions in the enterprise, with the objective of drawing up an employment equity plan covering a specified period. Designated employers with fewer than 150 employees are expected to submit a report every two years on their compliance with the EEA, while employers with more than 150 employees submit annual reports. These reports are public documents which must also be made available to the workers in the enterprise. Monitoring of compliance with the EEA and the implementation of employment equity plans are carried out by employees, trade unions, and the Labour Inspectorate. Labour inspectors can issue binding compliance orders and, when these are breached, the matter can be referred to the Labour Court, which is endowed with powers to levy fines. Another important body set up under the EEA, as noted above, is the CEE. The CEE is a corporatist body composed of representatives of organised labour, organised business and the state. The CEE conducts research on employment trends, norms, and benchmarks, with the objective of advising the Minister of Labour on the reduction of disproportional income differentials.

11.4   The effectiveness of federal character and B-B BEE

11.4.1   Trend analyses

As noted earlier, trend analyses within the Nigerian federal bureaucracy up to 2004 suggest that the FCP/FCC has not had the desired effect of promoting a more representative bureaucracy. Table 11.1 shows trends within the federal bureaucracy since the inception of the FCC. These figures are compiled and calculated by the FCC.

The three northern zones – which were to be the main beneficiaries of the FCC – have a smaller percentage of the bureaucracy in 2004 compared to 1996.[10] On the basis of these records, the FCC is clearly performing below expectation, incurring the wrath of its opponents without actually changing the situation of the marginalised. The explanation for these trends is that there was no new recruitment into the Civil Service between 1999 and 2005, so the FCC has just been tinkering at the margins of an already lopsided bureaucracy.

The FCC has faced a credibility crisis because of its poor showing so far. Some have expressed frustration that the FCC failed to stop

Table 11.1   Trends in representativeness of federal bureaucracies (all categories) 1996–2004 (per cent)

Zone	% in pop. (2005)	% of posts held							
		1996	1997	1998	1999	2000	2002	2003	2004
Northwest	25.56	12.3	10.4	10.4	10.9	10.4	9.5	10.1	9.5
Northeast	13.55	8.2	8.3	8.6	9.9	8.6	8.1	8.8	8.6
Northcentral	13.47	18.3	18.3	19.3	21.0	19.3	17.1	17.6	17.6
Southwest	19.7	24.5	24.9	24.7	20.7	24.9	25.9	24.2	24.4
Southeast	11.7	16.8	16.1	16.2	14.9	16.0	18.8	18.7	19.4
Southsouth	15.0	20.0	22.1	21.0	22.3	20.8	20.6	20.2	20.6

Source: Federal Character Commission, internal documents.

ethnic favouritism under President Obasanjo, who was accused of the 'Yorubalisation'[11] of the federal bureaucracy between 1999 and 2007. The late president Yar Adua also faced similar accusations of favouring Hausa-Fulani appointees between 2007 and 2009.[12]

A baseline study conducted by the South African DTI in 2007 gives a similarly bleak picture of the effectiveness of the B-B BEE in the three core areas of direct empowerment, human resources development and indirect empowerment. Of all the enterprises surveyed in the study, only 19.7 per cent claimed to have developed and implemented a B-B BEE plan (DTI, 2007b). Only 24.7 per cent claimed to have a formal scorecard from which they reported their compliance level. On the basis of the scores of individual enterprises, the study created five compliance categories: (1) 0 per cent – no compliance; (2) from just above 0 per cent to 50 per cent – low; (3) from just above 50 per cent to 80 per cent – moderate; (4) from just above 80 per cent to 100 per cent – good; and (5) those who have exceeded their targets, scoring more than 100 per cent – excellent.

On the criterion of *ownership*, the study found that 74.8 per cent fell into the 'no compliance' category. Despite this poor compliance, in 2006 the Department of Trade and Industry reported that at least 1,364 BEE deals worth R285 billion had been concluded between 1995 and 2005. Furthermore, from 2000 to 2006, 55 per cent of the top 40 companies on the Johannesburg Stock Exchange (JSE) had negotiated BEE deals worth more than 10 per cent of their assets; at least 10 per cent of the top 40 companies had entered into transactions worth 25 per cent of their assets.[13] It has also been claimed that Black ownership of the JSE top 100 companies went from 4 per cent in 1997 to 10 per cent in 2002

(Goniwe, 2004). In monetary terms, BEE deals increased by an annual average of 10 per cent between 1995 and 2002; this figure rose to 22.8 per cent between 2003 and 2008 (RSA, 2009: p. 18). Black ownership has thus progressed slowly and continues to encounter a number of problems. Black investors still run the risk of losing money in the deals.[14] Secondly, Black women's participation in ownership remains low; some suggest as low as 5 per cent of some BEE deals (Mlambo-Ngcuka, 2005). Finally, 'fronting' – whereby White owners continue to run an enterprise while conceding some supposed 'ownership' to Black collaborators – continues.

The second criterion for evaluating the B-B BEE is that of *human resource development* and *management control*. The 2003 Employment Equity Report by the CEE showed that Whites were still massively over-represented in the managerial cadres of industry (Table 11.2). However, the influence of affirmative action was still evident: according to the report, 'white males was the group with the biggest decline in representation in the work environment with African females gaining the most in terms of representation in employment in the large companies' (DOL, 2003: p. 14).

Commenting on the 2006 Employment Equity Report, Minister of Labour Membathisi Mdladlana lamented that progress towards a fairer representation of various communities within the workforce remained 'very slow' and 'the overall picture remains bleak' (Mdladlana, 2006). He also noted a declining trend of reporting by designated employers in breach of the law.

The third criterion for evaluating the progress of B-B BEE is *indirect empowerment*. Three indicators of this criterion, measured by the baseline survey, are preferential procurement, enterprise development, and

Table 11.2 South Africa: Occupational levels, gender and population group, 2003 (per cent)

Management level	Male				Female				Total
	African	Coloured	Indian	White	African	Coloured	Indian	White	
Top (15,515)	11	3	4	67	4	1	1	9	100
Senior (47,433)	10	4	5	58	4	2	1	15	100
Middle (258,122)	21	4	4	34	18	2	2	15	100

Source: Adapted from DOL (2003: p. 47).

socioeconomic development. A total of 85.4 per cent of surveyed enterprises had a 'no compliance' rating under preferential procurement. For enterprise development, 83.9 per cent had a 'no compliance' rating; the corresponding figure for socioeconomic development was 81 per cent.

11.4.2   The wider context of effectiveness

On the basis of the available trend evidence, both the FCP/FCC and the B-B BEE can be said to be relatively ineffective in achieving their specific targets. However, such a conclusion ignores the important fact that both policies are best understood as long-term processes, rather than snapshot outcomes. And both policies should be understood as the most obvious signs of their respective states' wider commitment to bringing about equity.

Despite its shortcomings, to dismiss the FCP/FCC as 'tribal character', as some commentators have done (Oyovbaire, 1983: p. 19), is untenable. Furthermore, the FCP/FCC has realised a number of important achievements, which should also be taken into consideration. Firstly, it has succeeded in creating new norms and procedures for the non-violent resolution of conflicts over ethnic and regional access: aggrieved communities do not have to resort to violence to get their concerns heard. Instead, the FCC provides an impartial and professional platform, through which complaints can be addressed.[15] In a country in which trust in democratic institutions is low and recourse to violence common,[16] this is an important achievement. Secondly, the FCC is increasingly generating the data through which the problem of representation can be objectively assessed, monitored and pronounced upon, away from the strident headlines of ethnic entrepreneurs. It is a credit to its professionalism that we now know as much as we do about trends within the federal bureaucracies. Previously, analysts would have been paralysed by competing partisan claims. Importantly, the pervasive *fear* of 'marginalisation' can now be calmed by a rational engagement with FCC data. Thirdly, through its oversight function, the FCC has positively changed the culture and norms of bureaucratic recruitment in Nigeria towards inclusive diversity. Heads of organisations are now subject to closer scrutiny. The full impact of this change will only be felt many decades down the line, when the current generation of ageing bureaucrats retire and new ones are appointed.[17] In this regard, the FCC has laid an important and valuable foundation.

On balance, therefore, the FCC has had a positive impact on Nigerian ethno-regional politics even as it has failed to deliver a representative bureaucracy. Real or imagined fears of 'domination' have not disappeared, but new, more constructive channels are being opened up for their resolution. This is not to suggest that all is well with the FCC or the wider political calculus of federal character within which it operates. There is the urgent need to address the numerous *implementation* issues raised in the criticism of the FCC, but the objective should be to find ways of improving its performance in the short-to-medium term.

For its part, the B-B BEE has suffered from a number of problems. First, the planners had unrealistic targets. Originally it was expected that the economy would be transformed and deracialised by 2014 (DTI, 2007a: p. 4). Undoing the evils of 300 years of segregation and apartheid in ten years is clearly an unrealistic proposition. Another such projection is that 52 per cent of all private business will change ownership under B-B BEE by 2018.[18]

Like the FCP in Nigeria, the B-B BEE in South Africa has faced scathing criticism. Firstly, the B-B BEE is accused of elitist consequences. For example, Moeletsi Mbeki, charged that the B-B BEE is more of a problem than a solution as it has only benefited ANC leaders.[19] Expanding numbers of unemployed Blacks have been left facing poverty and xenophobia, while the 'New Randlords' of the ANC enjoy the benefits of 'crony' capitalism (Russell, 2009: 173–4). Similarly, Ramotena Mabote claimed that for a fee, 'black people [are] using their melanin, occasionally their skills and mostly their networks, to validate white capital'.[20] A related criticism is that B-B BEE is stifling Black entrepreneurship by encouraging Black elites to 'settle for a slice of the action' while talented Blacks are 'shackled by the golden handcuffs of the corporate and public sector'.[21]

As might be expected, those in support of affirmative action have rebutted these criticisms. The government has admitted that while the earlier beneficiaries of BEE were six top Black companies with connections to the ANC government, the introduction of the Codes of Good Practice in 2004 had steered the B-B BEE process towards a broader base.[22] Other defenders have pointed out that those attacking affirmative action as elitist often put forward no alternative policy for addressing the skewed racial profile of the South African economy. It has even been suggested that what 'these critics are trying to run away from is [an]...empowerment that puts capital...in the hands of black people', preferring instead the diffusion of shares within the Black population in a manner which leaves White managerial control intact (Macozoma, 2005).

Saki Macozoma argues that elitist consequences are inherent in the capitalist nature of the South African transition and that the policy of B-B BEE was not designed as a panacea for all the ills of the country's economy. Its target is the deracialisation of that economy: 'Is the BEE programme achieving its objective of deracialising our economy? The answer is yes' (ibid.) In a similar vein, COSATU argued that 'dealing with discrimination may ultimately lead to the development of a new black bourgeoisie' (ANC, 2001). Others have also argued that the artificial compression of Black economic activities under apartheid led to artificially low levels of inequality within the Black population. Any policy which addressed this compression was bound to lead to greater inequalities within the Black population (Carter and May, 2001: pp. 1995–96).

The importance of both policies goes beyond the trend numbers, for they signal a commitment by the two states to address the yawning inequalities which have held back significant portions of both societies. Without such an obvious commitment, both societies could have faced serious inter-group conflicts. Until the critics of the philosophy of affirmative action in both countries put forward more appropriate policies for addressing these inequalities, the only obvious alternative seems to be social conflict.

11.5 Conclusion

Nancy Fraser suggests that there may be three dimensions to the search for 'participatory parity' by communities that have been historically disadvantaged: 'misrecognition', maldistribution and participation (Fraser, 2000). Basing her argument on Kant and Weber, she defines misrecognition as the relative distribution of honour, prestige and esteem within a community to the disadvantage of some groups. Maldistribution is about unequal group access to the labour markets, property regimes, and the structures of economic life, while participation is about unequal access to the political system. These three dimensions correspond to our notions of cultural, economic, and political horizontal inequalities.

One important contrast between Nigeria and South Africa relates to which dimensions of inequality are regarded as important. In both countries, there is the formal extension of full recognition to all individuals and groups. But this formal recognition is undermined in practice by the numerical and resource weight of the majority groups in Nigeria and by the long period of apartheid conditioning in South Africa. In both countries, however, cultural recognition is not an important dimension of the search for equity. In Nigeria, concern for equity is largely to do with the political dimension, specifically with political and bureaucratic appointments, while in South Africa formal liberal political participation is taken for granted, and the main concern is with maldistribution. In Nigeria, access to economic resources is still largely through the state, while South Africa has a more developed capitalist economic structure, which is less dependent on the state. Affirmative action in both countries reflects these divergent realities and concerns.

Another important contrast is the social unit in whose name claims are made. In Nigeria, the key claimants are ethnic and regional groups. However, religious affiliation has gradually become equally important. In South Africa, on the other hand, broad racial categories are the key claimants. This is not to suggest that intra-racial – ethnic – differences do not matter. For example, it is claimed that Zuma's Zulu co-ethnics see his rise to the presidency as 'their turn to have a share of the [empowerment] deals' (Russell, 2009: p. 178). Even if this claim were true, the ethnic factor is still relatively muted in the South African context. South Africa has an explicit concern with gender, which is lacking in Nigeria. The history of the liberation struggle has put the formal recognition of gender rights high on the South African agenda in a way that is not the case in Nigeria. But this is not to suggest that Nigerian women are any less successful in claiming their rights. The politics of gender equality is different in each country. Importantly, however, in South Africa data are collected on women's roles while in Nigeria they are not. In Nigeria data are collected strictly on territorial states, but, since these states overlap with ethnicities, ethnic origins and religious affiliation can often be determined through the data.

Both Nigeria and South Africa have so far promoted affirmative action in a way consistent with their histories and institutional logics. The process in South Africa has more corporatist and market-led elements than in Nigeria, where state institutions have more prominence. Similarly, the use of the quota model in Nigeria and of the trumping model in South Africa shows the relative levels of sophistication and capabilities of both economies and state institutions. The greater depth of the South African economy has also made possible the use of commercial verification agencies to certify compliance. Both countries are responding to felt needs for affirmative action and using existing institutional and societal resources to craft mechanisms for policy delivery.

In Nigeria, the concern with the political and the ethnic has tended to privilege elite claims to political offices in the politics of affirmative action. The established consensus around ethno-regional power-sharing has however been challenged and undermined by the decision of President Goodluck Jonathan to seek the office of the president in the 2011 elections. Wider socioeconomic inequalities, which are in some cases more acute than political inequalities, have been ignored. It was not until the formulation of the FCC Decree in 1996 that the 'second mandate', covering socioeconomic inequalities, was added to the agenda. As of 2009, no concrete steps have been taken to operationalise the second mandate. In South Africa, on the other hand, massive social expenditure, particularly in education, health, and pensions, has meant that greater attention is paid to socioeconomic inequalities. The *embourgeoisment* of the Black middle classes through B-B BEE has been accompanied by extensive social spending. The problem in South Africa is the high levels of unemployment, which undermine the potential returns to that social spending. The neoliberal context of wider economic policy has made it difficult to address this unemployment. Unfortunately, public debate in South Africa has been polarised between those wanting to address unemployment and poverty whilst ignoring the racialised nature of the economy, and those emphasising the racialised nature of the economy but downplaying rising poverty and unemployment.

South African B-B BEE bears a striking resemblance to the Nigerian indigenisation process of the 1970s, while the Nigerian FCP shows a remarkable similarity to the South African Employment Equity Act of the 1990s. In 1972 and 1977, Nigeria passed two Indigenisation Decrees aimed at indigenising swathes of the economy hitherto dominated by foreigners (see Rimlinger and Stremlau, 1972; Balabkins, 1982). This was seen as a struggle between all Nigerian aspirant middle classes on the one hand and foreigners on the other. This did not mean that intra-Nigerian divisions were not important. For example, the Yoruba middle classes were said to have had more than their fair share of the proceeds. On the other hand, in its concern with equitable access to jobs, the EEA resembles the FCP. The main difference is that the EEA deals with both state bureaucracies and private sector businesses, while the FCC has not been able to extend federal character beyond state institutions.

This brief comparison of the FCP and the B-B BEE points to some lessons the two countries can learn from each other's experience. B-B BEE has something to learn from the long-term trajectory of Nigeria's indigenisation. At the beginning, both suffered fairly identical problems of fronting, lagging targets, skills shortage, and compliance problems. As of 2009, however, Nigeria has managed to indigenise significant sections of its economy, hitherto controlled by foreign interests and management. Since the 1990s, Nigerian entrepreneurs have even entered the more sophisticated oil industry. Some own and operate oil fields along with the major international oil corporations.[23] Nigeria's experience with indigenisation suggests that indigenisation is a long *process* of economic change, starting from a concern with the control of medium-scale trading and ending with participation in the sophisticated heights of the oil industry.

That there has been difficulty in achieving a balanced bureaucracy in Nigeria from 1996 and employment equity in South Africa since 1998 suggests that public policy is a necessary, but not sufficient, element in addressing this issue. Families and communities must join the state in investing material and cultural resources in education and skills development in order to provide the human resources needed to make public policy on representative employment possible. Without such non-state involvement, the task is all the more difficult.

In South Africa, as in Nigeria, 'the question is not whether or not to have affirmative action. Have it we must, and in a deep and meaningful way. The issue is how best to handle affirmative action, how to ensure that it is conducted in a principled and effective manner'.[24] Still, the fact that it might be an unavoidable necessity is not to suggest that affirmative action is costless for individuals and groups. And this is why issues of principles and effectiveness are important in the wider public interest. The long-term consequences of affirmative action also need to be kept under constant review. In India, Malaysia, and Nigeria, for instance, affirmative action has led to heightened group prerogatives, while in the US and in South Africa it has contributed to greater intra-group inequality. In all instances, remedial action may become necessary in order to counter the unintended consequences of affirmative action. Societies cannot be run in perpetuity on affirmative action principles. Both countries must therefore craft sunset clauses and provisions into their policies.

Notes

1. Provisional figures for the 2005 census.
2. Ethnicity and religion were omitted in the 2005 census.
3. In the 1953 census, the north constituted 54 per cent of the population and the south 46 per cent. In the 2005 census, the corresponding figures were 52.58 per cent and 46.4 per cent respectively.
4. See www.jambng.com for comparative figures on university admissions.
5. *Tell Magazine,* 14 November 1994: p. 15.
6. See Alex Ekwueme,'What Nigeria Lost by Abacha's Untimely Death'. *Sunday Guardian,* 29 May 2005.
7. Cahn identifies four models: (1) showing preference among equally qualified candidates (the 'tiebreaking' model); (2) preferring a strong candidate to

an even stronger one (the 'plus factor' model); (3) preferring a merely qualified candidate to a strongly qualified candidate (the 'trumping' model); and (4) cancelling a search unless a qualified candidate of the preferred sort is available (the 'quota' model).

8. Ramotena Mabote, 'Screwed by BEE'. *Mail & Guardian Online*, 11 March 2005. http://www.mg.co.za/article/2005–03–11-screwed-by-bee.
9. Case no: 59251/2007, High Court of South Africa, Transvaal Provincial Division.
10. Federal Character Commission, internal documents.
11. 'Yorubalisation of Federal Appointments Real – Monguno'. *Sun News Online*, 15 April 15 2005.
12. 'Afenifere Alleges Marginalisation of Yoruba By Yar'Adua'. *Guardian News*. 5 January 2008; 'Benue Widows Protest Non-appointment of Akor as Customs Boss', *Guardian News,* 23 August 2009.
13. 'One Decade, R258bn in BEE Deals'. *Mail & Guardian Online,* 3 November. http://www.mg.co.za/article/2006–11–03-one-decade-r285bn-in-bee-deals.
14. Riaz Gardee, 'Understanding Sasol's BEE Offer'. *Mail & Guardian Online,* 26 June 2008. http://www.mg.co.za/article/2008–06–26-understanding-sasols-bee-offer.
15. An example is the case the Egbema Ijaw of Warri North Local Government Area took to the FCC in 2005. 'Federal Character Panel Seeks Balanced Itsekiri, Ijaw Representation'. Guardian News, 4 August 2005.
16. These are some of the messages that emerged from a sampling of mass attitudes by the Centre for Research on Inequality, Human Security and Ethnicity (CRISE) at the University of Oxford through perception surveys conducted in Lagos, Borno, Delta, Cross-Rivers and Kano States.
17. See 'Nigeria's Workforce is Ageing, Says Adegoroye'. *Guardian News,* 24 February 2006; M. Yayale Ahmed (Head of Service of the Federation), 2005, 'The Reform Process and its Positive Effects on the Public Service'.
18. A 2008 projection by Moody's Investors Service. See 'Black Economic Empowerment', www.southafrica.info/business/trends/empowerment/bee.htm 28 July 2008.
19. Moeletsi Mbeki, 'BEE More of a Problem Than a Solution'. *Mail & Guardian Online,* 24 June 2008. http://www.mg.co.za/article/2008–06–24-bee-more-of-a-problem-than-solution.
20. Ramotena Mabote, 'Screwed by BEE'. *Mail & Guardian Online,* 11 March 2005. http://www.mg.co.za/article/2005–03–11-screwed-by-bee.
21. Reg Rumney, 'Where BEE Damages'. *Mail & Guardian Online,* 16 March 2007.
22. 'One Decade, R258bn in BEE Deals'. *Mail & Guardian Online,* 3 November 2006, http://www.mg.co.za/article/2006-11-03-one-decade-r285bn-in-bee-deals.
23. Mike Awoyinfa, 'We've Never Felt This Insecure, Not Even During the Civil War: Interview with Former Oil Minister Jubril Aminu'. *Sun News Online,* 1 August 2009.
24. Mike Awoyinfa, 'We've Never Felt This Insecure, Not Even During the Civil War: Interview with Former Oil Minister Jubril Aminu'. *Sun News Online,* 1 August 2009.

References

Adamu, F. (2003) 'Globalisation and Economic Glocalisation in Northern Nigeria'. Paper presented at the Development Studies Association annual conference *Globalisation and Development*, Glasgow, 9–12 September.

Afolayan, A.A. (1983) 'Population'. In J.S. Oguntoyinbo, O.O. Areola and M. Filani (eds) *A Geography of Nigerian Development* (Ibadan: Heinemann).

ANC (African National Congress) (2001) 'Black Economic Empowerment, ETC Discussion Document'. *Umrabulo* 13 (4th Quarter). Online: www.anc.org.za/ancdocs/pubs/umrabulo/13/umrabulo13n.html.

ANC (African National Congress) (nd) *Affirmative Action and the New Constitution*. Online: www.anc.org.za/ancdocs/policy/affirm.html (accessed 30 June 2009).

Balabkins, N. (1982) *Indigenization and Economic Development: The Nigerian Experience* (Greenwich, CT: JAI Press).

Bangura, Y. (ed.) (2006) *Ethnic Inequalities and Public Sector Governance* (Basingstoke: Palgrave Macmillan).

Bergman, B.R. (1996) *In Defense of Affirmative Action* (New York: BasicBooks).

Cahn, S.M. (2002) 'Introduction'. In Steven M. Cahn (ed.) *The Affirmative Action Debate* (New York: Routledge).

Carter, M.R., and J. May (2001) 'One Kind of Freedom: Poverty Dynamics in Post-apartheid South Africa'. *World Development* 29 (12): 1987–2006.

CDC (Constitution Drafting Committee) (1977) *Report of the Constitution Drafting Committee*, Vol. 1 (Lagos: Government Printers).

DOL (Department of Labour) (2003) *Employment Equity Report* (Pretoria: Department of Labour).

DTI (Department of Trade and Industry) (2007a) *A Strategy for Broad-Based Black Economic Empowerment* (Pretornia: Department of Trade and Industry). Online: http://www.dti.gov.za/bee/complete.pdf (accessed 30 June 2009).

DTI (Department of Trade and Industry) (2007b) *BBBEE Progress Baseline Report* (Pretoria: Department of Trade and Industry). Online: www.dti.gov.za/bee/BaselineReport.htm.

FCC (Federal Character Commission) (1996) *First Annual Report* (Abuja: Federal Character Commission).

Federal Office of Statistics (FOS) (1995/1996) *General Household Survey 1995/1996, National Report* (Lagos: FOS).

Fraser, N. (2000) 'Rethinking Recognition'. *New Left Review* 3 (May/June): 107–120.

Galadanchi, H.S. (2007) *Overview of Maternal Mortality in Northern Nigeria* (Kano: Development Research and Projects Centre).

Goniwe, M. (2004) 'Speech During the Debate on the State of the Nation Address'. Online:www.anc.org.za/ancdocs/speeches/2004/sp0210j.html.

Hamalai, L. (1994) 'Distribution of Industrial Enterprises in Nigeria and National Unity'. In A. Mahadi, G.A. Kwanashie and A.M. Yakubu (eds) Nigeria: The State of the Nation and the Way Forward (Kaduna: Arewa House).

Hoogeveen, J., and B. Ozler (2005) 'Not Separate, Not Equal: Poverty and Inequality in Post-Apartheid South Africa'. *William Davidson Institute Working Paper* No. 739 (Ann Arbor, MI: University of Michigan Business School).

Jibril, M. (1991) 'Minority-Languages and Lingua Francas in Nigerian Education'. In E.N. Emenanjo (ed.) *Multilingualism, Minority Languages and Language Policy in Nigeria* (Agbor: Central Books).

Kirk-Greene, A.H.M. (1975) *The Genesis of the Nigerian Civil War and the Theory of Fear* (Uppsala: Nordic African Institute).

Krislor, S. (1974) *Representative Bureaucracy* (Engelwood Cliffs, NJ: Prentice-Hall).

Langer, A. (2007) 'The Peaceful Management of Horizontal Inequalities in Ghana'. *CRISE Working Paper No. 25* (Oxford: Centre for Research on Inequality, Human Security and Ethnicity, University of Oxford).

Leibbrandt, M., H. Bhorat and I. Woolard (1999) 'Understanding Contemporary Household Inequality in South Africa'. *DPRU Working Paper* No. 99/25.

Macozoma, S. (2005) 'Can a Capitalist System Produce Socialist Results?' *Umrabulo* 22 (first Quarter). Online: http://www.anc.org.za/show.php?doc= ancdocs/pubs/umrabulo/umrabulo22/capitalist.html.

McIntyre, D.I. and L. Gilson (2000) 'Redressing Dis-advantage: Promoting Vertical Equity within South Africa'. *Health Care Analysis* 8: 235–58.

Mdladlana, M. (2006) *Launch of the 6th Commission for Employment Equity Annual Report Speech Given by Minister of Labour Membathisi Mdladlana*, Laboria House, Pretoria, 11 September.

Mlambo-Ngcuka, P. (2005) 'Adding Value at the Rock Face: Empowerment Lessons from the Mining Sector'. *Umrabulo* 22 (first Quarter). Online: www.anc.org.za/ancdocs/pubs/umrabulo/umrabulo22/adding.html.

Mustapha, A.R. (2009) 'Institutionalising Ethnic Representation: How Effective is Affirmative Action in Nigeria?'. *Journal of International Development* 21 (4): 561–76.

Mustapha, A.R. (2002) 'Coping With Diversity: The Nigerian State in Historical Perspective'. In A.I. Samatar and A.I. Samatar (eds) *The African State: Reconsiderations* (Portsmouth, NH: Heinemann).

Mustapha, A.R. (1999) 'Back to the Future?: Multi-Ethnicity and the State in Africa'. In L. Basta and J. Ibrahim (eds) *Federalism and Decentralization in Africa: The Multicultural Challenge* (Fribourg: Institute of Federalism, University of Fribourg).

Mustapha, A.R. (1986) 'The National Question and Radical Politics in Nigeria'. *Review of African Political Economy* 37: 81–96.

O'Connell, J. (1967) 'Political Integration: The Nigerian Case'. In A. Hazelwood (ed.) *African Integration and Disintegration* (Oxford: Oxford University Press).

Oyovbaire, S.E. (1983) 'Structural Change and Political Processes in Nigeria'. *African Affairs* 82 (326): 19.

Pennock, J.R. (1968) 'Political Representation: An Overview'. In J.R. Pennock and J.W. Chapman (eds) *Representation: Yearbook of the American Society for Political and Legal Philosophy* (New York: Atherton Press).

Rimlinger, G.V., and C.C. Stremlau (1972) *Indigenization and Management Development in Nigeria* (Lagos: Nigerian Institute of Management).

RSA (Republic of South Africa) (2009) *Development Indicators 2009* (Pretoria: The Presidency, Republic of South Africa).

Russell, A. (2009) *After Mandela: The Battle for the Soul of South Africa* (London: Hutchinson).

Soludo, C. (2007) *Preserving Stability and Accelerating Growth*. Central Bank of Nigeria, Speech by the Governor, 16 January.

SSA (Statistics South Africa) (2007) *Mid-year Population Estimates, South Africa: 2007* (Pretoria: Statistics South Africa). Online:http://www.statssa.gov.za/PublicationsHTML/P03022007/html/P03022007.html.

Stewart, F. (ed.) (2008) *Horizontal Inequalities and Conflict: Understanding Group Violence in Multiethnic Societies* (Basingstoke: Palgrave Macmillan).

Frances Stewart: A Select Bibliography

Monographs

(2001) *War and Underdevelopment*, Vol. 1: *The Economic and Social Causes of Conflict*; Vol. 2: *Country Experience*, with E.V.K. FitzGerald and others (Oxford: Oxford University Press).

(1999) *Conflict and Growth in Africa: Kenya, Tanzania and Uganda*, with J. Klugman and B. Neyapti (Paris: OECD) (also French version).

(1995) *Adjustment and Poverty: Options and Choices* (London: Routledge).

(1992) *North-South and South-South: Essays on International Economics* (London: Macmillan).

(1987) *Adjustment with a Human Face*, with G.A. Cornia and R. Jolly (Oxford: Oxford University Press) (translated into French, Spanish, Italian and German).

(1986) *Economic Policies and Agricultural Performance: The Case of Tanzania* (Paris: OECD).

(1985) *Planning to Meet Basic Needs* (London: Macmillan).

(1982) *International Cooperation, A Framework for Change*, with A. Sengupta (Oxford: Frances Pinter).

(1981) *First Things First, Meeting Basic Human Needs in Developing Countries*, with P. Streeten and others (Oxford: Oxford University Press).

(1977) *Technology and Underdevelopment* (London: Macmillan); (1978) 2nd ed. and paperback; (1983) *Tecnologia y Subdesarollo*, Spanish ed. (Mexico City: Fondo de Cultura Económica).

Edited Books

(2008) *Horizontal Inequalities and Conflict: Understanding Group Violence in Multiethnic Societies* (Basingstoke: Palgrave Macmillan).

(2008) *Post-Conflict Economic Recovery. Enabling Local Ingenuity*, with J. Ohiorhenuan (New York: UNDP).

(2007) *Defining Poverty in the Developing World*, with R. Saith and B. Harriss-White (Basingstoke: Palgrave Macmillan).

(2006) *Globalization, Violent Conflict and Self-Determination*, with E.V.K. FitzGerald and R. Venugopal (Basingstoke: Palgrave Macmillan).

(2002) *Group Behaviour and Development: Is the Market Destroying Cooperation?*, with J. Heyer and R. Thorp (Oxford: Oxford University Press).

(2000) *War, Hunger and Displacement: The Origin of Humanitarian Emergencies*, Vol. 1: *War and Displacement in Developing Countries*; Vol. 2: *Weak States and Vulnerable Economies: The Origins of Humanitarian Emergencies in Developing Economies*, with E.W. Nafziger and R. Väyrynen (Oxford: Oxford University Press).

(1997) *Global Development Fifty Years after Bretton Woods, Essays in Honour of Gerald K. Helleiner*, with R. Culpeper and A. Berry (London: Macmillan).
(1995) *Economic and Political Reform in Developing Countries*, with O. Morrissey (London: Macmillan).
(1994) *Market Forces and World Development*, with R. Prendergast (Basingstoke: Macmillan).
(1992) *Alternative Development Strategies in Sub-Saharan Africa*, with S. Lall and S. Wangwe (Basingstoke: Macmillan).
(1990) *The Other Policy: The Influence of Policies on Technology Choice and Small Business Development*, with H. Thomas and T. de Wilde (London: Intermediate Technology Publications).
(1987) *Macro-Policies for Appropriate Technology* (London: Westview).
(1986) *Theory and Reality in Development*, with S. Lall (London: Macmillan).
(1983) *Work, Income and Inequality: Payments Systems in the Third World* (London: Macmillan).
(1982) *The Economics of New Technology in Developing Countries*, with J. James (Oxford: Frances Pinter).
(1975) *Employment, Income Distribution and Development* (London: Frank Cass).

Articles in Journals

(2009) 'Horizontal Inequality: Two Types of Trap'. *Journal of Human Development and Capabilities* 10 (3): 315–40.
(2006) 'Human Development: Beyond the Human Development Index', with G. Ranis and E. Samman. *Journal of Human Development* 7 (3): 323–58.
(2005) 'When and How Far is Group Formation a Route out of Chronic Poverty?', with R. Thorp and A. Heyer. *World Development* 33 (6): 907–20.
(2005) 'Groups and Capabilities'. *Journal of Human Development* 6 (2): 185–204.
(2004) 'Development and Security'. *Conflict, Security and Development* 4 (3): 261–88.
(2003) 'Global Governance: The Case for a World Economic and Social Council', with S. Daws. *Finance and the Common Good* 15.
(2003) 'Conflict and the Millennium Development Goals'. *Journal of Human Development* 4 (3): 325–52.
(2003) 'Does it Matter That We Do Not Agree on the Definition of Poverty? A Comparison of Four Approaches', with C. Ruggeri Laderchi and R. Saith. *Oxford Development Studies* 31 (3): 243–74; shortened version in UNDP, *Poverty in Focus* (December 2006); (2006) edited version in M. McGillivray and M. Clarke (eds) *Understanding Human Well-being* (Tokyo: United Nations University Press).
(2003) 'Decentralization and Human Development in Argentina', with N. Habibi, C. Huang, D. Miranda, V. Murillo, G. Ranis and M. Sarkar. *Journal of Human Development* 4 (1): 73–101.
(2002) 'Crecimiento Económico y Desarollo Humano en Américan Latina', with G. Ranis. *Revista de la Cepal* 78: 7–24.
(2002) 'Amartya Sen's Contribution to Development Thinking', with S. Deneulin. *Studies in Comparative International Development* 37 (2): 61–70; (2009) repr. in S.J. Shapiro, M. Tadajewski and C.J. Shultz (eds) *Macromarketing* (New Delhi: Sage Publications).

(2002) 'Root Causes of Violent Conflict in Developing Countries'. *British Medical Journal* 324: 342–45.

(2001) 'The Debt Relief Initiative for Poor Countries: Good News for the Poor?', with G. Ranis. *World Economics* 2 (3): 111–26.

(2001) 'Income Distribution and Development'. *Mahbub ul Haq Human Development Review* 1 (1): 1–14.

(2000) 'Crisis Prevention: Tackling Horizontal Inequalities'. *Oxford Development Studies* 28 (3): 245–62.

(2000) 'Strategies for Success in Human Development', with G. Ranis. *Journal of Human Development* 1 (1): 49–70.

(2000) 'Globalization, Liberalization, and Inequality: Real Causes', with A. Berry. *Challenge: The Magazine of Economic Affairs* 43 (1): 44–93.

(2000) 'Economic Growth and Human Development', with A. Ramirez and G. Ranis. *World Development* 28 (2): 197–220.

(1999) 'Aid in the 21st Century: Reconciling the Real and the Desirable'. *Development* 42 (3): 16–21.

(1999) 'Computable General Equilibrium Models, Adjustment and the Poor in Africa', with L. De Maio and R. van der Hoeven. *World Development* 27 (3): 453–70.

(1999) 'V-Goods and the Role of the Urban Informal Sector in Development', with G. Ranis. *Economic Development and Cultural Change* 47 (2): 259–88; also in (1999) G. Barba Navaretti, R. Faini and G. Zanalda (eds) *Labour Markets, Poverty and Development* (Oxford: Clarendon Press).

(1999) 'The Asian Crisis and Human Development', with G. Ranis. *IDS Bulletin* 30 (1): 108–19.

(1998) 'Food Aid During Conflict: Can One Reconcile its Humanitarian, Economic and Political Economy Effects?' *American Journal of Agricultural Economics* 80 (3): 560–65.

(1997) 'Growth and Human Development: Pakistan in a Comparative Perspective', with G. Ranis. *The Pakistan Development Review* 36 (4): 333–52; (2002) repr. in P. Athukorala (ed.) *The Economic Development of South Asia* (Cheltenham: Edgar Elgar).

(1997) 'Civil Conflict in Developing Countries over the Last Quarter of a Century: An Empirical Overview of Economic and Social Consequences', with F.P. Humphreys and N. Lea. *Oxford Development Studies* 25 (1): 11–42.

(1996) 'Groups for Good or Ill'. *Oxford Development Studies* 24 (1): 9–25.

(1996) 'Globalisation and Education'. *International Journal of Educational Development* 16 (4): 327–33.

(1995) 'Basic Needs, Capabilities and Human Development'. *Greek Economic Review* 17 (2): 83–96; published in revised form in A. Offer (ed.) *In Pursuit of the Quality of Life*, Oxford: Oxford University Press (1996).

(1995) 'The Governance and Mandates of the International Financial Institutions'. *IDS Bulletin* 26 (4): 28–35.

(1994) 'Decentralisation in Indonesia'. with G. Ranis. *Bulletin of Indonesian Economic Studies* 30 (3): 41–72.

(1993) 'Two Errors of Targeting', with G.A. Cornia. *Journal of International Development* 5 (5): 459–96; (1995) repr. in D. van der Walle and K. Nead (eds) *Public Spending and the Poor* (Baltimore; London: John Hopkins University Press); (2003) repr. as 'Subsidios Alimentarios: dos Errores de Focalización'. *Revista de Comercio Exterior* (June).

(1993) 'War and Underdevelopment: Can Economic Analysis Help Reduce the Costs?' *Journal of International Development* 5 (4): 357–80; (1995) repr. in P. Terhal and J.G. de Vries (eds) *Development Transformation and State Policy*, Silver Jubilee Volume, Centre for Development Planning, Erasmus University, Rotterdam (New Delhi: Manohar).

(1993) 'Rural Non-agricultural Activities in Development: Theory and Application', with G. Ranis. *Journal of Development Economics* 40 (1): 75–102.

(1991) 'Are Adjustment Policies in Africa Consistent with Long-run Development Needs?' *Development Policy Review* 9 (4): 413–36; (1994) repr. in W. van der Geest (ed.) *Negotiating Structural Adjustment in Africa* (London: James Currey).

(1991) 'The Many Faces of Adjustment'. *World Development* 19 (12): 1847–64; (1992) repr. in P. Mosley (ed.) *Development Finance and Policy Reform* (Basingstoke; New York: Macmillan; St Martin's Press).

(1991) 'A Note on "Strategic" Trade Theory and the South'. *Journal of International Development* 3 (4): 467–84.

(1991) 'The Role of the South in a Chaotic World'. *Development* 34 (2): 40–5.

(1991) 'How Significant are Externalities for Development?', with E. Ghani. *World Development* 19 (6): 569–94.

(1990) 'The Fiscal System, Adjustment and the Poor', with G.A. Cornia. *Ricerche Economiche* 44 (2–3): 349–73; (1991) repr. as 'Sistema Fiscal, Ajuste y Pobreza'. *Colección Estudios CIEPLAN* 31: 77–106 (numero especial, marzo).

(1989) 'Basic Needs Strategies, Human Rights, and the Right to Development'. *Human Rights Quarterly* 11 (3): 347–75.

(1989) 'Recession, Structural Adjustment and Infant Health: The Need for a Human Face'. *Transactions of the Royal Society of Tropical Medicine and Hygiene* 83: 30–1.

(1988) 'Adjustment with a Human Face: The Role of Food Aid'. *Food Policy* 13 (1): 18–26.

(1987) 'Money and South-South cooperation'. *Third World Quarterly* 9 (4): 1184–205; repr. in N. Sopiee, B.A. Hamzah and C.H. Leong (eds) *Crisis and Response: The Challenge to South-South Economic Co-operation* (Kuala Lumpur: Institute of Strategic and International Studies Malaysia).

(1987) 'Back to Keynesianism: Reforming the IMF'. *World Policy Journal* 4 (3): 465–83.

(1986) 'Food Aid: Pitfalls and Potential'. *Food Policy* 11 (4): 311–22; (1986) repr. in *Food Aid and the Well-Being of Children in the Developing World* (New York: UNICEF-World Food Programme).

(1986) 'Trade Strategies for Development', with E. Ghani. *Economic and Political Weekly* 21 (34): 1501–10.

(1985) 'Mapping World Trade', with E. Ghani. *Development* 28 (4): 4–15.

(1985) 'The Fragile Foundations of the Neo-classical Approach to Development Economics'. *Journal of Development Studies* 21 (2): 282–92.

(1985) 'The International Debt Situation and North South Negotiations'. *World Development* 13 (2): 191–205; (1988) repr. in H. Singer, N. Hatti and R. Tandon (eds) *Resource Transfer and the Debt Trap* (New Delhi: Ashish Publishing House); and in C. Wilbur (ed.) *The Political Economy of Development and Underdevelopment*, 4th ed. (New York: Random House).

(1984) 'Inflation and Recovery'. *Journal of Development Planning* 14: 27–56.

(1984) 'Alternative Conditionality'. *Development* 27: 64–75.

(1983) 'Macro-policies for Appropriate Technology, an Introductory Classification'. *International Labour Review* 122 (3): 279–93; (1985) repr. in J. James and S. Watanabe (eds) *Technology, Institutions and Government Policies* (London: Macmillan).

(1983) 'Brandt II – the Mirage of Collective Action in a Self-serving World'. *Third World Quarterly* 5 (3): 640–49; (1987) repr. in T. Miljan (ed.) *The Political Economy of North-South Relations* (Peterborough, Canada: Broadview Press).

(1981) 'Arguments for the Generation of Technology by Less-developed Countries'. *The Annals of the American Academy of Political and Social Science* 458 (1): 97–109.

(1981) 'New Products: A Discussion of the Welfare Effects of the Introduction of New Products in Developing Countries', with J. James. *Oxford Economic Papers* 33 (1): 81–107.

(1980) 'A New Currency for Trade Among Developing Countries', with M. Stewart. *Trade and Development* 2: 69–82.

(1980) 'The Brandt Report'. *Overseas Development Institute Review* 1 (April): 65–9; repr. in R. Jolly and S. P. Joekes (eds) *Britain on Brandt,* a Special Issue of *Institute of Development Studies Review* (April): 36–38.

(1979) 'Raising Wages in the Controlled Sector: A Comment on Elliot', with J. Weeks. *Journal of Development Studies* 16 (1): 88–93.

(1979) 'Country Experience in Providing for Basic Needs'. *Finance and Development* 16 (4): 23–6; (1980) repr. in *Poverty and Basic Needs* (Washington, DC: World Bank).

(1978) 'Paul Beckerman: a Comment'. *World Development* 6 (4): 545–48.

(1978) 'Inequality, Technology and Payments Systems'. *World Development* 6 (3): 275–93.

(1978) 'Social Cost-Benefit Analysis in Practice: Some Reflections in the Light of Case Studies Using Little-Mirrlees Techniques'. *World Development* 6 (2): 153–65.

(1977) 'Technology and Underdevelopment'. *Overseas Development Institute Review* 1: 92–105.

(1976) 'Strategies for Development: Poverty, Income Distribution, and Growth', with P. Streeten. *Oxford Economic Papers* 28 (3): 381–405; (1979) repr. in O. Muñoz Gomá (ed.) *Distribución del Ingreso en América Latina* (Buenos Aires: El Cid Editor); and (1980) in K. W. Thee (ed.) *Pembangunan Ekonomi dan Pemerataan* (Jakarta: LP3ES).

(1975) 'The Employment Effects of Wage Changes in Poor Countries', with J. Weeks. *Journal of Development Studies* 11 (2): 93–107.

(1975) 'A Note on Social Cost-benefit Analysis and Class Conflict in LDCs'. *World Development* 3 (1): 31–9; (1979) repr. in C. Wilber (ed.) *The Political Economy of Development and Underdevelopment,* 2nd ed. (New York: Random House).

(1974) 'Technology and Employment in LDCs'. *World Development* 2 (3): 17–46; (1974) repr. in E. Edwards (ed.) *Employment in Developing Nations* (New York: Columbia University Press); and (2001) in A.K. Dutt (ed.) *The Political Economy of Development* (Cheltenham: Edward Elgar).

(1973) 'Economic Development and Labour Use: A Comment'. *World Development* 1 (12): 25–8.

(1973) 'Adjustment Assistance: A Proposal'. *World Development* 1 (6): 43–7.

(1972) 'Choice of Technique in Developing Countries'. *Journal of Development Studies* 9 (1): 99–121.

(1972) 'Little-Mirrlees Methods and Project Appraisal', with P. Streeten. *Bulletin of the Oxford University Institute of Economics and Statistics* 34 (1): 75–92.

(1971) 'Conflicts Between Output and Employment Objectives in Developing Countries', with P. Streeten. *Oxford Economic Papers* 23 (2): 147–69; (1983) repr. in M.P. Todaro (ed.) *The Struggle for Economic Development* (New York: Longman).

(1971) 'Foreign Capital, Domestic Savings and Economic Development: A Comment'. *Bulletin of the Oxford University Institute of Economics and Statistics* 33 (2): 138–48.

(1971) 'Appropriate, Intermediate or Inferior Economics'. *Journal of Development Studies* 7 (3): 321–29.

Chapters in Books

(2009) 'Addressing Discrimination and Inequality Among Groups'. In J. von Brau, R. Vargas Hill and R. Pandya-Lorch (eds) *The Poorest and Hungry* (Washington, DC: IFPRI).

(2009) 'Macro Adjustment Policies and Horizontal Inequalities', with A. Langer. In P. Arestis and J. Eatwell (eds) *Issues in Global Development: Essays in Honour of Ajit Singh* (London: Palgrave).

(2009) 'Country Patterns of Behavior on Broader Dimensions of Human Development', with G. Ranis and E. Samman. In K. Basu and R. Kanbur (eds) *Arguments for a Better World* (Oxford: OUP).

(2009) 'Policies towards Horizontal Inequalities in Post-Conflict Reconstruction'. In T. Addison and T. Brück (eds) *Making Peace Work: The Challenges of Social and Economic Reconstruction* (London: Palgrave).

(2008) 'Successful Transition Towards a Virtuous Cycle of Human Development and Economic Growth: Country Studies' with G. Ranis and Y. Dong. In K. Haq and R. Ponzio (eds) *Pioneering the Human Development Revolution, An Intellectual Biography of Mahbub ul Haq* (New Delhi: OUP).

(2007) 'Dynamic Links between the Economy and Human Development', with G. Ranis. In J.A. Ocampo, K.S. Jomo and S. Khan (eds) *Policy Matters: Economic and Social Policies to Sustain Equitable Development* (London: Zed Books).

(2007) 'Motivations for Conflict: Groups and Individuals', with G.K. Brown. In C. Crocker, F. Osler Hampson and P. Aall (eds) *Leashing the Dogs of War: Conflict Management in a Divided World* (Washington, DC: US Institute of Peace Press). Book received an Outstanding Academic Title award from CHOICE, a review publication of the Association of College and Research Libraries.

(2007) 'Do We Need a New "Great Transformation"? Is One likely'. In G. Mavrotas and A. Shorrocks (eds) *Advancing Development* (London: Palgrave Macmillan).

(2007) 'Basic Needs Approach'. In D.A. Clark (ed.) *The Elgar Companion to Development Studies* (Cheltenham: Edward Elgar).

(2006) 'The Evolution of Economic Ideas: From Import Substitution to Human Development'. In E.V.K. FitzGerald and R. Thorp (eds) *Economic Doctrines in Latin America* (London: Palgrave Macmillan).

(2006) 'Do PRSPs Empower Poor Countries and Disempower the World Bank, or Is It the Other Way Round?' In G. Ranis, J.R. Vreeland and S. Kosack (eds) *Globalization and the Nation State* (London: Routledge).

(2005) 'Poverty Reduction Strategy Papers Within the Human Rights Perspective', with M. Wang. In P. Alston and M. Robinson (eds) *Human Rights and Development* (Oxford: Oxford University Press).

(2005) 'The Priority of Human Development', with G. Ranis. In E. Hershberg and C. Thornton (eds) *The Development Imperative* (New York: Social Science Research Council).

(2004) 'Evaluating Evaluation in a World of Multiple Goals, Interests and Models'. In G.K. Pitman, O.N. Feinstein and G.K. Ingram (eds) *Evaluating Development Effectiveness* (World Bank Series on Evaluation and Development 7) (New Brunswick, NJ: Transaction Publishers).

(2004) 'Economic Growth and Human Development in Latin America', with G. Ranis. In G. Indart (ed.) *Economic Reforms, Growth and Inequality in Latin America: Essays in Honour of Albert Berry* (Aldershot: Ashgate).

(2003) 'Income Distribution and Development'. In J. Toye (ed.) *Trade and Development: Directions for the 21st Century* (Cheltenham: Edward Elgar).

(2002) 'Dynamic Interactions between the Macro Environment, Development Thinking and Group Behaviour'. In J. Heyer, F. Stewart and R. Thorpe (eds) *Group Behaviour and Development* (Oxford: Oxford University Press).

(2002) 'Why Groups Matter'. In E.V.K. FitzGerald (ed.) *Social Institutions and Economic Development* (Dordrecht: Kluwer Academic Publications).

(2002) 'Conflict in South Asia: Prevalence, Costs and Policies'. In K. Haq (ed.) *The South Asian Challenge* (Oxford: Oxford University Press).

(2002) 'Horizontal Inequalities as a Source of Conflict'. In F.O. Hampson and D.M. Malone (eds) *From Reaction to Conflict Prevention: Opportunities for the UN System* (Boulder, CO: Lynne Rienner Publishers).

(2001) 'Le Cause Profonde dei Conflitti: Indicazioni per le Politiche di Pace'. In R. Papini (ed.) *Globalizzazione: Solidarietà o Esclusione?* (Naples: Edizioni Scientifiche Italiane).

(2001) 'Horizontal Inequalities: A Neglected Dimension of Development'. *WIDER Annual Lectures 5*, December 2001, WIDER, Helsinki; (2005) repr. in G.A. Cornia, M. Pohjola and A. Shorrocks (eds) *Wider Perspectives on Global Development* (Basingstoke: Palgrave Macmillan).

(2001) 'Aid In The Twenty-First Century: Reconciling the Real and the Desirable'. In S. Storm and C.W.M. Naastepad (eds) *Globalization and Economic Development: Essays in Honour of J. George Waardenburg* (Cheltenham: Edgar Elgar).

(2001) 'Adjustment and Poverty in Asia: Old Solutions and New Problems'. In W. Mahmud (ed.) *Adjustment and Beyond: The Reform Experience in South Asia* (Basingstoke: Palgrave).

(2000) 'Civil Wars in Sub-Saharan Africa: Counting the Economic and Social Cost'. In D. Ghai (ed.) *Renewing Social and Economic Progress in Africa: Essays in Memory of Philip Ndegwa* (Basingstoke; New York: Macmillan; St Martin's Press).

(1999) 'Growth and Human Development: Comparative Latin American Experience', with G. Ranis. *Institutional Reforms, Growth and Human Development in Latin America* (YCIAS Working Paper Series) (New Haven, CT: Yale Center for International and Area Studies).

(1999) 'Globalization, Liberalization, and Inequality: Expectations and Experience', with A. Berry. In A. Hurrell and N. Woods (eds) *Inequality, Globalization, and World Politics* (Oxford: Oxford University Press).

(1999) 'Democracy, Conflict and Development – Three Cases', with M. O'Sullivan. In G. Ranis, S.-C. Hu and Y.-P. Chu (eds) *The Political Economy of Comparative Development into the 21st Century: Essays in Memory of John C.H. Fei* (Cheltenham: Edward Elgar).

(1999) 'The Asian Crisis: Social Consequences and Policies'. In *Structural Aspects of the East Asian Crisis* (Paris: OECD).

(1999) 'The Evolution of Development Economics and Gustav Ranis' Role', with A. Berry. In G. Saxonhouse and T.N. Srinivasan (eds) *Development, Duality, and the International Economic Regime: Essays in Honor of Gustav Ranis* (Ann Arbor, MI: University of Michigan Press).

(1998) 'Consumption, Globalization and Theory: Why There Is a Need for Radical Reform'. In *Consumption for Human Development* (Background Papers for the Human Development Report) (New York: HDRO-UNDP).

(1998) 'An Economic and Social Security Council', with S. Daws. In D. Sapsford and J.-R. Chen (eds) *Development Economics and Policy: the Conference Volume to Celebrate the 85th Birthday of Professor Sir Hans Singer* (Basingstoke: Macmillan).

(1997) 'Comment on "John Williamson and the Washington Consensus Revisited" '. In L. Emmerij (ed.) *Economic and Social Development into the XXI Century* (Washington, DC: Inter-American Development Bank).

(1997) 'The Urban Informal Sector within a Global Economy', with G. Ranis. In U. Kirdar (ed.) *Cities Fit for People* (New York: United Nations Publications).

(1997) 'Market Liberalisation and Income Distribution: The Experience of the 1980s', with A. Berry. In R. Culpeper, A. Berry and F. Stewart (eds) *Global Development Fifty Years after Bretton Woods* (Basingstoke: Palgrave Macmillan).

(1996) 'The IMF and the Global Economy', with E.V.K. FitzGerald. Memorandum submitted to the Treasury Committee on The International Monetary Fund, Minutes of Evidence, 4 November (London: HMSO).

(1996) 'Trade and Industrial Policy in Africa', with S. Lall. In B. Ndulu, N. van der Walle et al., *Agenda for Africa's Economic Renewal* (Washington, DC: Overseas Development Council); a shortened version also appeared in *Development* 39 (2): 64–7.

(1995) 'Why We Need a Structured Market'. In G.K. Helleiner, S. Abrahamian, E. Bacha, R. Lawrence and P. Malan (eds) *Poverty, Prosperity and the World Economy: Essays in Memory of Sidney Dell* (Basingstoke: Macmillan).

(1995) 'Biases in Global Markets: Can the Forces of Inequity and Marginalisation Be Modified'. In M. ul Haq, R. Jolly, P. Streeten and K. Haq (eds) *The UN and the Bretton Woods Institutions: New Challenges for the Twenty-First Century* (Basingstoke: Macmillan).

(1995) 'The Social Impact of Globalisation and Marketisation'. In U. Kirdar and L. Silk (eds) *People: From Impoverishment to Empowerment* (New York: New York University Press).

(1994) 'Education and Development: The Experience of the 1980s and Lessons for the 1990s'. In R. Prendergast and F. Stewart (eds) *Market Forces and World Development* (Basingstoke: Macmillan).

(1994) 'Conflict and Development: What Kinds of Policies Can Reduce the Damage of War?', with K. Wilson. In G. Tansey, K. Tansey and P. Rogers (eds)

A World Divided: Militarism and Development after the Cold War (London: Earthscan Publications).

(1993) 'How Well Did the World Bank Meet the Needs of the 1980s'. In M. Nissanke and A. Hewitt (eds) *Economic Crisis in Developing Countries* (Oxford: Pinter Publishers).

(1993) 'The Role of the South in a Chaotic World'. In A. Carty and H. Singer (eds) *Conflict and Change in the 1990s: Ethics, Laws and Institutions* (Basingstoke: Macmillan).

(1992) 'Tackling Malnutrition: What Can Targeted Nutritional Interventions Achieve?', with G. Kumar. In B. Harriss, S. Guhan and R. Cassen (eds) *Poverty in India: Research and Policy* (Bombay: Oxford University Press).

(1992) 'Short-term Policies for Long-term Development'. In G.A. Cornia, R. van der Hoeven and T. Mkandawire (eds) *Africa's Recovery in the 1990s* (Basingstoke; New York: Macmillan; St Martin's Press).

(1992) 'Can Adjustment Programmes Incorporate the Interests of Women?' In H. Afshar and C. Dennis (eds) *Women and Adjustment Policies in the Third World* (Basingstoke: Macmillan).

(1991) 'Externalities, Development and Trade', with E. Ghani. In G.K. Helleiner (ed.) *Trade Policy, Industrialization and Development* (Oxford: Oxford University Press).

(1990) 'Technology Transfer for Development'. In R.E. Evenson and G. Ranis (eds) *Science and Technology: Lessons for Development Policy* (Boulder, CO: Westview).

(1989) *Engendering Adjustment for the 1990s: Report of a Commonwealth Expert Group on Women and Structural Adjustment* (co-author) (London: Commonwealth Secretariat).

(1989) 'Summary of Discussions and Suggestions for Future Research'. In B. Salome (ed.) *Fighting Urban Unemployment in Developing Countries* (Paris: OECD).

(1989) 'Comment on R. Sah and J.E. Stiglitz'. In G. Calvo, R. Findlay, P. Kouri and J. de Macedo (eds) *Debt, Stabilisation and Development* (Oxford: Basil Blackwell).

(1989) 'Inequality in Developing Countries: A Comment on Ferge'. In M. Bulmer, J. Lewis and D. Piachaud (eds) *The Goals of Social Policy* (London: Unwin Hyman).

(1988) 'Do Third World Countries Benefit from Counter-trade?', with H.V. Singh. In S. Dell (ed.) *Policies for Development* (Basingstoke: Macmillan).

(1988) 'Technology: Major Issues for Policy in the 1980s'. In H. Singer, N. Hatti and R. Tandon (eds) *Technology Transfer by Multinationals* (New Delhi: Ashish Publishing House).

(1987) 'Technical Change in the North: Some Implications for the South'. In L. Pasinetti and P. Lloyd (eds) *Structural Change, Economic Interdependence and World Development*, Vol. 3: *Structural Change and Adjustment in the World Economy* (Basingstoke: Macmillan).

(1986) 'Basic Needs Achievements in Sub-Saharan Africa: A Macro-economic Approach'. In *The Challenge of Employment and Basic Needs in Africa, Essays in Honour of Shyam B. L. Nigam and to mark the tenth anniversary of JASPA* (Nairobi: Oxford University Press).

(1986) 'Alternative Trading Strategies', with E. Ghani. In P. Ekins (ed.) *The Living Economy* (London: Routledge and Kegan Paul).

(1984) 'New Theories of International Trade: Some Implications for the South'. In H. Kierzkowski (ed.) *Monopolistic Competition and International Trade* (Oxford: Oxford University Press).

(1984) 'Facilitating Indigenous Technical Change in Third World Countries'. In M. Fransman and K. King (eds) *Technological Capability in the Third World* (London: Macmillan).

(1984) 'Introduction'. In R. Kaplinsky, *Sugar Processing: The Development of a Third World Technology* (London: Intermediate Technology Publications).

(1983) 'Work and Welfare'. In P. Streeten and H. Maier (eds) *Human Resources, Employment and Development: Proceedings of the Sixth World Congress of the International Economic Association held in Mexico City, 1980*, Vol. 2: *Concepts, Measurement and Long-Run Perspective* (London: Macmillan).

(1982) 'Industrialisation, Technical Change and the International Division of Labour'. In G.K. Helleiner (ed.) *For Good or Evil: Economic Theory and North-South Negotiations* (Buffalo: University of Toronto Press).

(1982) 'The New International Economic Order and Basic Needs: Conflicts and Complementarities'. In C. Brundenius and M. Lundahl (eds) *Development Strategies and Basic Needs in Latin America* (Boulder, CO: Westview Press).

(1981) 'Technology Transfer and North-South Relations: Some Current Issues'. In J.S. Szyliowicz (ed.) *Technology and International Affairs* (New York: Praeger).

(1981) 'Taxation and the Control of Transfer Pricing'. In R. Murray (ed.) *Multinationals Beyond the Market* (Brighton: Harvester Press).

(1981) 'Taxation and Technology Transfer'. In T. Sagafi-nejad, R. Moxon and H.V. Perlmutter (eds) *Controlling Technology Transfer* (New York: Pergamon Press).

(1979) 'Employment and Choice of Technique'. In D. Ghai and M. Godfrey (eds) *Essays on Employment in Kenya* (Nairobi: Kenya Literature Bureau).

(1979) 'The Tripartite Agreements in Kenya'. In D. Ghai and M. Godfrey (eds) *Essays on Employment in Kenya* (Nairobi: Kenya Literature Bureau).

(1979) 'International Technology Transfer: Issues and Policy Options'. *World Bank Staff Working Paper* No. 344; (1981) repr. in P. Streeten and R. Jolly (eds) *Recent Issues in World Development* (Oxford: Pergamon).

(1979) 'International Mechanisms for Appropriate Technology'. In A.S. Bhalla (ed.) *Towards Global Action for Appropriate Technology* (Oxford: Pergamon).

(1978) 'Employment Policies'. In R. Cassen and M. Wolfson (eds) *Planning for Growing Populations* (Paris: OECD).

(1976) 'International Action for Appropriate Technology', with A.S. Bhalla. In *Background Papers for the Tripartite World Conference on Employment, Income Distribution and Social Progress and the International Division of Labour, Geneva, June 1976*, Vol. 2: *International Strategies for Employment* (Geneva: International Labour Office).

(1976) 'Capital Goods in Developing Countries'. In A. Cairncross and M. Puri (eds) *Employment, Income Distribution and Development Strategy* (London: Macmillan); (1991) repr. in K. Martin (ed.) *Strategies of Economic Development: Readings in the Political Economy of Industrialisation* (Basingstoke: Macmillan); (1981) abridged version in I. Livingstone (ed.) *Development Economics and Policy: Readings* (London: Allen and Unwin).

(1975) 'The Direction of International Trade: Gains and Losses for the Third World'. In G.K. Helleiner (ed.) *A World Divided: The Less Developed Countries in the International Economy* (Cambridge: Cambridge University Press); (1979) Spanish tr. in *Hacia un Nuevo Orden Económico Internacional?* (Economico International Siglo Veintiuno Editores).

(1975) 'Kenya, Strategies for Development'. In G. Routh et al. (eds) *Development Paths in India and China* (London: Macmillan); (1981) repr. in T. Killick (ed.) *Papers on the Kenyan Economy* (Nairobi; London: Heinemann Educational).

(1973) 'The Control of Profits'. In *Employment, Incomes and Equality: A Strategy for Increasing Productive Employment in Kenya* (ILO Mission Report on Kenya, Technical Paper 17) (Geneva: International Labour Office).

(1969) 'Transfer of Economic Concepts from Highly Developed to Less Developed Countries'. In K.B. Madhava (ed.) *International Development 1969* (Proceedings of the Eleventh World Conference of the Society for International Development, New Delhi, India, 14–17 November 1969) (Dobbs Ferry, NY: Oceana Publications).

Author Index

Subject Index

U

Unemployment, 143, 158, 173, 181, 186–8, 193, 195, 247, 260–1, 271
  youth, 238, 247–8
  unemployment insurance/pay, 154, 180
  see also employment
United Nations Children's Fund (UNICEF), 12, 27
United Nations Industrial Development Organisation (UNIDO), 8, 24, 48
United Nations Research Institute for Social Development (UNRISD), 149
United States Agency for International Development (USAID), 143
Universalism(ist)(istic), 12, 132, 159–60
Uruguay, 173–4, 176–7, 183–4, 187–9, 194
  Frente Amplio, 174

V

Value
  change(s), 10, 128, 134–9, 145
  drivers of values, 129, 135, 145
  formation, 127–8, 134, 139
  framework(s), 128, 130, 138
Vázquez, Tabaré, 173
Vellu, Samy, 226
Venezuela, 173–9, 183, 186, 194
Violence, 4, 14–17, 37, 208–11, 218, 231, 233–5, 239, 241, 243, 245, 267
  see also group conflict, violent conflict

W

Ward, Barbara, 29
Welfare state(s), 12, 138, 142–4, 149–54, 156–65, 195
  developmental welfare state(s), 150, 155, 161, 164
  universalistic welfare state, 160
Wilson, Harold, 20–1
World Bank (WB), 12, 25, 31, 143
World Trade Organization (WTO), 52
World Values Survey (WVS), 211

Z

Zia-ul-Haq, President Muhammad, 25